足球竞赛规则
2016/2017

中国足球协会　审定

人民体育出版社

国际足球联合会

地址：Münstergasse, 9, 8001 Zurich, Switzerland
电话：+41（0）44 245 1886
传真：+41（0）44 245 1887
网址：www.theifab.com

未经国际足球理事会允许，本规则的部分或全部章节不得复制或翻译。本书中文内容如有歧义，以相应英文版本内容为准。

2016年6月1日生效

前　言

国际足球理事会作为《足球竞赛规则》相关决策的全球性机构，每年都要对《足球竞赛规则》进行修订和调整。为提高《足球竞赛规则》的时效性，中国足球协会也同时对《足球竞赛规则》英文版本进行翻译和审定，受到国内广大裁判工作者、教练员、运动员，以及足球爱好者的欢迎。

为适应当今足球运动的迅猛发展，提高《足球竞赛规则》的科学性和可读性，使其更易于理解和统一执行，自2014年起，国际足球理事会开始着手对《足球竞赛规则》进行结构性调整和修订，在第127次、第128次和第129次国际足球理事会年度大会上，陆续通过了相关内容的修订决定。在正式颁布的《足球竞赛规则》2016/2017中，国际足球理事会对原有规则章节结构、条文内容、语言措辞等方面进行了大面积的修订。为与最新足球竞赛规则保持同步，确保规则执行的一致性，经国际足球理事会授权，中国足球协会对英文版《足球竞赛规则》2016/2017进行了翻译和审定。本书包含了国际足球理事会《足球竞赛规则》2016/2017的全部章节和说明内容，同时加入了国际足球理事会关于竞赛规则的最新决议，这些决议作为对新规则的补充说明，以及后续规则版本的简要介绍。

中国足球协会希望通过《足球竞赛规则》2016/2017（中英文对照）的出版，更好地服务于各类足球工作者，以及喜爱和关心足球运动的各界人士，作为学习、掌握和正确运用足球竞赛规则的规范参考。

本次《足球竞赛规则》主要由刘虎、陈亮力翻译，段明洋审校修改，毛鹤鸣参与了部分内容的修订工作。

中国足球协会裁判委员会
2017年4月

Contents

- 5 History of The IFAB
- 7 Structure and working of The IFAB
- 9 Background to the current Law revision

11 Notes on the Laws of the Game

12 Laws of the Game 2016/2017
- 13 01 The Field of Play
- 22 02 The Ball
- 24 03 The Players
- 30 04 The Players' Equipment
- 33 05 The Referee
- 40 06 The Other Match Officials
- 46 07 The Duration of the Match
- 48 08 The Start and Restart of Play
- 50 09 The Ball In and Out of Play
- 51 10 Determining the Outcome of a Match
- 55 11 Offside
- 58 12 Fouls and Misconduct
- 67 13 Free Kicks
- 70 14 The Penalty Kick
- 73 15 The Throw-in
- 75 16 The Goal Kick
- 77 17 The Corner Kick

目　录

5　国际足球理事会历史
7　国际足球理事会组织机构及职能
9　新版本修订背景

11 足球竞赛规则注解

12 足球竞赛规则 2016/2017
　13　第 一 章　比赛场地
　22　第 二 章　球
　24　第 三 章　队员
　30　第 四 章　队员装备
　33　第 五 章　裁判员
　40　第 六 章　其他比赛官员
　46　第 七 章　比赛时间
　48　第 八 章　比赛开始与恢复
　50　第 九 章　比赛进行与停止
　51　第 十 章　确定比赛结果
　55　第十一章　越位
　58　第十二章　犯规与不正当行为
　67　第十三章　任意球
　70　第十四章　罚球点球
　73　第十五章　掷界外球
　75　第十六章　球门球
　77　第十七章　角球

79 Law changes 2016/2017
- 80 Outline summary of Law changes
- 84 Details of all Law changes

126 Glossary
- 127 Football bodies
- 128 Football terms
- 137 Referee terms

138 Practical Guidelines for Match Officials
- 139 Introduction
- 140 Positioning, Movement and Teamwork
- 153 Body language, Communication and Whistle
- 159 Other advice
  - Advantage
  - Allowance for time lost
  - Holding an opponent
  - Offside
  - Treatment/assessment after a caution/sending-off offence

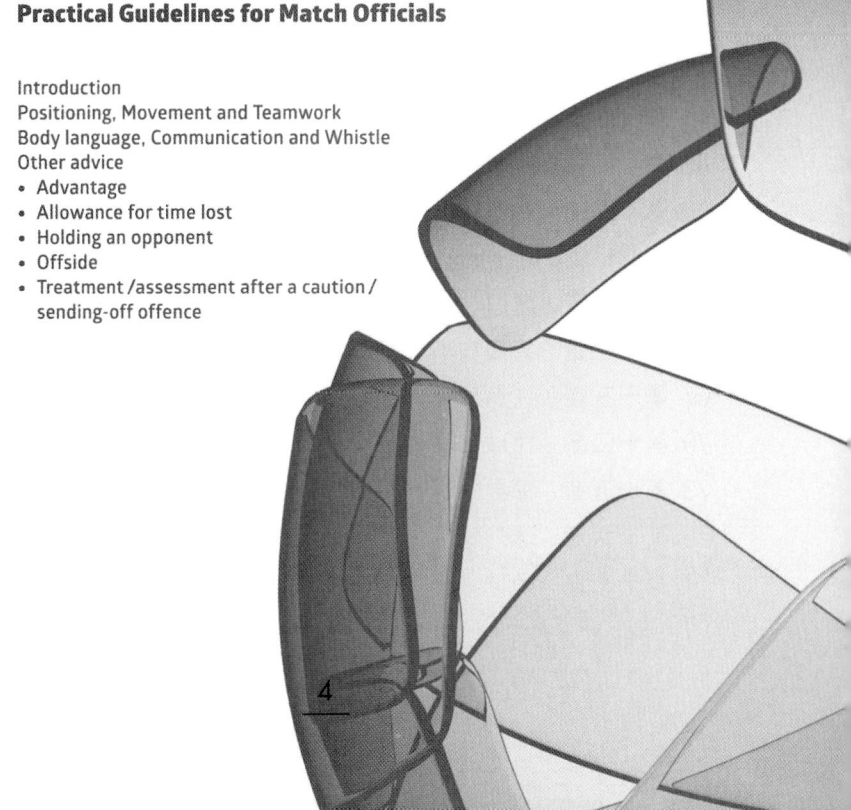

79 竞赛规则变更内容 2016/2017
80 规则变更概要
84 规则变更详解（按规则章节排序）

126 术语汇编
127 足球机构
128 足球术语
137 裁判术语

138 比赛官员实践指南
139 引言
140 选位、移动与团队配合
153 肢体语言、沟通与哨音
159 其他建议
- 有利
- 对损耗时间的补足
- 使用手臂等部位拉扯、阻止对方队员行动
- 越位
- 出现可警告/罚令出场的犯规后对受伤队员的治疗/伤势评估

168 附录　国际足球理事会第131次年度工作会议决议

History of The IFAB

The IFAB is the universal decision-making body for the Laws of the Game of association football. Its objectives are to safeguard, compile and amend the Laws as they apply within the scope of world football as organised by FIFA, which includes ensuring that the Laws are uniformly applied worldwide and monitored accordingly, and that organised football is practised consistently.

The IFAB was formed when two representatives from each of the football associations of England, Scotland, Wales and Northern Ireland met on 2 June 1886. The brainchild of the English FA, the new body was created to draw up a uniform set of Laws at a time when each country applied different rules. Once established as the guardians of the Laws of the Game, The IFAB's role was and remains to preserve, monitor, study and where appropriate improve the Laws.

The game of football spread rapidly and in 1904 seven nations met in Paris to form FIFA, Fédération Internationale de Football Associations, which joined The IFAB in 1913.

The IFAB has overseen many Law changes since the creation of the first set of official Laws in 1863. For example, offside is probably the most amended Law e.g. originally a player in front of the ball was offside. The goal area first appeared in 1869, followed by corner kicks in 1872, and the first penalty kick was awarded in 1891 - until 1902 it could be taken from any point along a line 12 yards from the goal. The 1912 decision to prohibit goalkeepers from handling the ball outside the penalty area led to an increase in the number of goals and from 1920 players could not be offside from throw-ins.

国际足球理事会历史

国际足球理事会是负责《足球竞赛规则》相关决策的全球性机构。其任务是保障、编撰、修订国际足球联合会组织下的足球竞赛规则，包括其在世界范围内的统一施行，以及相应的监管，以确保足球运动的一致性。

1886年6月2日，英格兰、苏格兰、威尔士和北爱尔兰足球协会各两名代表经过会晤，发起成立了国际足球理事会。新成立的国际足球理事会在当时各国执行不同足球规则的情况下，应英格兰足球协会的倡议，编写了统一的足球竞赛规则。自成立之日起，国际足球理事会就担当着《足球竞赛规则》守护者的角色，至今仍承担着保护、监管、研究并在需要时修订规则的任务。

足球运动迅猛发展，1904年，由7个国家在巴黎发起成立了国际足球联合会。国际足球联合会于1913年加入国际足球理事会。

自1863年第一套官方足球竞赛规则诞生以来，国际足球理事会已经审核了多项规则修改。例如，越位规则可能是修改最多的部分，最初队员处在球前即视为越位；球门区于1869年出现；角球于1872年出现；1891年出现了历史上第一例球点球判罚——直至1902年，球点球可在距球门12码的任一位置罚出；1912年，守门员被禁止在罚球区外用手触球，这一变化让进球数大幅提高；从1920年开始，队员在掷界外球的情况下不被判罚越位。

Steadily, The IFAB changed the game and the mind-set of those who played and watched it. The change prohibiting goalkeepers from handling deliberate 'back-passes', introduced after the 1990 FIFA World Cup Italy™, and the 1998 ruling that red cards be awarded for serious tackles from behind are good examples of that shift in attitude.

In October 2010 The IFAB reconsidered the introduction of goal line technology (GLT) and agreed to a two-year period of comprehensive testing. In July 2012 The IFAB made the historic decisions to approve GLT and the use of Additional Assistant Referees.

March 2016 was also an historic AGM when a testing phase for Video Assistant Referees was approved along with the most comprehensive revision of the Laws of the Game in The IFAB's history.

国际足球理事会稳步地推动着足球运动的发展变化，改变着从事和观赏足球运动的人们的观念。1990年意大利世界杯引入了禁止守门员用手触及故意"回传球"，以及1998年规定从身体后侧严重抢截犯规应出示红牌等，都是对足球运动认识和态度的转变。

2010年10月，国际足球理事会再次考虑引入球门线技术，并同意开展一项为期两年的全面测试。2012年7月，国际足球理事会做出历史性决定，通过了球门线技术和附加助理裁判员的使用。

2016年3月，在国际足球理事会年度大会上，同样见证了历史性的时刻，会议通过了录像辅助裁判的阶段测试，以及国际足球理事会历史上最全面地修订的《足球竞赛规则》。

Structure and working of The IFAB

In 2012 The IFAB started a reform process which concluded on 13 January 2014 when The IFAB became an autonomous association under Swiss Law and approved the statutes that define the purpose, structure and responsibilities of The IFAB and its bodies. To ensure the work of The IFAB is transparent, democratic and modern, an executive secretariat, led by the Secretary of The IFAB, was introduced.

Whilst The IFAB composition remained unchanged, the reform saw the formation of the Football Advisory Panel and Technical Advisory Panel consisting of experts from across the world of football. These panels aim to improve the consultation process and foster a more proactive approach to the development of the Laws.

Annual General Meeting (AGM)

The AGM takes place in February or March in England, Scotland, Wales and Northern Ireland in strict rotation, as well as a location decided by FIFA in FIFA World Cup™ years. AGM decisions on the Laws of the Game are binding on confederations and national football associations as from 1 June. However, confederations and national football associations whose current season or competition has not ended by 1 June may delay the change(s) until the beginning of their next season or end of the competition; those which start before 1 June may apply them once The IFAB has issued the official circular announcing any changes.

No alteration to the Laws of the Game can be made by any confederation or national football association (including competitions) unless it has been passed by The IFAB.

国际足球理事会组织机构及职能

2012年国际足球理事会开始改组,并于2014年1月13日根据瑞士法律,规范了国际足球理事会及其附属机构的宗旨、组织结构及职责,成为具有独立自主权的组织。为确保国际足球理事会的工作透明化、民主化和现代化,由国际足球理事会秘书长主持的执行秘书处开始运行。

尽管国际足球理事会的构成结构没有发生变化,然而由足球领域的专家组成的足球顾问组和技术顾问组的成型则是改革的见证。顾问组旨在改进议事程序,建立对《足球竞赛规则》完善和发展的主动机制。

年度大会

年度大会每年二三月轮流在英格兰、苏格兰、威尔士、北爱尔兰,以及国际足联在世界杯年份指定的地点举行。年度大会就《足球竞赛规则》做出的决议,从当年6月1日起,对各洲际联合会和国家足球协会具有约束力。不过,如果洲际联合会和国家足球协会组织的现阶段赛季或竞赛,在6月1日尚未结束,可在下一赛季开始或本次竞赛结束时执行。在6月1日前开赛的赛季或赛事,也可以执行国际足球理事会正式发布的任何规则变动。

除国际足球理事会批准外,各洲际联合会或国家足球协会(包括赛事方)不得修改《足球竞赛规则》。

Annual Business Meeting (ABM)
The ABM is the preparatory meeting for the AGM and is held in November. The ABM can consider items submitted by any confederation or national football association and may approved experiments and trials. However, changes to the Laws must be approved at the AGM.

Technical Subcommittee (TSC)
The IFAB TSC consists of experts from the four British FAs, FIFA and The IFAB and is responsible for considering potential Law changes and overseeing trials approved by the ABM and AGM.

Advisory Panels
The Football Advisory Panel (FAP) and Technical Advisory Panel (TAP) consist of experts from across the world of football, who support The IFAB's work on the Laws of the Game. They include former players, coaches and referees from different confederations and football bodies . FAP provides perspectives from players and coaches while TAP assesses technical details and possible impacts on refereeing of any Law changes.

年度工作会议

年度工作会议是年度大会的筹备会议，在每年11月举行。年度工作会议可以商议由各洲际联合会或国家足球协会提交的议案，并可批准实验和测试计划。然而，有关《足球竞赛规则》的变动必须经年度大会审议通过。

技术附属委员会

国际足球理事会技术附属委员会，由4个英国足协、国际足球联合会和国际足球理事会的专家组成，负责商议可能做出的规则变动，以及监督由年度大会和年度工作会议批准的测试。

顾问组

足球顾问组和技术顾问组由全世界足球领域的专家组成，协助国际足球理事会对《足球竞赛规则》进行修订。这些专家来自不同洲际联合会和足球机构的退役球员、教练员和裁判员。足球顾问组从球员和教练员的角度提出建议，而技术顾问组就任何规则上的变动，对技术细节和裁判员执法可能带来的影响进行评估。

Background to the current Law revision

The authority for the current revision of the Laws of the Game is found in the minutes of the 127th, 128th and 129th AGMs. The TSC started work in autumn 2014 and the minutes of the 129th AGM on 28th February 2015 record that:

"…the aim of the revision is to make the Laws of the Game more accessible and more easily understood by everyone in football and increase consistency of understanding, interpretation and application."

The revision has focussed on making the Laws appropriate for the modern game at all levels. The major areas of change are:

- **More simple structure** – Law and Law Interpretation have been combined so all the information for each Law is in the same place
- **Updated titles** – some Laws have been renamed to reflect their content and allow inclusion of text not previously assigned to a Law e.g. Law 6: 'The Assistant Referees' has become 'The Other Match Officials' to allow inclusion of Fourth Officials, Additional Assistant Referees etc.
- **English and phraseology** – unnecessary words have been removed and a more consistent use of words and phrases makes the Laws more readable, helps translation and reduces confusion and misunderstandings. Contradictions and unnecessary repetitions have been removed. The Laws are now 'gender neutral', reflecting the importance of women in football today
- **Updated content** – some changes bring the Laws up to date with modern football e.g. the increased number of substitutes

新版本修订背景

在国际足球理事会第127次、第128次和第129次年度大会上，通过了对现版本《足球竞赛规则》的修订。技术附属委员会在2014年秋季已经开始着手修订工作，并在2015年2月28日举行的第129次年度大会的纪要中明确，"……修订规则的主要目的，是为了使规则更加易于被足球领域的所有人理解和接受，提高理解、翻译和运用上的统一性"。

本次修订注重使竞赛规则适用于当代足球各级别水平的比赛。主要修订内容体现在以下几个方面：

- 更简明的结构——规则正文与诠释部分合二为一，使得每章的所有信息归纳在同一部分中。
- 标题的修订——部分章节的标题已被更改，以体现该章节的实际内容，并将此前未归类的部分进行了归纳。例如，第6章"助理裁判员"改为"其他比赛官员"，以将第四官员、附加助理裁判员等归纳为一类。
- 语言和措辞——删除了不必要的词语，以及矛盾之处和重复措辞，使用了更为统一规范的词语和词组，增强规则的可读性，减少翻译时的混淆和误解。现版本《足球竞赛规则》适用于男子和女子足球运动，体现了当代足球运动中女性的重要性。
- 内容的修订——部分修订内容使得《足球竞赛规则》与时俱进，适应当代足球，例如增加队员替换的人数。

Two important 'new' sections have been introduced:

- **Law changes explained** – this section gives the 'old' text, the 'new' text and an explanation for each Law change
- **Glossary** – this is a list of definitions of important words/phrases which are sometimes misunderstood and/or difficult to translate

The IFAB believes that this revision makes the Laws of the Game more accessible and more easily understood by everyone involved or interested in football. This should lead to increased consistency of understanding, interpretation and application so there are fewer disputes and controversies resulting from conflicting interpretations.

The IFAB acknowledges with grateful thanks the work on this revision by the Technical Subcommittee:

- David Elleray (Project lead, The IFAB)
- Neale Barry (The FA)
- Jean-Paul Brigger (FIFA)
- Massimo Busacca (FIFA)
- William Campbell (Irish FA)
- Ray Ellingham (FA of Wales)
- John Fleming (Scottish FA)
- Fernando Tresaco Gracia (FIFA)

本版规则引入两个重要的"新"篇章：
- 规则变更详解—这一部分将新旧版本内容进行对照，并就各处变动做出了相应说明。
- 术语汇编—这一部分是对容易误解和/或难以翻译的词语/词组进行了具体定义。

国际足球理事会相信，本次修订能够使所有足球参与者或爱好者理解《足球竞赛规则》。同时，提高《足球竞赛规则》的理解、翻译和运用的一致性，减少因对规则翻译的不一致所造成的歧义。

国际足球理事会对在修订工作中做出贡献的技术附属委员会成员表示由衷的感谢，他们是：
- 戴维·埃勒雷David Elleray（项目主管，国际足联）
- 尼尔·巴里 Neale Barry（英格兰足球协会）
- 让-保罗·布里格Jean-Paul Brigger（国际足联）
- 马西莫·布萨卡Massimo Busacca（国际足联）
- 威廉·坎贝尔William Campbell（爱尔兰足球协会）
- 雷·埃林汉姆Ray Ellingham（威尔士足球协会）
- 约翰·弗莱明John Fleming（苏格兰足球协会）
- 费尔南多·特雷萨科·格拉西亚Fernando TresacoGracia（国际足联）

Notes on the Laws of the Game

Modifications

Subject to the agreement of the national football association concerned and provided the principles of these Laws are maintained, the Laws may be modified in their application for matches for players of under 16 years of age, for women footballers, for veteran footballers (over 35 years of age) and for players with disabilities, in any or all of the following ways:

- size of the field of play
- size, weight and material of the ball
- width between the goalposts and height of the crossbar from the ground
- duration of the periods of play
- substitutions

Further modifications are only allowed with the consent of The IFAB.

Official languages

The IFAB publishes the Laws of the Game in English, French, German and Spanish. If there is any divergence in the wording, the English text is authoritative.

Key

The main Law changes are underlined and highlighted in the margin.

足球竞赛规则注解

规则内容的调整

在不违背规则主旨的前提下，经会员协会同意，可以对规则某些条款做适当调整，以适应16岁以下队员的比赛、女子足球比赛、年长足球运动员（35岁以上）和伤残人士参与的比赛。该调整可涉及如下某一（或全部）方面：

- 球场的大小。
- 比赛球的大小、质量及制作材料。
- 两门柱间的宽度及地面到球门横梁的高度。
- 比赛时间。
- 替换人数。

如要做进一步调整，须经国际足球理事会批准。

官方语言

国际足球理事会使用英文、法文、德文和西班牙文出版《足球竞赛规则》，如果不同语言文字出现任何歧义，则以英文版文字为准。

提示

规则的主要变更部分在文中以下画线的方式标出。

Laws of the Game
2016/2017

足球竞赛规则
2016/2017

01. The Field of Play

1. **Field surface**

   The field of play must be a wholly natural or, if competition rules permit, a wholly artificial playing surface except where competition rules permit an integrated combination of artificial and natural materials (hybrid system).

   The colour of artificial surfaces must be green.

   Where artificial surfaces are used in competition matches between representative teams of national football associations affiliated to FIFA or international club competition matches, the surface must meet the requirements of the FIFA Quality Programme for Football Turf or the International Match Standard, unless special dispensation is given by The IFAB.

2. **Field markings**

   The field of play must be rectangular and marked with continuous lines which must not be dangerous. These lines belong to the areas of which they are boundaries.

   Only the lines indicated in Law 1 are to be marked on the field of play.

   The two longer boundary lines are touchlines. The two shorter lines are goal lines.

   The field of play is divided into two halves by a halfway line, which joins the midpoints of the two touchlines.

   The centre mark is at the midpoint of the halfway line. A circle with a radius of 9.15 m (10 yds) is marked around it.

第一章　比赛场地

1. 场地表面

比赛场地必须为全天然草皮。若竞赛规程允许，可使用全人造草皮。此外，如果竞赛规程允许，可使用人造和天然结合材料制成的整体草皮（混合系统）。

人造草皮场地的表面必须为绿色。

除国际足球理事会特许外，在国际足联所属的国家协会代表队之间、国际俱乐部之间比赛中使用的人造草皮场地，必须达到《国际足联足球场地质量项目》或《国际比赛标准》的要求。

2. 场地标识

比赛场地形状必须为长方形，且由不具危险性的连续标线标示。这些标线作为边界线是其所标示区域的一部分。

只有在第一章中提及的标线可以标画在比赛场地内。

两条较长的边界线为边线，两条较短的边界线为球门线。

比赛场地由一条连接两侧边线中点的中线划分为两个半场。

中线的中心位置为中点。以中点为圆心画一个半径为9.15米（10码）的圆圈。

Marks may be made off the field of play 9.15 m (10 yds) from the corner arc at right angles to the goal lines and the touchlines.

All lines must be of the same width, which must not be more than 12 cm (5 ins). The goal lines must be of the same width as the goalposts and the crossbar.

Where artificial surfaces are used, other lines are permitted provided they are a different colour and clearly distinguishable from the football lines.

A player who makes unauthorised marks on the field of play must be cautioned for unsporting behaviour. If the referee notices this being done during the match, the player is cautioned when the ball next goes out of play.

3. Dimensions

The touchline must be longer than the goal line.

- Length (touchline):
  minimum   90 m (100 yds)
  maximum   120 m (130 yds)

- Length (goal line):
  minimum   45 m (50 yds)
  maximum   90 m (100 yds)

4. Dimensions for international matches

- Length (touchline):
  minimum   100 m (100 yds)
  maximum   110 m (120 yds)

- Length (goal line):
  minimum   64 m (70 yds)
  maximum   75 m (80 yds)

Competitions may determine the length of the goal line and touchline within the above dimensions.

可在比赛场地外，距角球弧9.15米（10码）处，分别做垂直于球门线和边线的标记。

所有标线宽度必须一致，且不得超过12厘米（5英寸）。球门线、球门柱和横梁的宽度必须一致。

允许其他标线出现在人造草皮的场地上，但其颜色必须有别于足球比赛场地使用的标线，且区分明显。

在比赛场地内制造未经许可标记的队员，必须以非体育行为予以警告。如果裁判员在比赛进行中发现此类情况，则在随后比赛停止时警告相关队员。

3. 场地尺寸

边线必须长于球门线。

- 长度（边线）：
  最短 90米（100码）
  最长 120米（130码）

- 长度（球门线）：
  最短 45米（50码）
  最长 90米（100码）

4. 国际比赛场地尺寸

- 长度（边线）：
  最短 100米（110码）
  最长 110米（120码）

- 长度（球门线）：
  最短 64米（70码）
  最长 75米（80码）

竞赛方可以在上述尺寸范围内规定球门线和边线的长度。

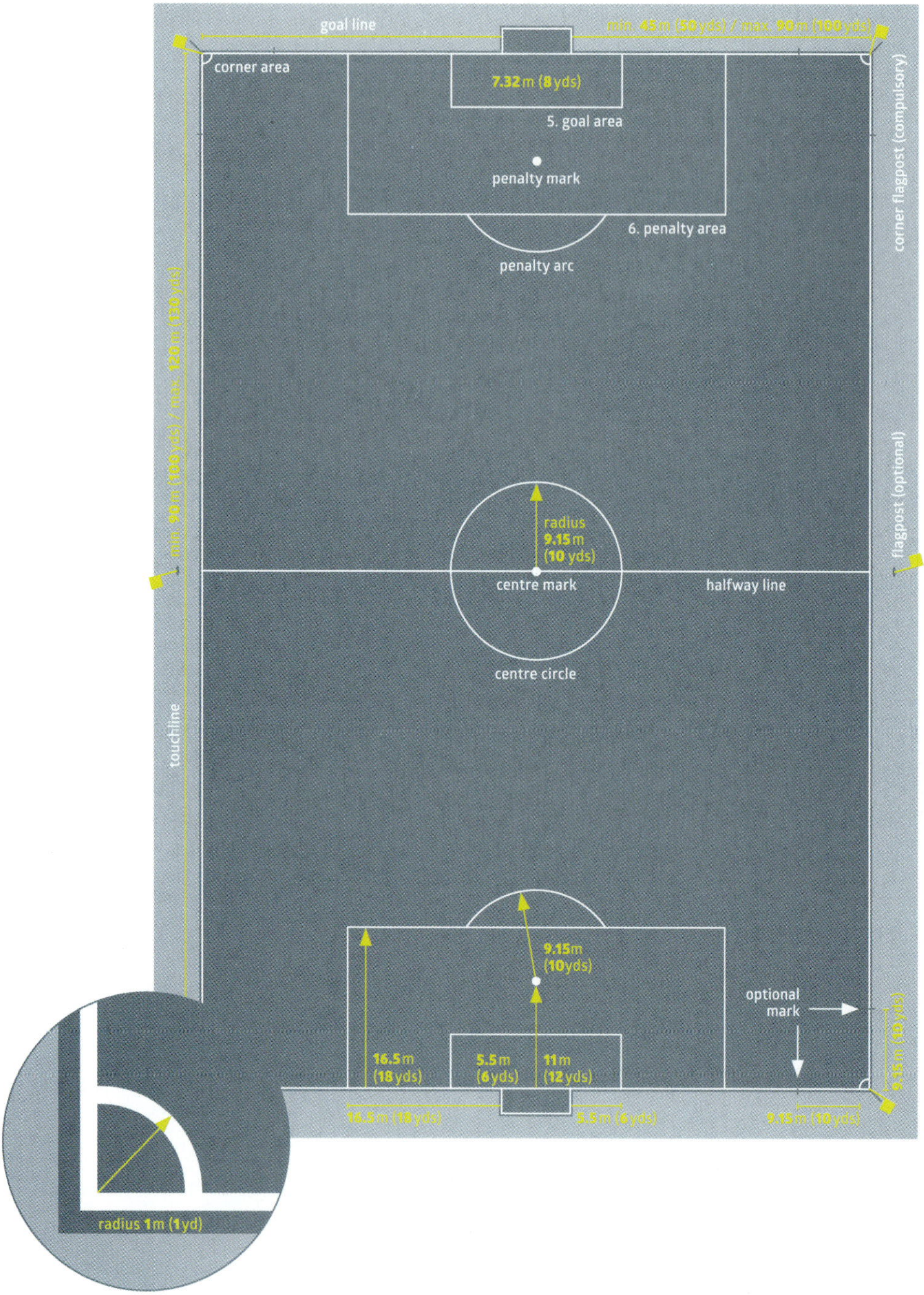

goal line
min. 45m (50yds) / max. 90m (100yds)
corner area
7.32m (8yds)
5. goal area
penalty mark
6. penalty area
penalty arc
corner flagpost (compulsory)
min. 90m (100yds) / max. 120m (130yds)
radius
9.15m
(10 yds)
centre mark
halfway line
flagpost (optional)
centre circle
touchline
9.15m
(10yds)
optional
mark
16.5m
(18yds)
5.5m
(6yds)
11m
(12yds)
9.15m (10yds)
16.5m (18yds)
5.5m (6yds)
9.15m (10yds)
radius 1m (1yd)

15

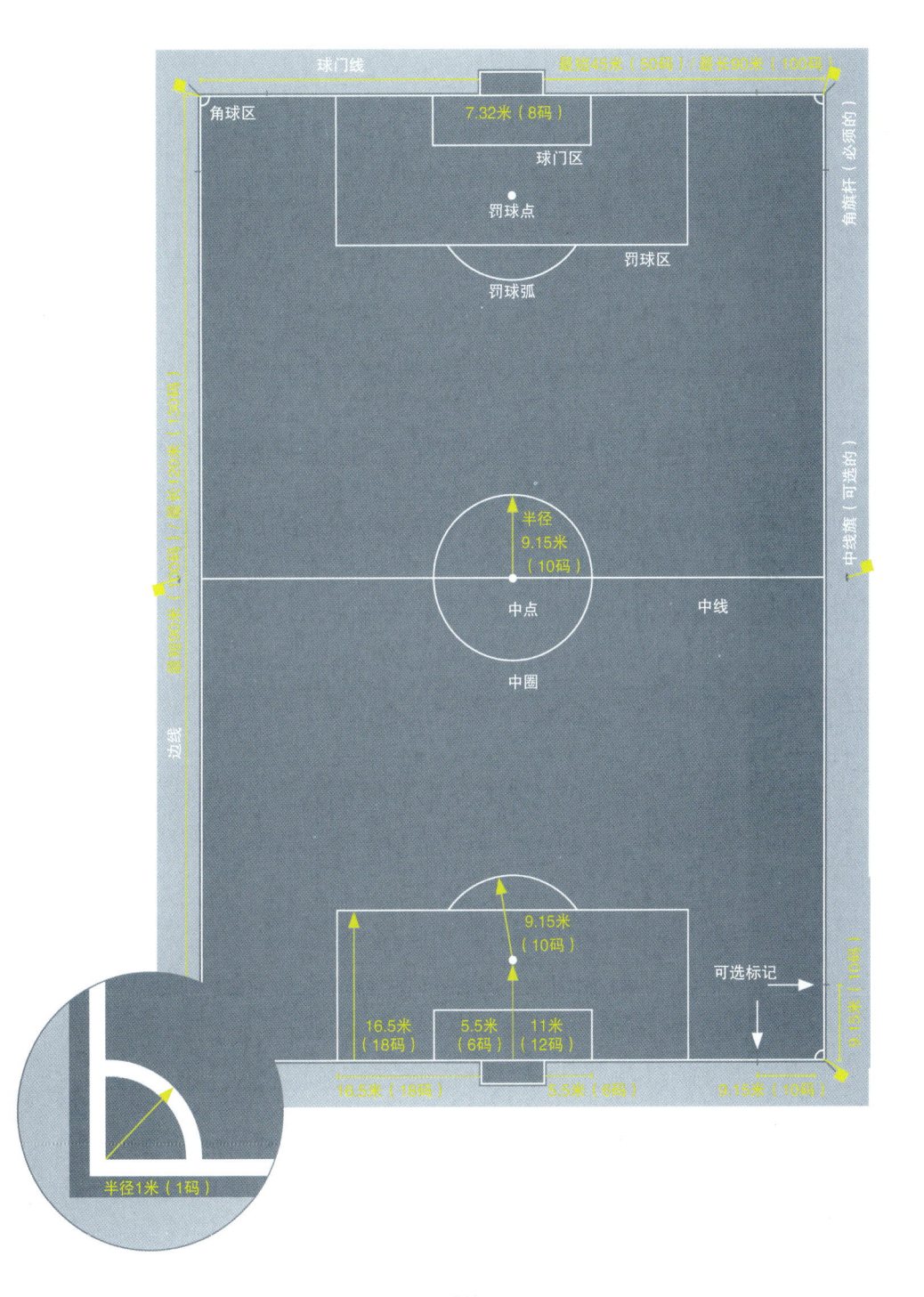

5. **The goal area**

    Two lines are drawn at right angles to the goal line, 5.5 m (6 yds) from the inside of each goalpost. These lines extend into the field of play for 5.5 m (6 yds) and are joined by a line drawn parallel with the goal line. The area bounded by these lines and the goal line is the goal area.

6. **The penalty area**

    Two lines are drawn at right angles to the goal line, 16.5 m (18 yds) from the inside of each goalpost. These lines extend into the field of play for 16.5 m (18 yds) and are joined by a line drawn parallel with the goal line. The area bounded by these lines and the goal line is the penalty area.

    Within each penalty area, a penalty mark is made 11 m (12 yds) from the midpoint between the goalposts.

    An arc of a circle with a radius of 9.15 m (10 yds) from the centre of each penalty mark is drawn outside the penalty area.

7. **The corner area**

    The corner area is defined by a quarter circle with a radius of 1 m (1 yd) from each corner flagpost drawn inside the field of play.

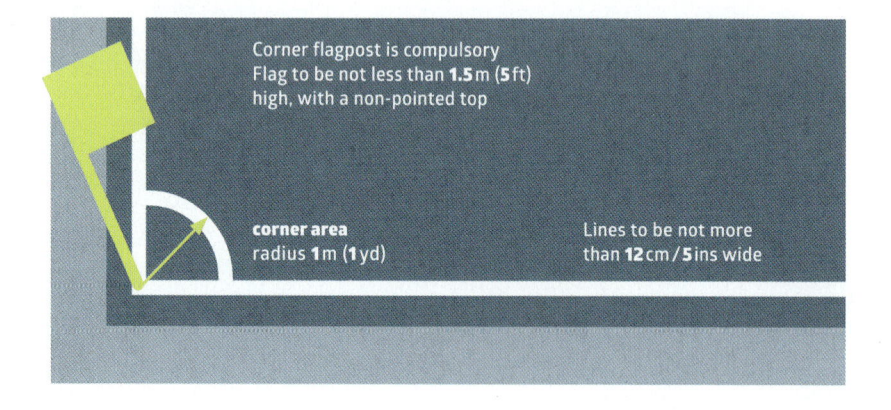

Corner flagpost is compulsory
Flag to be not less than **1.5** m (**5** ft) high, with a non-pointed top

corner area
radius **1** m (**1** yd)

Lines to be not more than **12** cm / **5** ins wide

5. 球门区

从距两根球门柱内侧5.5米（6码）处，画两条垂直于球门线的标线。这两条标线向比赛场地内延伸5.5米（6码），与一条平行于球门线的标线相连接。由这些标线和球门线围成的区域是球门区。

6. 罚球区

从距两根球门柱内侧16.5米（18码）处，画两条垂直于球门线的标线。这两条标线向比赛场地内延伸16.5米（18码），与一条平行于球门线的标线相连接。由这些标线和球门线围成的区域是罚球区。

在每个罚球区内，距两根球门柱之间的中点11米（12码）处，设置一个罚球点。

在每个罚球区外，以罚球点为圆心，画一段半径为9.15米（10码）的圆弧。

7. 角球区

在比赛场地内，以各角旗杆为圆心，画一半径为1米的四分之一圆，这部分区域为角球区。

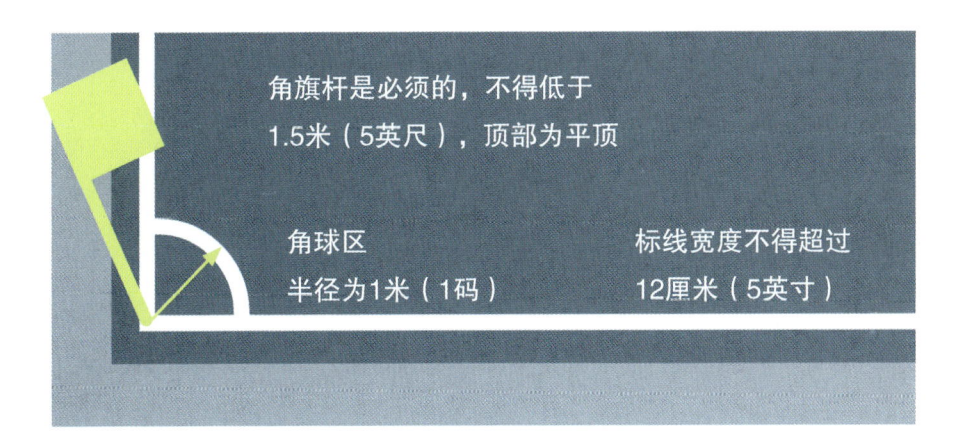

角旗杆是必须的，不得低于1.5米（5英尺），顶部为平顶

角球区
半径为1米（1码）

标线宽度不得超过12厘米（5英寸）

8. **Flagposts**

    A flagpost, at least 1.5 m (5 ft) high, with a non-pointed top and a flag must be placed at each corner.

    Flagposts may be placed at each end of the halfway line, at least 1 m (1 yd) outside the touchline.

9. **The technical area**

    The technical area relates to matches played in stadiums with a designated seated area for team officials and substitutes as outlined below:

    - the technical area should only extend 1 m (1 yd) on either side of the designated seated area and up to a distance of 1 m (1 yd) from the touchline
    - markings should be used to define the area
    - the number of persons permitted to occupy the technical area is defined by the competition rules
    - the occupants of the technical area:
        - are identified before the start of the match in accordance with the competition rules
        - must behave in a responsible manner
        - must remain within its confines except in special circumstances, e.g. a physiotherapist/doctor entering the field of play, with the referee's permission, to assess an injured player
    - only one person at a time is authorised to convey tactical instructions from the technical area

8. 旗杆

必须在比赛场地各角竖立高度不低于1.5米（5尺）的平顶旗杆。

可在中线两端、边线外不少于1米处竖立旗杆。

9. *技术区域*

技术区域是指设在场地内，与比赛相关，供球队官员和替补队员使用的有座席的区域，描述如下：

- 技术区域仅可从座席区域两侧向外扩展1米（1码），向前扩展到距边线至少1米（1码）。
- 应用标线标示出该区域。
- 允许占用技术区域的人员数量由竞赛规程决定。
- 占用技术区域的人员：
  - 需依据竞赛规程，在比赛开始前审核确认。
  - 举止必须得当。
  - 必须留在限定区域内。除特殊情况外，如理疗师/医生经裁判员许可后进入比赛场地内查看受伤队员伤情。
- 同一时刻仅允许1人在技术区域内进行战术指导。

10. Goals

A goal must be placed on the centre of each goal line.

A goal consists of two vertical posts equidistant from the corner flagposts and joined at the top by a horizontal crossbar. The goalposts and crossbar must be made of approved material. They must be square, rectangular, round or elliptical in shape and must not be dangerous.

The distance between the inside of the posts is 7.32 m (8 yds) and the distance from the lower edge of the crossbar to the ground is 2.44 m (8 ft).

The position of the goalposts in relation to the goal line must be in accordance with the graphics.

The goalposts and the crossbar must be white and have the same width and depth, which must not exceed 12 cm (5 ins).

If the crossbar becomes displaced or broken, play is stopped until it has been repaired or replaced in position. If it can not be repaired the match must be abandoned. A rope or any flexible or dangerous material may not replace the crossbar. Play is restarted with a dropped ball.

Nets may be attached to the goals and the ground behind the goal; they must be properly supported and must not interfere with the goalkeeper.

Safety
Goals (including portable goals) must be firmly secured to the ground.

10. 球门

必须在两条球门线的中央，各放置一个球门。

球门由两根距角旗杆等距离的直立球门柱和一根连接球门柱顶部的水平横梁组成。球门柱和横梁必须由经批准的材料制成。其形状必须为正方形、矩形、圆形或椭圆形，且不具危险性。

两根球门柱内侧之间的距离为7.32米（8码），从横梁下沿至地面的距离为2.44米（8英尺）。

球门柱与球门线的位置关系必须符合图例所示（见下页）。

球门柱和横梁颜色必须为白色，且宽度和厚度必须一致，不得超过12厘米（5英寸）。

如果横梁移位或折损，则停止比赛直至横梁修复或归位。如果无法修复，则必须中止比赛。不得用绳、任何弹性或危险性材料代替横梁使用。比赛以坠球方式恢复。

球门网可系在球门和球门后的地面上，并且必须适当撑开，不得影响守门员的活动。

安全性

球门（包括可移动式球门）必须牢固地固定在地面上。

2.44 m (8 ft)

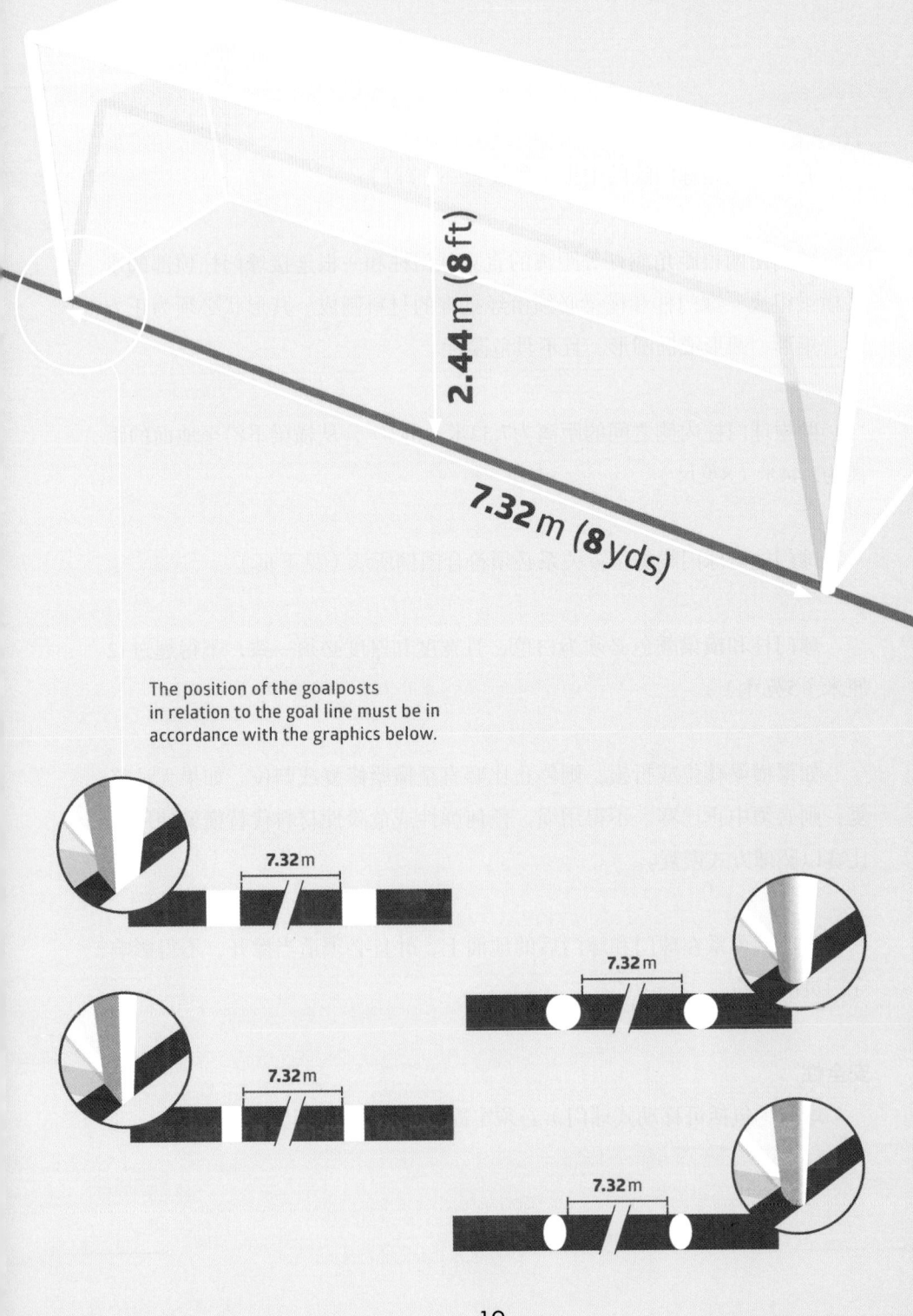

7.32 m (8 yds)

The position of the goalposts in relation to the goal line must be in accordance with the graphics below.

7.32 m

7.32 m

7.32 m

7.32 m

2.44米（8英尺）

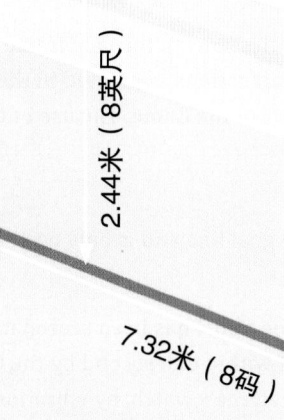

7.32米（8码）

球门柱和球门线的位置关系必须符合如下图示：

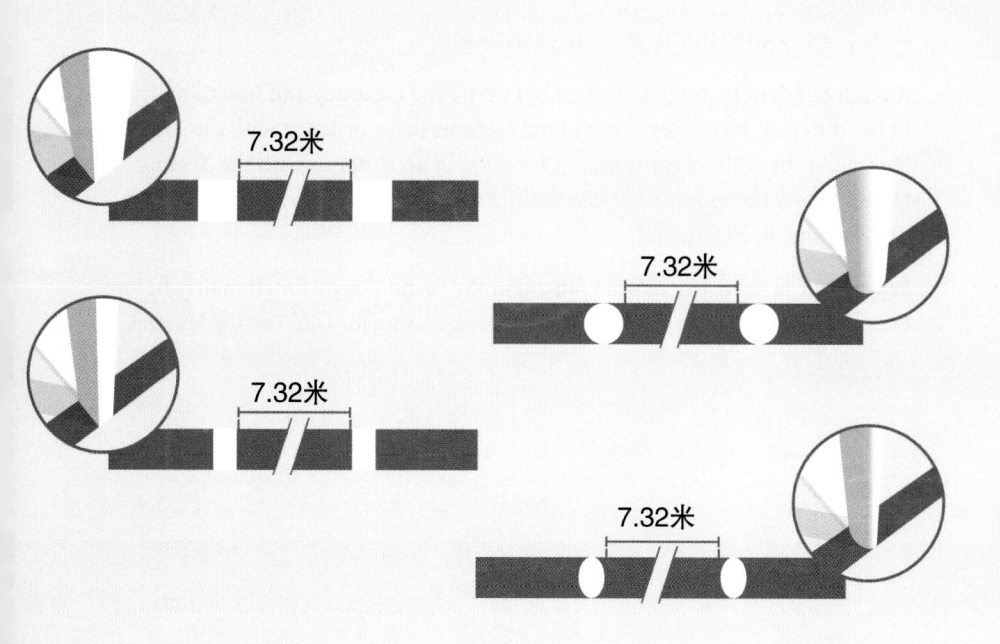

7.32米

7.32米

7.32米

7.32米

11. Goal Line Technology (GLT)

GLT systems may be used to verify whether a goal has been scored to support the referee's decision.

Where GLT is used, modifications to the goal frame may be permitted in accordance with the specifications stipulated in the FIFA Quality Programme for GLT and with the Laws of the Game. The use of GLT must be stipulated in the competition rules.

Principles of GLT

GLT applies solely to the goal line and is only used to determine whether a goal has been scored.

The indication of whether a goal has been scored must be immediate and automatically confirmed within one second by the GLT system only to the match officials (via the referee's watch, by vibration and visual signal).

Requirements and specifications of GLT

If GLT is used in competition matches, the competition organisers must ensure that the system is certified according to one of the following standards:

- FIFA Quality PRO
- FIFA Quality
- IMS - INTERNATIONAL MATCH STANDARD

An independent testing institute must verify the accuracy and functionality of the different technology providers' systems in accordance with the Testing Manual. If the technology does not function in accordance with the Testing Manual, the referee must not use the GLT system and must report this to the appropriate authority.

Where GLT is used, the referee must test the technology's functionality before the match as set out in the FIFA Quality Programme for GLT Testing Manual.

11. 球门线技术（GLT）

球门线技术系统可以用于帮助裁判员判定进球与否。

若比赛中使用球门线技术，则允许对球门框架进行改造，但需遵循《国际足联球门线技术质量项目》和《足球竞赛规则》的具体要求。如果使用球门线技术，必须在竞赛规程中注明。

球门线技术原则

球门线技术仅用于在球门线上判定进球与否。

有关进球与否的提示信号，必须在1秒钟内由球门线技术系统即时自动确认，该信息仅可传送给比赛官员（通过裁判员手表的震动和可视信号）。

球门线技术规定及要求

如果在比赛中使用球门线技术，竞赛组织方必须确保该系统符合如下任一标准：
- 国际足联专业品质。
- 国际足联品质。
- 国际比赛标准。

独立测试机构必须按照测试手册的要求，检测不同技术提供方系统的准确性和功能性。如果该技术未能达到测试手册要求的功能，则裁判员不得使用该球门线技术系统，且必须向相关机构报告。

使用球门线技术时，裁判员必须在赛前按照《国际足联质量项目——球门线技术测试手册》的要求，对该技术的功能进行测试。

12. Commercial advertising

No form of commercial advertising, whether real or virtual, is permitted on the field of play, on the ground within the area enclosed by the goal nets or the technical area, or on the ground within 1 m (1 yd) of the boundary lines from the time the teams enter the field of play until they have left it at half-time and from the time the teams re-enter the field of play until the end of the match. Advertising is not permitted on the goals, nets, flagposts or their flags and no extraneous equipment (cameras, microphones, etc.) may be attached to these items.

In addition, upright advertising must be at least:

- 1 m (1 yd) from the touchlines of the field of play
- the same distance from the goal line as the depth of the goal net
- 1 m (1 yd) from the goal net

13. Logos and emblems

The reproduction, whether real or virtual, of representative logos or emblems of FIFA, confederations, national football associations, competitions, clubs or other bodies is forbidden on the field of play, the goal nets and the areas they enclose, the goals, and the flagposts during playing time. They are permitted on the flags on the flagposts.

12. 商业广告

从球队进入比赛场地起至上半场结束离开，下半场重新进入比赛场地至比赛结束，任何形式的商业广告，无论是实体的还是虚拟的，都不允许出现在比赛场地内、球门网围合区域内的地面上，以及技术区域，或在场地边界线外1米以内的地面上。同样，广告也不得出现在球门、球门网、旗杆或旗杆的旗帜上，也不可将外部设备（如照相机、麦克风等）附着在这些场地器材上。

此外，直立的广告必须：
- 距离比赛场地边线至少1米（1码）。
- 距离球门线的距离至少等同于球门网的纵深。
- 距球门网至少1米。

13. 标志和图案

在比赛进行期间，国际足联、洲际足球联合会、国家足球协会、竞赛方、俱乐部，以及其他机构的代表性标志或图案的复制品，无论是实体还是虚拟形式，都禁止出现在比赛场地内、球门网及其围合区域、球门和旗杆上，但可出现在旗杆的旗帜上。

02. The Ball

1. Qualities and measurements

All balls must be:

- spherical
- made of suitable materiaal
- of a circumference of between 70 cm (28 ins) and 68 cm (27 ins)
- between 450 g (16 oz) and 410 g (14 oz) in weight at the start of the match
- of a pressure equal to 0.6 – 1.1 atmosphere (600 – 1,100 g/cm^2) at sea level (8.5 lbs/sq in – 15.6 lbs/sq in)

All balls used in matches played in an official competition organised under the auspices of FIFA or confederations must bear one of the following:

- FIFA Quality PRO
- FIFA Quality
- IMS - INTERNATIONAL MATCH STANDARD

Balls carrying previous quality marks such as "FIFA Approved", "FIFA Inspected" or "International Matchball Standard" may be used in aforementioned competitions until 31 July 2017.

Each mark indicates that it has been officially tested and meets the specific technical requirements for that mark which are additional to the minimum specifications stipulated in Law 2 and must be approved by The IFAB. The institutes conducting the tests are subject to the approval of FIFA.

Where goal line technology (GLT) is used, balls with integrated technology must carry one of the above listed quality marks.

第二章 球

1. 质量与测量

所有比赛用球必须：

- 是球形。
- 由合适的材料制成。
- 周长为68厘米（27英寸）至70厘米（28英寸）。
- 重量在比赛开始时为410克（14盎司）至450克（16盎司）。
- 气压处于0.6～1.1个海平面（标准）大气压力（600～1100克/平方厘米、8.5～15.6磅/平方英寸）。

由国际足联、洲际联合会主办的正式赛事中，使用的所有比赛用球必须印有如下标志之一：

- 国际足联专业品质
- 国际足联品质
- 国际比赛标准

此前印有"国际足联批准""国际足联监制"或"国际比赛用球标准"标志的球，仍可用于上述赛事直至2017年7月31日。

印有这些标志即表明该球已通过官方测试，符合与标志相对应的具体技术规定。这些标志是本章对比赛用球最低要求的补充，其使用也必须得到国际足球理事会批准。相关的检测机构也要得到国际足联的认证。

在使用球门线技术（GLT）时，含有集成技术的比赛用球必须印有上述三种标志之一。

National football association competitions may require the use of balls bearing one of these marks.

In matches played in an official competition organised under the auspices of FIFA, confederations or national football associations, no form of commercial advertising is permitted on the ball, except for the logo/emblem of the competition, the competition organiser and the authorised manufacturer's trademark. The competition regulations may restrict the size and number of such markings.

2. Replacement of a defective ball

If the ball becomes defective:

- play is stopped and
- restarted by dropping the replacement ball where the original ball became defective

If the ball becomes defective at a kick-off, goal kick, corner kick, free kick, penalty kick or throw-in the restart is re-taken.

If the ball becomes defective during a penalty kick or kicks from the penalty mark as it moves forward and before it touches a player, crossbar or goalposts the penalty kick is retaken.

The ball may not be changed during the match without the referee's permission.

3. Additional balls

Additional balls which meet the requirements of Law 2 may be placed around the field of play and their use is under the referee's control.

国家足球协会的赛事可以要求使用印有这些标志之一的比赛用球。

在由国际足联、洲际联合会或国家足球协会主办的正式比赛中，除赛事标志和图案、赛事组织方和授权制造商商标外，任何形式的商业广告均不允许出现在比赛用球上。竞赛规程可限定这些标识的大小和数量。

2. 坏球的更换

如果比赛用球出现破损：

- 停止比赛。
- 用更换的比赛用球在原球出现破损处以坠球恢复比赛。

如果比赛用球在开球、球门球、角球、任意球、罚球点球或掷界外球时出现破损，则以重新执行的方式恢复比赛。

如果比赛用球在罚球点球或球点球决胜期间，在被踢出并向前移动后，触及队员、横梁或球门柱之前出现破损，则重罚该球点球。

在比赛中未经裁判员许可，不得更换比赛用球。

3. 其他比赛用球

符合第二章规定的其他比赛用球可放置在比赛场地周围，在裁判员管理下使用。

03. The Players

1. Number of players

A match is played by two teams, each with a maximum of eleven players; one must be the goalkeeper. A match may not start <u>or continue</u> if either team has fewer than seven players.

If a team has fewer than seven players because one or more players has deliberately left the field of play, the referee is not obliged to stop play and the advantage may be played, but the match must not resume after the ball has gone out of play if a team does not have the minimum number of seven players.

If the competition rules state that all players and substitutes must be named before kick-off and a team starts a match with fewer than eleven players, only the players and substitutes named in the starting line-up may take part in the match upon their arrival.

2. Number of substitutions

Official competitions

A maximum of three substitutes may be used in any match played in an official competition organised under the auspices of FIFA, confederations or national football associations.

The competition rules must state how many substitutes may be named, from three to a maximum of twelve.

第三章 队员

1. 场上队员人数

　　一场比赛由两队参加，每队最多可有11名上场队员，其中1名必须为守门员。如果任何一队场上队员人数少于7人，则比赛不得开始或继续。

　　如果某队因1名或多名场上队员故意离开比赛场地，而造成队员人数少于7人，则裁判员不必停止比赛，可掌握有利继续比赛，但随后比赛停止时，如果某队场上队员人数仍不足7人，则比赛不得恢复。

　　如果竞赛规程规定，在比赛开始前必须提交所有上场队员和替补队员名单，而一队以不足11名上场队员的情况开始比赛，则只有在提交名单内的上场队员和替补队员可在到达赛场后参加比赛。

2. 替换人数
正式赛事

　　由国际足联、洲际联合会或国家足球协会主办的正式比赛中，每队最多可使用3名替补队员。

　　竞赛规程必须明确可提名的替补队员人数，从3名到最多不超过12名。

Other matches
In national "A" team matches, a maximum of six substitutes may be used.

In all other matches, a greater number of substitutes may be used provided that:

- the teams reach agreement on a maximum number
- the referee is informed before the match

If the referee is not informed, or if no agreement is reached before the match, each team is allowed a maximum of six substitutes.

Return substitutions
The use of return substitutions is only permitted in the lowest levels (grassroots/recreational) of football, subject to the agreement of the national football association.

3. Substitution procedure
The names of the substitutes must be given to the referee before the start of the match. Any substitute not named by this time may not take part in the match.

To replace a player with a substitute, the following must be observed:

- the referee must be informed before any substitution is made
- the player being substituted receives the referee's permission to leave the field of play, unless already off the field
- the player being replaced is not obliged to leave at the halfway line and takes no further part in the match, except where return substitutions are permitted
- if a player who is to be replaced refuses to leave, play continues

The substitute only enters:

- during a stoppage in play
- at the halfway line
- after the player being replaced has left
- after receiving a signal from the referee

其他比赛

在国家A队之间的比赛中，每队最多可使用6名替补队员。

其他所有比赛，遵从如下规定即可增加替换人数：

- 双方球队就替换人数上限达成一致。
- 比赛开始前告知裁判员。

如果赛前未告知裁判员、双方球队未达成一致，则每队最多可使用6名替补队员。

返场替换（已替换下场的队员重新上场比赛）

返场替换仅允许在最低级别的足球比赛中使用（草根/娱乐），前提是得到国家足球协会的同意。

3. 替换程序

替补队员名单必须在赛前向裁判员提交。任何未在此阶段提交名单的替补队员不得参加该场比赛。

替补队员替换场上队员时，必须遵从如下规定：

- 替换前必须通知裁判员。
- 被替换的队员经裁判员许可离开比赛场地，除非他已在比赛场地外。
- 被替换的队员不必经中线离开比赛场地。除非允许返场替换，否则他不得再次参加该场比赛。
- 如果被替换的队员拒绝离开比赛场地，则比赛继续。

替补队员遵从如下规定方可进入比赛场地：

- 在比赛停止时。
- 从中线处。
- 被替换的队员已离开比赛场地。
- 在得到裁判员信号后。

The substitution is completed when a substitute enters the field of play; from that moment, the substitute becomes a player and the replaced player becomes a substituted player.

Substitutes can take any restart provided they first enter the field of play.

If a substitution is made during the half-time interval or before extra time, the procedure must be completed before the match restarts.

All substituted players and substitutes are subject to the referee's authority whether they play or not.

4. Changing the goalkeeper

Any of the players may change places with the goalkeeper if:

- the referee is informed before the change is made
- the change is made during a stoppage in play

5. Infringements and sanctions

If a named substitute starts a match instead of a named player and the referee is not informed of this change:

- the referee allows the named substitute to continue playing
- no disciplinary sanction is taken against the named substitute
- the named player can become a named substitute
- the number of substitutions is not reduced
- the referee reports the incident to the appropriate authorities

If a player changes places with the goalkeeper without the referee's permission, the referee:

- allows play to continue
- cautions both players when the ball is next out of play

For any other infringements of this Law:

- the players are cautioned
- play is restarted with an indirect free kick, from the position of the ball when play was stopped

当替补队员进入比赛场地，替换程序即为完成。从此时起，替补队员成为场上队员、被替换的队员成为已替换下场的队员。

如果由替换上场的队员执行任一恢复比赛的程序，他必须先进入比赛场地。

如果在中场休息或加时赛开始前进行队员替换，替换程序必须在比赛恢复前完成。

所有已替换下场的队员和替补队员，无论其是否上场参赛，裁判员均可对其行使职权。

4. 更换守门员

任何场上队员都可与守门员互换位置：

- 互换位置前告知裁判员。
- 在比赛停止时互换位置。

5. 违规与处罚

如果一名被提名的替补队员在未告知裁判员的情况下，取代被提名的上场队员开始比赛：

- 裁判员允许该名替补队员继续比赛。
- 不必对该名替补队员执行纪律处罚。
- 原先被提名的上场队员视为被提名的替补队员。
- 替换人数不做削减。
- 裁判员向相关机构报告此事件。

如果一名场上队员未经裁判员允许与守门员互换位置，裁判员：

- 允许比赛继续。
- 在随后比赛停止时警告这两名队员。

对于其他任何违反本章条文的情况：

- 警告相关队员。
- 在比赛停止时球所在地点，以间接任意球恢复比赛。

6. Players and substitutes sent off

A player who is sent off:

- before submission of the team list can not be named on the team list in any capacity
- after being named on the team list and before kick-off may be replaced by a named substitute, who can not be replaced; the number of substitutions the team can make is not reduced
- after the kick-off can not be replaced

A named substitute who is sent off before or after the kick-off may not be replaced.

7. Extra persons on the field of play

The coach and other officials named on the team list (with the exception of players or substitutes) are team officials. Anyone not named on the team list as a player, substitute or team official is an outside agent.

If a team official, substitute, substituted or sent off player or outside agent enters the field of play the referee must:

- only stop play if there is interference with play
- have the person removed when play stops
- take appropriate disciplinary action

If play is stopped and the interference was by:

- a team official, substitute, substituted or sent off player, play restarts with a direct free kick or penalty kick
- an outside agent, play restarts with a dropped ball

If a ball is going into the goal and the interference does not prevent a defending player playing the ball, the goal is awarded if the ball enters the goal (even if contact was made with the ball) unless the ball enters the opponents' goal.

6. 场上队员和替补队员被罚令出场

上场队员被罚令出场：
- 在球队名单提交前被罚令出场，不得以任何身份列入球队名单内。
- 在提交球队名单后，比赛开始前被罚令出场，可由被提名的替补队员取代，替补队员名单不得增补，球队的替换人数不做削减。
- 在比赛开始后被罚令出场，不得被替换。

被提名的替补队员在比赛开始前或比赛开始后被罚令出场，替补队员名单均不得增补。

7. 比赛场地内多出的人员

列入球队名单的教练员和其他官员（上场队员和替补队员除外）视为球队官员。除球队名单内的上场队员、替补队员以及球队官员外，其他任何人员视为场外因素。

如果球队官员、替补队员、已替换下场或被罚令出场的队员，以及场外因素进入比赛场地内，裁判员必须：
- 当存在干扰比赛的情况才可停止比赛。
- 在比赛停止时，责令无关人员离开比赛场地。
- 采取相应的纪律措施。

如果比赛停止是由如下干扰造成：
- 球队官员、替补队员、已替换下场或被罚令出场的队员，则以直接任意球或球点球恢复比赛。
- 场外因素，则以坠球恢复比赛。

如果球将要进门时，干扰因素没有阻止防守队员处理球，随后球进门，则进球有效（即便干扰因素与球发生接触），除非球进入对方球门。

8. **Player outside the field of play**

    If, after leaving the field of play with the referee's permission, a player re-enters without the referee's permission, the referee must:

    - stop play (not immediately if the player does not interfere with play or if the advantage can be applied)
    - caution the player for entering the field of play without permission
    - order the player to leave the field of play

    If the referee stops play, it must be restarted:

    - with an indirect free kick from the position of the ball when play was stopped or
    - in accordance with Law 12 if the player infringes this Law

    A player who crosses a boundary line as part of a playing movement, does not commit an infringement.

9. **Goal scored with an extra person on the field of play**

    If, after a goal is scored, the referee realises, before play restarts, an extra person was on the field of play when the goal was scored:

    - the referee must disallow the goal if the extra person was:
        - a player, substitute, substituted player, sent off player or team official of the team that scored the goal
        - an outside agent who interfered with play unless a goal results as outlined above in 'extra persons on the field of play'

    Play is restarted with a goal kick, corner kick or dropped ball.

    - the referee must allow the goal if the extra person was:
        - a player, substitute, substituted player, sent off player or team official of the team that conceded the goal
        - an outside agent who did not interfere with play

8. 比赛场地外的队员

如果一名场上队员经裁判员允许离开比赛场地，随后未经裁判员许可重新进入比赛场地内，裁判员必须：

- 停止比赛（如果该名队员未干扰比赛或出现可掌握有利的情况，不必立即停止比赛）。
- 以未经允许进入比赛场地为由警告该名队员。
- 责令该名队员离开比赛场地。

如果裁判员停止比赛，比赛必须：
- 在比赛停止时球所在地点以间接任意球恢复。
- 若该名队员违反规则第十二章条文，则按相应程序恢复。

场上队员在正常比赛移动中越过边界线，不应视为违反规则。

9. 比赛场地内多出人员时出现进球

如果裁判员在进球后，比赛恢复前意识到进球时比赛场地内有多出的人员：

- 如果多出的人员是如下人员，裁判员必须判定进球无效：
  - 进球队一方的场上队员、替补队员、已替换下场或被罚令出场的队员及球队官员。
  - 干扰了比赛的场外因素，除非进球符合本章第7条"比赛场地内多出的人员"的说明。

以球门球、角球或坠球恢复比赛。

- 如果多出的人员是如下人员，裁判员必须判定进球有效：
  - 被进球队一方的场上队员、替补队员、已替换下场或被罚令出场的队员及球队官员。
  - 没有干扰比赛的场外因素。

In all cases, the referee must have the extra person removed from the field of play.

If, after a goal is scored and play has restarted, the referee realises an extra person was on the field of play when the goal was scored, the goal can not be disallowed. If the extra person is still on the field the referee must:

- stop play
- have the extra person removed
- restart with a dropped ball or free kick as appropriate

The referee must report the incident to the appropriate authorities.

10. Team captain

The team captain has no special status or privileges but has a degree of responsibility for the behaviour of the team.

无论何种情况，裁判员必须责令多出的人员离开比赛场地。

如果裁判员在出现进球，且已经恢复比赛后意识到发生进球时比赛场地内有多出的人员，则不得取消进球。如果多出的人员仍在比赛场地内，裁判员必须：
- 停止比赛。
- 责令多出的人员离开比赛场地。
- 以坠球或相应的任意球方式恢复比赛。

裁判员必须向相关机构报告此事件。

10. 球队队长
球队队长并不享有特殊身份或权力，但他对球队的行为需承担一定责任。

04. The Players' Equipment

1. Safety

A player must not use equipment or wear anything that is dangerous.

All items of jewellery (necklaces, rings, bracelets, earrings, leather bands, rubber bands, etc.) are forbidden and must be removed. Using tape to cover jewellery is not permitted.

The players must be inspected before the start of the match and substitutes before they enter the field of play. If a player is wearing or using unauthorised/dangerous equipment or jewellery the referee must order the player to:

- remove the item
- leave the field of play at the next stoppage if the player is unable or unwilling to comply

A player who refuses to comply or wears the item again must be cautioned.

2. Compulsory equipment

The compulsory equipment of a player comprises the following separate items:

- a shirt with sleeves
- shorts
- socks – tape or <u>any material applied or worn externally</u> must be the same colour as that part of the sock it is applied to <u>or covers</u>
- shinguards – these must be made of a suitable material to provide reasonable protection and covered by the socks
- footwear

Goalkeepers may wear tracksuit bottoms.

第四章 队员装备

1. 安全性

队员不得使用或佩戴具有危险性的装备或任何物件。

禁止佩戴任何类型的珠宝首饰（项链、指环、手镯、耳坠、皮质带、橡胶带等），如有佩戴必须移除。不允许用胶带覆盖珠宝首饰。

上场队员必须在比赛开始前、替补队员则在进入比赛场地前接受检查。如果场上队员穿戴或使用了未授权/具有危险性的装备或珠宝首饰，裁判员必须令其：

- 移除相关物件。
- 如果队员暂时无法或不愿将物件摘除，则需在随后比赛停止时，离开比赛场地摘除。

拒绝摘除或再次穿戴相关物件的队员，必须对其予以警告。

2. 必要装备

场上队员的必要装备包括如下单独分开的物件：

- 有袖上衣。
- 短裤。
- 护袜——胶带或任何附着、外套的材料，其颜色必须与所附着或包裹部分的护袜颜色一致。
- 护腿板——护腿板必须由能提供一定保护的合适材料制成，由护袜完全包裹。
- 鞋子。

守门员可穿着长裤。

A player whose footwear or shinguard is lost accidentally must replace it as soon as possible and no later than when the ball next goes out of play;
if before doing so the player plays the ball and/or scores a goal, the goal is awarded.

3. **Colours**
   - The two teams must wear colours that distinguish them from each other and the match officials
   - Each goalkeeper must wear colours that are distinguishable from the other players and the match officials
   - If the two goalkeepers' shirts are the same colour and neither has another shirt, the referee allows the match to be played

   Undershirts must be the same colour as the main colour of the shirt sleeve; undershorts/tights must be the same colour as the main colour of the shorts or the lowest part of the shorts – players of the same team must wear the same colour.

4. **Other equipment**

   Non-dangerous protective equipment, for example headgear, facemasks and knee and arm protectors made of soft, lightweight padded material is permitted as are goalkeepers' caps and sports spectacles.

   Where head covers are worn, they must:

   - be black or the same main colour as the shirt (provided that the players of the same team wear the same colour)
   - be in keeping with the professional appearance of the player's equipment
   - not be attached to the shirt
   - not be dangerous to the player wearing it or any other player (e.g. opening/closing mechanism around neck)
   - not have any part(s) extending out from the surface (protruding elements)

   The use of any form of electronic communication between players (including substitutes/substituted and sent off players) and/or technical staff is not permitted.

意外脱落鞋子或护腿板的场上队员，必须在随后比赛停止前尽快整理好装备，如果该名队员在整理好装备前触球且/或射门得分，则进球有效。

3. 着装颜色
- 队员的着装颜色必须有别于对方球队和比赛官员。
- 双方守门员着装颜色必须有别于其他场上队员和比赛官员。
- 如果双方守门员的上衣颜色相同且无法更换，裁判员允许比赛进行。

上衣内衣颜色必须与衣袖主色一致；内衬裤/紧身裤颜色必须与短裤主色或短裤底部颜色一致——同队场上队员必须颜色统一。

4. 其他装备
可允许佩戴不具危险性的保护器具，如软性、轻质材料制成的头罩、面具、护膝和护臂，类似的还包括守门员球帽和运动眼镜等。

如需佩戴头巾，其必须：
- 为黑色或与上衣主色一致（同队场上队员必须颜色统一）。
- 设计合乎球员装备专业形象。
- 不得与上衣相连。
- 不会对佩戴者个人和其他队员构成危险（如在颈部有可开合的装置）。
- 不能有任何部分凸出头巾表面（突出表面的部件）。

不允许队员（包括替补队员/已替换下场和被罚令出场队员）和／或技术人员使用任何形式的电子通讯设备。

Where electronic performance and tracking systems (EPTS) are used (subject to the agreement of the national football association/competition organiser):

- they must not be dangerous
- information and data transmitted from the devices/systems is not permitted to be received or used in the technical area during the match

Equipment must not have any political, religious or personal slogans, statements or images. Players must not reveal undergarments that show political, religious, personal slogans, statements or images, or advertising other than the manufacturer's logo. For any infringement the player and/or the team will be sanctioned by the competition organiser, national football association or to be justified by FIFA.

5. Infringements and sanctions

For any infringement of this Law play need not be stopped and the player:

- is instructed by the referee to leave the field of play to correct the equipment
- leaves when play stops, unless the equipment has already been corrected

A player who leaves the field of play to correct or change his equipment must:

- have the equipment checked by a match official before being allowed to re-enter
- only re-enter with the referee's permission (which may be given during play)

A player who enters without permission must be cautioned and if play is stopped to issue the caution, an indirect free kick is awarded from the position of the ball when play was stopped.

使用表现跟踪电子系统（EPTS）时（遵从国家足球协会/赛事组织方规定）：
- 相关系统必须不具备危险性。
- 在比赛中，不允许在技术区域内接收或使用该装置/系统传送的信息和数据。

队员装备不得带有任何政治性、宗教性、个人化的标语、言论或图像。队员不得展示内衣、裤上带有任何政治性、宗教性、个人化的标语、言论或图像，以及生产商标志以外的广告。任何违反规定的队员和/或球队将由赛事组织方、国家足球协会或国际足联处理。

5. 违规与处罚

无需为任何违反本章条文的行为停止比赛，违规的场上队员：
- 由裁判员引导离开比赛场地调整装备。
- 除非已经调整好装备，否则需在比赛停止时离开比赛场地。

离开比赛场地调整或更换装备的队员必须：
- 由一名比赛官员在其被许可重新进入比赛场地前检查好装备。
- 只可在裁判员许可后重新进入比赛场地（可在比赛进行中）。

未经裁判员允许进入比赛场地的队员必须予以警告，如果因警告而停止比赛，则在比赛停止时球所在地点以间接任意球恢复比赛。

05. The Referee

1. **The authority of the referee**
   Each match is controlled by a referee who has full authority to enforce the Laws of the Game in connection with the match.

2. **Decisions of the referee**
   Decisions will be made to the best of the referee's ability according to the Laws of the Game and the 'spirit of the game' and will be based on the opinion of the referee who has the discretion to take appropriate action within the framework of the Laws of the Game.

   The decisions of the referee regarding facts connected with play, including whether or not a goal is scored and the result of the match, are final.

   The referee may not change a decision on realising that it is incorrect or on the advice of another match official if play has restarted or the referee has signalled the end of the first or second half (including extra time) and left the field of play or terminated the match.

   If a referee is incapacitated, play may continue under the supervision of the other match officials until the ball is next out of play.

3. **Powers and duties**
   The referee:

   - enforces the Laws of the Game
   - controls the match in cooperation with the other match officials
   - acts as timekeeper, keeps a record of the match and provides the appropriate authorities with a match report, including information on disciplinary action and any other incidents that occurred before, during or after the match
   - supervises and/or indicates the restart of play

第五章　裁判员

1. 裁判员的权力

每场比赛由一名裁判员掌控，他有全部权力去执行与比赛相关的竞赛规则。

2. 裁判员的决定

裁判员依据《足球竞赛规则》和"足球运动精神"，尽自身最大能力，在规则框架内酌情考量，做出自己认为最合适的决定。

裁判员根据与比赛相关的事实所做出的决定，包括进球与否以及比赛的结果，都是最终的决定。

如果裁判员本人，或经其他比赛官员建议后意识到自己决定错误，而比赛已经恢复，或裁判员已经示意上下半场结束（包括加时赛）并离开比赛场地，或已经中止了比赛，则不可更改判罚决定。

如果裁判员无法继续执法，比赛可在其他比赛官员的监管下继续进行，直到随后比赛停止。

3. 权力和职责

裁判员：
- 执行《足球竞赛规则》。
- 与其他比赛官员协作管理比赛。
- 记录比赛时间、比赛成绩、并向相关机构提交比赛报告，报告内容包括赛前、赛中、赛后发生的纪律处罚信息及任何其他事件。
- 监管和/或示意比赛恢复。

Advantage
- allows play to continue when an infringement or offence occurs and the non-offending team will benefit from the advantage and penalises the infringement or offence if the anticipated advantage does not ensue at that time or within a few seconds

Disciplinary action
- punishes the more serious offence, in terms of sanction, restart, physical severity and tactical impact, when more than one offence occurs at the same time
- takes disciplinary action against players guilty of cautionable and sending-off offences
- has the authority to take disciplinary action from entering the field of play for the pre-match inspection until leaving the field of play after the match ends (including kicks from the penalty mark). If, before entering the field of play at the start of the match, a player commits a sending-off offence, the referee has the authority to prevent the player taking part in the match (see Law 3.6); the referee will report any other misconduct
- has the power to show yellow or red cards from entering the field of play at the start of the match until after the match has ended, including during the half-time interval, extra time and kicks from the penalty mark
- takes action against team officials who fail to act in a responsible manner and may expel them from the field of play and its immediate surrounds
- acts on the advice of other match officials regarding incidents that the referee has not seen

Injuries
- allows play to continue until the ball is out of play if a player is only slightly injured
- stops play if a player is seriously injured and ensures that the player is removed from the field of play. An injured player may not be treated on the field of play and may only re-enter after play has restarted; if the ball is in play, re-entry must be from the touchline but if the ball is out of play, it may be from any boundary line. Exceptions to the requirement to leave the field of play are only when:

有利
- 当犯规或违规情况发生时，未犯规或违规的一队能从有利原则中获益，则允许比赛继续。如果预期的有利没有在那一时刻或随后几秒内出现，则判罚最初的犯规或违规。

纪律处罚
- 当多种犯规同时发生时，从纪律处罚、比赛恢复方式、身体接触程度和战术影响等方面考量，判罚相对严重的犯规。
- 对应被警告和罚令出场的队员执行纪律处罚。
- 从进入比赛场地开始赛前检查直至比赛结束（包括球点球决胜）离开比赛场地，裁判员均有权执行纪律处罚。如果在开赛进入场地前，一名上场队员犯有可被罚令出场的犯规，裁判员有权阻止其参加该场比赛（详见第三章第6条），并将任何其他不正当行为上报。
- 从开赛前进入比赛场地直至比赛结束，包括中场休息、加时赛和球点球决胜期间，裁判员都有权出示红黄牌。
- 向对自己行为不负责任的球队官员采取处罚措施，可将其驱逐出比赛场地及其周边区域。
- 对于自己未看到的情况，根据其他比赛官员的建议做出判罚决定。

受伤
- 如果队员仅是轻微受伤，则允许比赛继续直至比赛停止。
- 如果队员严重受伤，则停止比赛，确保受伤队员离开比赛场地。受伤队员不可在比赛场地内接受治疗，在比赛恢复后才可重新进入比赛场地；如果比赛在进行中，受伤队员必须从边线处入场；比赛停止时，则可从任一边界线入场。当发生如下情况时，不必遵循离场治疗的规定：

- a goalkeeper is injured
- a goalkeeper and an outfield player have collided and need attention
- players from the same team have collided and need attention
- a severe injury has occurred
- <u>a player is injured as the result of a physical offence for which the opponent is cautioned or sent off (e.g. reckless or serious foul challenge), if the assessment/treatment is completed quickly</u>

- ensures that any player bleeding leaves the field of play. The player may only re-enter on receiving a signal from the referee, who must be satisfied that the bleeding has stopped and there is no blood on the equipment
- if the referee has authorised the doctors and /or stretcher bearers to enter the field of play, the player must leave on a stretcher or on foot. A player who does not comply, must be cautioned for unsporting behaviour
- if the referee has decided to caution or send off a player who is injured and has to leave the field of play for treatment, the card must be shown before the player leaves
- if play has not been stopped for another reason, or if an injury suffered by a player is not the result of an infringement of the Laws of the Game, play is restarted with a dropped ball

Outside interference
- stops, suspends or abandons the match for any infringements of the Laws or because of outside interference e.g. if:

  - the floodlights are inadequate
  - an object thrown by a spectator hits a match official, a player or team official, the referee may allow the match to continue, or stop, suspend or abandon it depending on the severity of the incident
  - a spectator blows a whistle which interferes with play - play is stopped and restarted with a dropped ball
  - an extra ball, other object or animal enters the field of play during the match, the referee must:

- 守门员受伤时。
- 守门员与其他队员发生碰撞，需要引起关注时。
- 同队队员发生碰撞，需要引起关注时。
- 出现严重受伤时。
- 场上队员因遭受对方队员有身体接触，且可被警告或罚令出场的犯规（如鲁莽或严重犯规性质的抢截）而受伤，其伤情能够在短时间完成评估/得到治疗时。
- 确保任何流血的队员离开比赛场地。必须在其流血已被止住、装备没有血迹的情况下，经裁判员示意后，才可重新进入比赛场地。
- 如果裁判员已经指示医生和/或担架手进入比赛场地，受伤队员必须在担架上或自行离开比赛场地。未遵从该条文的受伤队员必须以非体育行为予以警告。
- 如果裁判员已经决定要对需要离场接受治疗的受伤队员予以警告或罚令出场，必须在其离场前出示红黄牌。
- 如果不是因为类似原因而暂停比赛，或队员受伤并不是因违反竞赛规则造成的，则以坠球恢复比赛。

场外干扰

- 裁判员可就任何违反规则的情况或场外干扰等原因暂停、中断或中止比赛，如：
- 比赛场地照明灯光不足。
- 观众掷入的物品击中比赛官员、参赛队员或球队官员，裁判员就事件的严重程度决定继续、暂停、中断或中止比赛。
- 观众鸣哨干扰比赛——裁判员停止比赛，随后以坠球恢复比赛。
- 比赛进行中，多余的球、其他物品或动物出现在场内，裁判员必须：

> stop play (and restart with a dropped ball) only if it interferes with play unless the ball is going into the goal and the interference does not prevent a defending player playing the ball, the goal is awarded if the ball enters the goal (even if contact was made with the ball) unless the ball enters the opponents' goal
> allow play to continue if it does not interfere with play and have it removed at the earliest possible opportunity

- allows no unauthorised persons to enter the field of play

4. Referee's equipment
Compulsory equipment:
- Whistle(s)
- Watch(es)
- Red and yellow cards
- Notebook (or other means of keeping a record of the match)

Other equipment
Referees may be permitted to use:

- Equipment for communicating with other match officials – buzzer/beep flags, headsets etc.
- EPTS or other fitness monitoring equipment

Referees and other match officials are prohibited from wearing jewellery or any other electronic equipment.

5. Referee signals
Refer to graphics for approved referee signals.

In addition to the current 'two armed' signal for an advantage, a similar 'one arm' signal is now permitted as it is not always easy for referees to run with both arms extended.

> 只有当其干扰了比赛，裁判员才停止比赛（随后以坠球恢复比赛），除非球将要进门，干扰因素没有阻止防守队员处理球，且随后球进门，则视为进球有效（即便干扰因素与球发生接触），除非球进入另一方球门。
> 如果其未干扰比赛，则裁判员允许比赛继续，并尽早将其移出比赛场地。
- 未经授权的人员不得进入比赛场地。

4. 裁判员的装备

必要装备：
- 一个或多个口哨。
- 一块或多块手表。
- 红黄牌。
- 记录簿（或其他可记录比赛情况的用具）。

其他装备

可允许裁判员使用：
- 与其他比赛官员进行交流的设备——振动/蜂鸣信号旗、耳麦等。
- 表现跟踪电子系统或其他体质监测设备。

禁止裁判员和其他比赛官员佩戴珠宝首饰或任何其他电子设备。

5. 裁判员的示意信号

参见裁判员示意信号图例。

除现行的"双手"示意有利信号外，"单手"示意有利现在也允许，因为裁判员展开双臂跑动并不轻松。

Indirect free kick

Direct free kick

Advantage (1)

Advantage (2)

间接任意球　　　　　　　　直接任意球

有利（1）　　　　　　　　有利（2）

Penalty kick

Red and **Yellow** card

Corner kick

Goal kick

罚球点球

红牌、黄牌

角球

球门球

6. Liability of Match Officials

A referee or other match official is not held liable for:

- any kind of injury suffered by a player, official or spectator
- any damage to property of any kind
- any other loss suffered by any individual, club, company, association or other body, which is due or which may be due to any decision taken under the terms of the Laws of the Game or in respect of the normal procedures required to hold, play and control a match.

Such decisions may include a decision:

- that the condition of the field of play or its surrounds or that the weather conditions are such as to allow or not to allow a match to take place
- to abandon a match for whatever reason
- as to the suitability of the field equipment and ball used during a match
- to stop or not to stop a match due to spectator interference or any problem in spectator areas
- to stop or not to stop play to allow an injured player to be removed from the field of play for treatment
- to require an injured player to be removed from the field of play for treatment
- to allow or not to allow a player to wear certain clothing or equipment
- where the referee has the authority, to allow or not to allow any persons (including team or stadium officials, security officers, photographers or other media representatives) to be present in the vicinity of the field of play
- any other decision taken in accordance with the Laws of the Game or in conformity with their duties under the terms of FIFA, confederation, national football association or competition rules or regulations under which the match is played

6. 比赛官员的责任

裁判员或其他比赛官员不对如下情况承担责任：
- 参赛队员、官员或观众任何形式的受伤。
- 任何形式的财产损失。
- 由于或可能由于根据竞赛规则，或按照正常程序要求做出的维持、继续和管理比赛的决定，对任何个人、俱乐部、公司、协会或其他机构所造成的任何损失。

这些决定可能包括：
- 就比赛场地及其周边环境，或天气状况决定是否进行比赛。
- 因无论何种原因决定中止比赛。
- 比赛场地器材和比赛用球是否适合在比赛中使用。
- 根据观众的影响或观众区域的任何问题，决定是否停止比赛。
- 是否停止比赛将受伤队员移至场外治疗。
- 要求受伤队员移至场外治疗。
- 是否允许队员穿着某种服装或佩戴某种设备。
- 在有权时，决定是否允许任何人员（包括球队或球场官员、安保人员、摄像师或者其他媒体代表）出现在比赛场地附近区域。
- 根据竞赛规则或国际足联、洲际联合会、国家足球协会条款，或比赛所涉及的竞赛规程履行职责时所做出的决定。

06. The Other Match Officials

Other match officials (two assistant referees, fourth official, two additional assistant referees and reserve assistant referee) may be appointed to matches. They will assist the referee in controlling the match in accordance with the Laws of the Game but the final decision will always be taken by the referee.

The match officials operate under the direction of the referee. In the event of undue interference or improper conduct, the referee will relieve them of their duties and make a report to the appropriate authorities.

With the exception of the reserve assistant referee, they assist the referee with offences and infringements when they have a clearer view than the referee and they must submit a report to the appropriate authorities on any serious misconduct or other incident that occurred out of the view of the referee and the other match officials. They must advise the referee and other match officials of any report being made.

The match officials assist the referee with inspecting the field of play, the balls and players' equipment (including if problems have been resolved) and maintaining records of time, goals, misconduct etc.

Competition rules must state clearly who replaces a match official who is unable to start or continue and any associated changes. In particular, it must be clear whether, if the referee is unable to continue, the fourth official or the senior assistant referee or senior additional assistant referee takes over.

第六章　其他比赛官员

可选派其他比赛官员（两名助理裁判员、一名第四官员、两名附加助理裁判员，以及候补助理裁判员）执法比赛。他们根据竞赛规则协助裁判员管理比赛，但最终决定必须由裁判员做出。

比赛官员在裁判员的领导下履行各自职责。如果出现不当的干涉或行为，裁判员可解除其职权，并向相关机构提交报告。

除候补助理裁判员外，当其他比赛官员的观察角度比裁判员更好时，需提示裁判员发生的犯规和违规情况，并就裁判员或其他比赛官员视线范围外发生的任何严重不当行为或其他事件，向有关机构提交报告。在完成报告前，必须与裁判员和其他比赛官员商议。

其他比赛官员协助裁判员检查比赛场地、比赛用球及队员装备（包括再次检查相关问题是否已被解决），以及记录比赛时间、进球、不正当行为等。

竞赛规程必须明确由谁替换不能开始或继续执法的比赛官员，以及任何相应产生的更替。尤其要明确，当裁判员不能继续执法时，是由第四官员、第一助理裁判员，还是第一附加助理裁判员替换。

1. **Assistant referees**

    They indicate when:

    - the whole of the ball leaves the field of play and which team is entitled to a corner kick, goal kick or throw-in
    - a player in an offside position may be penalised
    - a substitution is requested
    - at penalty kicks, the goalkeeper moves off the goal line before the ball is kicked and if the ball crosses the line; if additional assistant referees have been appointed the assistant referee takes a position in line with the penalty mark

    The assistant referee's assistance also includes monitoring the substitution procedure.

    The assistant referee may enter the field of play to help control the 9.15m (10 yards) distance.

2. **Fourth official**

    The fourth official's assistance also includes:

    - supervising the substitution procedure
    - checking a player's/substitute's equipment
    - the re-entry of a player following a signal/approval from the referee
    - supervising the replacement balls
    - indicating the minimum amount of additional time the referee intends to play at the end of each half (including extra time)
    - informing the referee of irresponsible behaviour by any technical area occupant

3. **Additional assistant referees**

    The additional assistant referees may indicate:

    - when the whole of the ball passes over the goal line, including when a goal is scored
    - which team is entitled to a corner kick or goal kick
    - whether, at penalty kicks, the goalkeeper moves off the goal line before the ball is kicked and if the ball crosses the line

1. 助理裁判员

当出现如下情况时，给予示意：
- 球的整体离开比赛场地，应由哪一队踢角球、球门球或掷界外球。
- 处于越位位置的队员可被判罚越位。
- 申请队员替换。
- 在罚球点球时，守门员是否在球被踢出前离开球门线，以及球是否越过球门线。如果比赛选派附加助理裁判员，则助理裁判员的选位应在与罚球点齐平的位置上。

助理裁判员的协助也包括监管队员替换程序。
助理裁判员可进入比赛场地管理9.15米（10码）的距离。

2. 第四官员

第四官员的协助包括：
- 监管队员替换程序。
- 检查场上队员/替补队员的装备。
- 在裁判员示意/同意后让场上队员重新进入比赛场地。
- 监管用于更换使用的比赛用球。
- 在各半场（包括加时赛）结束时，展示裁判员将要补足的最短补时时间。
- 将技术区域人员的不当行为告知裁判员。

3. 附加助理裁判员

附加助理裁判员需示意：
- 当球的整体越过球门线，包括进球得分时。
- 哪一队踢角球或球门球。
- 在罚球点球时，守门员是否在球被踢出前离开球门线，以及球是否越过球门线。

4. **Reserve assistant referee**
   The only duty of a reserve assistant referee is to replace an assistant referee or fourth official who is unable to continue.

5. **Assistant referee signals**

Substitution

Attacking free kicks

Defending free kicks

4. 候补助理裁判员

候补助理裁判员的唯一任务是替换不能继续执法的助理裁判员或第四官员。

5. 助理裁判员的信号

替换队员

攻方踢任意球

守方踢任意球

Throw-in for **attacke**r

Throw-in for **defender**

Corner kick

Goal kick

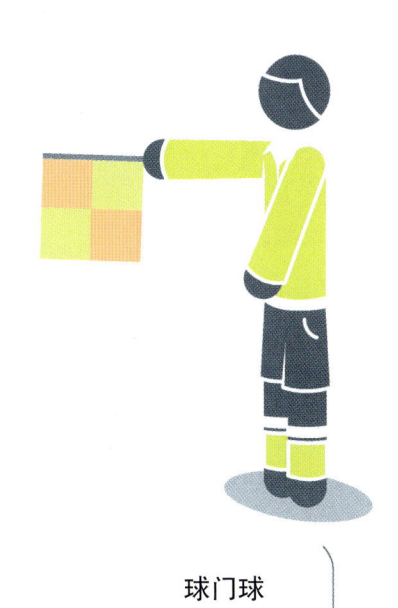

攻方掷界外球 守方掷界外球

角球 球门球

1 — Offside

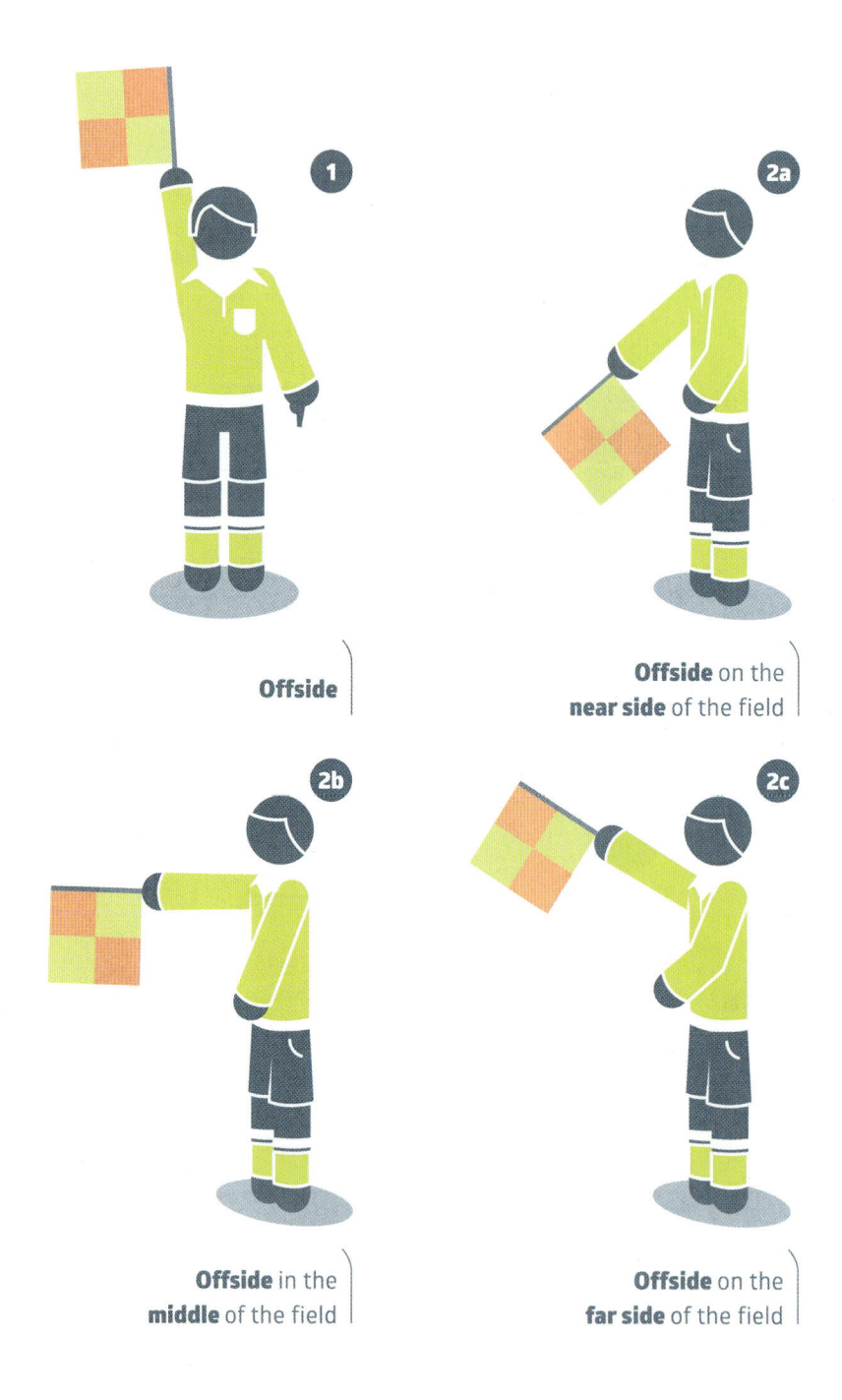

2a — **Offside** on the **near side** of the field

2b — **Offside** in the **middle** of the field

2c — **Offside** on the **far side** of the field

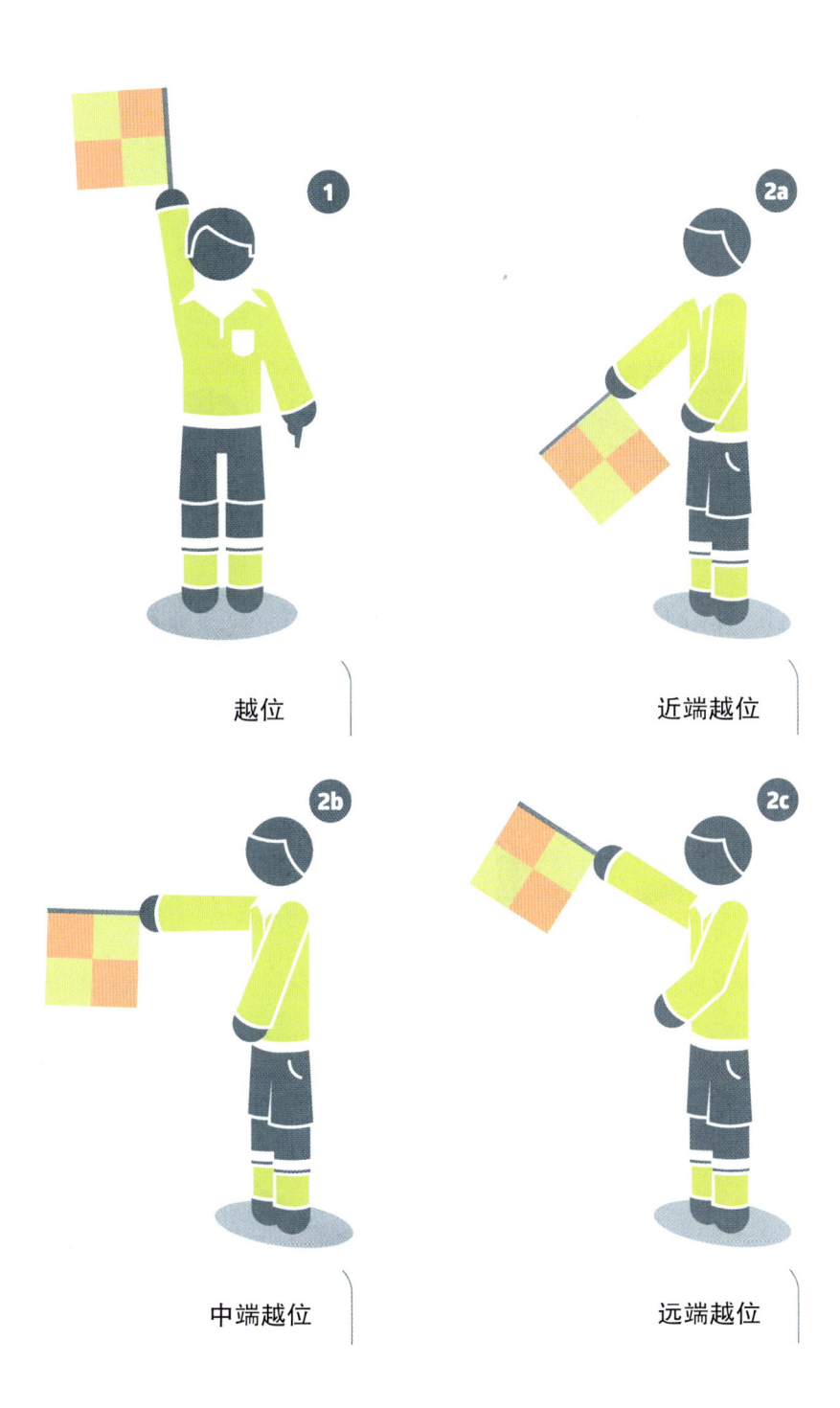

越位

近端越位

中端越位

远端越位

6. Additional assistant referee signals

goal
(unless the ball has very clearly passed over the goal line)

6. 附加助理裁判员的信号

进球
（除非球明显越过球门线）

07. The Duration of the Match

1. Periods of play

A match lasts for two equal halves of 45 minutes which may only be reduced if agreed between the referee and the two teams before the start of the match and is in accordance with competition rules.

2. Half-time interval

Players are entitled to an interval at half-time, not exceeding 15 minutes. Competition rules must state the duration of the half-time interval and it may be altered only with the referee's permission.

3. Allowance for time lost

Allowance is made by the referee in each half for all time lost in that half through:

- substitutions
- assessment and/or removal of injured players
- wasting time
- disciplinary sanctions
- stoppages for drinks or other medical reasons permitted by competition rules
- any other cause, including any significant delay to a restart (e.g. goal celebrations)

The fourth official indicates the minimum additional time decided by the referee at the end of the final minute of each half. The additional time may be increased by the referee but not reduced.

The referee must not compensate for a timekeeping error during the first half by changing the length of the second half.

第七章 比赛时间

1. 比赛阶段
　　一场比赛分为两个45分钟相同时长的半场。依照竞赛规程，在比赛开始前经裁判员和双方球队同意后，方可缩短各半场比赛时长。

2. 中场休息
　　队员享有中场休息的权利，休息时间不得超过15分钟。竞赛规程必须明确中场休息的时长，在经裁判员许可的情况下方可调整中场休息时长。

3. 对损耗时间的补足
　　裁判员对每半场所有因如下情况而损耗的时间予以补足：
- 队员替换。
- 对受伤队员的伤情评估和/或将其移出比赛场地。
- 浪费的时间。
- 纪律处罚。
- 竞赛规程允许的因补水或其他医疗原因造成的暂停。
- 任何其他原因，包括任何明显延误比赛恢复的情况（如庆祝进球）。

　　第四官员在每半场最后一分钟结束时展示裁判员决定的最短补时时间。裁判员可增加补时时间，但不得减少。

　　裁判员不得因上半场计时失误而改变下半场的比赛时长。

4. **Penalty kick**

   If a penalty kick has to be taken or retaken, the half is extended until the penalty kick is completed.

5. **Abandoned match**

   An abandoned match is replayed unless the competition rules or organisers determine otherwise.

4. 罚球点球

如需执行罚球点球或重罚球点球，应延长该半场时长直至罚球点球程序完成。

5. 中止的比赛

除非竞赛规程规定，或主办方另有决议，否则中止的比赛需进行重赛。

08. The Start and Restart of Play

A kick-off starts both halves of a match, both halves of extra time and restarts play after a goal has been scored. Free kicks (direct or indirect), penalty kicks, throw-ins, goal kicks and corner kicks are other restarts (see Laws 13 – 17).
A dropped ball is the restart when the referee stops play and the Law does not require one of the above restarts.

If an infringement occurs when the ball is not in play this does not change how play is restarted.

1. **Kick-off**
   Procedure
   - the team that wins the toss of a coin decides which goal it will attack in the first half
   - their opponents take the kick-off
   - the team that wins the toss takes the kick-off to start the second half
   - for the second half, the teams change ends and attack the opposite goals
   - after a team scores a goal, the kick-off is taken by their opponents

   For every kick-off:

   - all players must be in their own half of the field of play
   - the opponents of the team taking the kick-off must be at least 9.15 m (10 yds) from the ball until it is in play
   - the ball must be stationary on the centre mark
   - the referee gives a signal
   - the ball is in play when it is kicked and clearly moves
   - a goal may be scored directly against the opponents from the kick-off

第八章　比赛开始与恢复

一场比赛各半场、加时赛各半场、进球后均以开球恢复比赛。任意球（直接或间接任意球）、罚球点球、掷界外球、球门球和角球是其他恢复比赛的方式（详见规则第十三章至第十七章）。当裁判员暂停比赛，而规则未明确以上述任何一种方式恢复比赛时，以坠球恢复比赛。

比赛停止时发生的违规违例行为，不会改变随后恢复比赛的方式。

1. 开球

程序

- 掷硬币猜中的一队决定上半场进攻方向。
- 另一队开球。
- 掷硬币猜中的一队在下半场开球开始比赛。
- 下半场，双方球队交换半场和进攻方向。
- 当一队进球后，由另一队开球。

所有的开球:

- 所有场上队员必须处在本方半场内。
- 开球队的对方队员必须距球至少9.15米（10码）直至比赛开始。
- 球必须放定在中点上。
- 裁判员给出信号。
- 当球被踢且明显移动时，比赛即为开始。
- 开球可直接射入对方球门得分。

Infringements and sanctions

If the player taking the kick-off touches the ball again before it has touched another player an indirect free kick, or for deliberate handball a direct free kick, is awarded.

In the event of any other infringement of the kick-off procedure the kick-off is retaken.

2. Dropped ball
Procedure

The referee drops the ball at the position where it was when play was stopped, unless play was stopped inside the goal area in which case the ball is dropped on the goal area line which is parallel to the goal line at the point nearest to where the ball was when play was stopped.

The ball is in play when it touches the ground.

Any number of players may contest a dropped ball (including the goalkeepers); the referee cannot decide who may contest a dropped ball or its outcome.

Infringements and sanctions

The ball is dropped again if it:

- touches a player before it touches the ground
- leaves the field of play after it touches the ground, without touching a player

If a dropped ball enters the goal without touching at least two players play is restarted with:

- a goal kick if it enters the opponents' goal
- a corner kick if it enters the team's goal

违规与处罚

如果开球队员在其他场上队员触及球前再次触球，则判罚间接任意球，如果故意用手触球，则判罚直接任意球。

对于其他任何违反开球程序的情况，应重新开球。

2. 坠球

程序

裁判员在比赛停止时球所在地点执行坠球，除非比赛停止时球在球门区内，在此情况下，应在与球门线平行的球门区线上、在比赛停止时距球最近的地点执行坠球。

当球触及地面，比赛即为恢复。

所有场上队员均可参与坠球（包括守门员）。裁判员不得决定由谁参与坠球或坠球的结果。

违规与处罚

出现如下情况时，需重新坠球：
- 球在触及地面前被队员触及。
- 球在触及地面后，未经队员触及而离开比赛场地。

如果坠球后，球未经至少两名场上队员触及而进入球门：

- 球进入对方球门，则以球门球恢复比赛。
- 球进入本方球门，则以角球恢复比赛。

09. The Ball in and out of Play

1. **Ball out of play**

   The ball is out of play when:

   - it has wholly passed over the goal line or touchline on the ground or in the air
   - play has been stopped by the referee

2. **Ball in play**

   The ball is in play at all other times, including when it rebounds off a match official, goalpost, crossbar or corner flagpost and remains in the field of play.

第九章　比赛进行与停止

1. 比赛停止
当出现如下情况时，比赛即为停止：
- 球的整体从地面或空中越过球门线或边线。
- 裁判员停止了比赛。

2. 比赛进行
所有其他时间，均为比赛进行中，包括球从比赛官员、球门柱、横梁或角旗杆弹回，且仍在比赛场地内。

10. Determining the Outcome of a Match

1. **Goal scored**

   A goal is scored when the whole of the ball passes over the goal line, between the goalposts and under the crossbar, provided that no offence or infringement of the Laws of the Game has been committed by the team scoring the goal.

   If a referee signals a goal before the ball has passed wholly over the goal line, play is restarted with a dropped ball.

2. **Winning team**

   The team scoring the greater number of goals is the winner. If both teams score no goals or an equal number of goals the match is drawn.

   When competition rules require a winning team after a drawn match or home-and-away tie, the only permitted procedures to determine the winning team are:

   - away goals rule
   - extra time
   - kicks from the penalty mark

3. **Kicks from the penalty mark**

   Kicks from the penalty mark are taken after the match has ended and unless otherwise stated, the relevant Laws of the Game apply.

   Procedure
   Before kicks from the penalty mark start

   - Unless there are other considerations (e.g. ground conditions, safety etc.), the referee tosses a coin to decide the goal at which the kicks will be taken which may only be changed for safety reasons or if the goal or playing surface becomes unusable

第十章 确定比赛结果

1. 进球得分

当球的整体从球门柱之间及横梁下方越过球门线，且进球队未犯规或违规时，即为进球得分。

如果裁判员在球的整体还未越过球门线时示意进球，则以坠球恢复比赛。

2. 获胜队

进球数较多的队伍为获胜队。如果双方球队没有进球或进球数相等，则该场比赛为平局。

当竞赛规程规定一场比赛出现平局，或主客场进球数相同时必须有一方取胜，仅允许采取如下方式决定获胜队：

- 客场进球规则。
- 加时赛。
- 球点球决胜。

3. 球点球决胜

在比赛结束后执行球点球决胜程序，除非有其他规定，否则按竞赛规则相关内容执行。

程序

球点球决胜开始前

- 裁判员通过掷硬币决定球点球决胜使用的球门，除非有其他考虑（如场地条件、安全性等）。只有因为安全原因，或在球门、场地草皮无法正常使用的情况下，才可更换球点球决胜使用的球门。

Goal

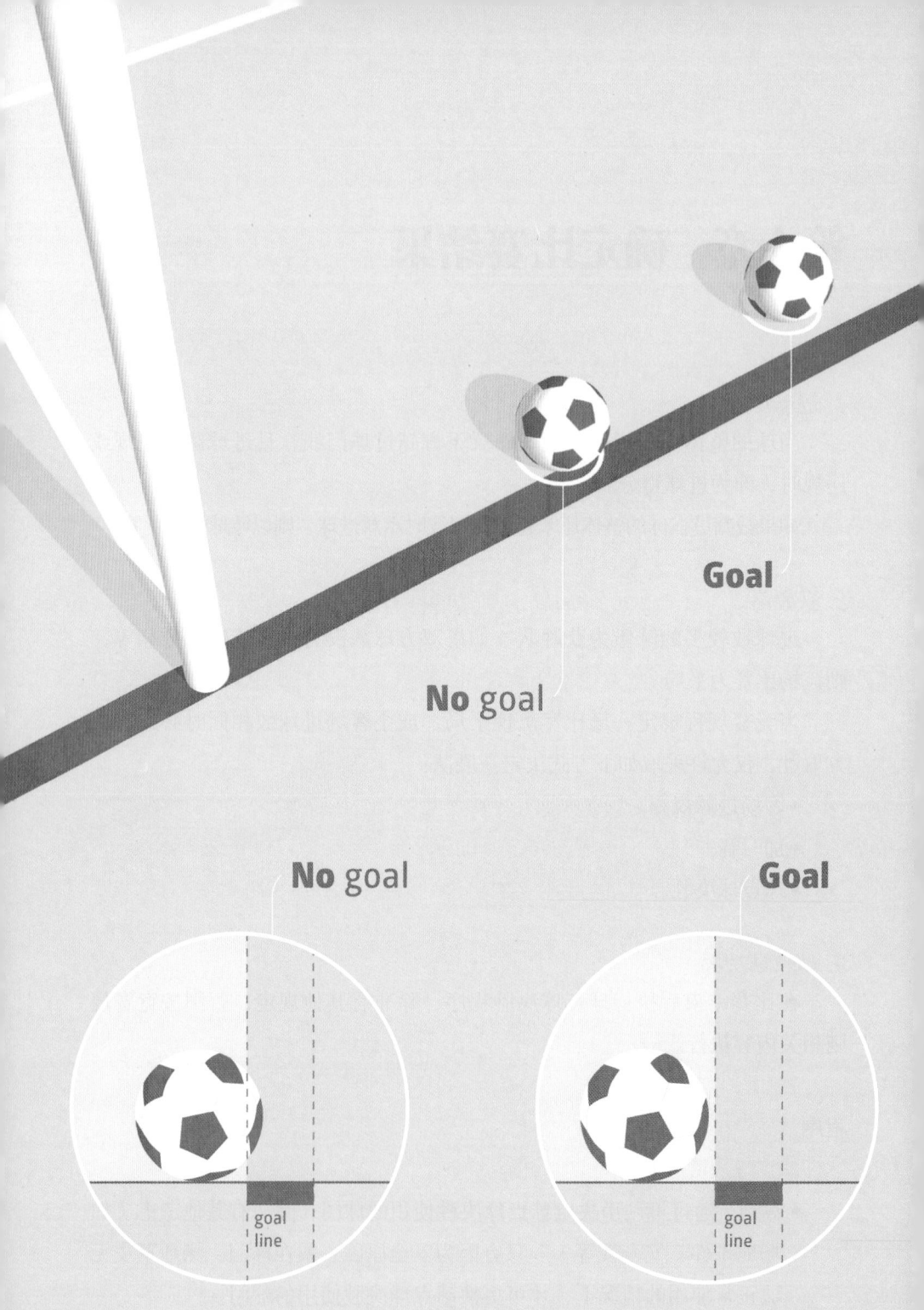

No goal

No goal

Goal

goal line

goal line

进球

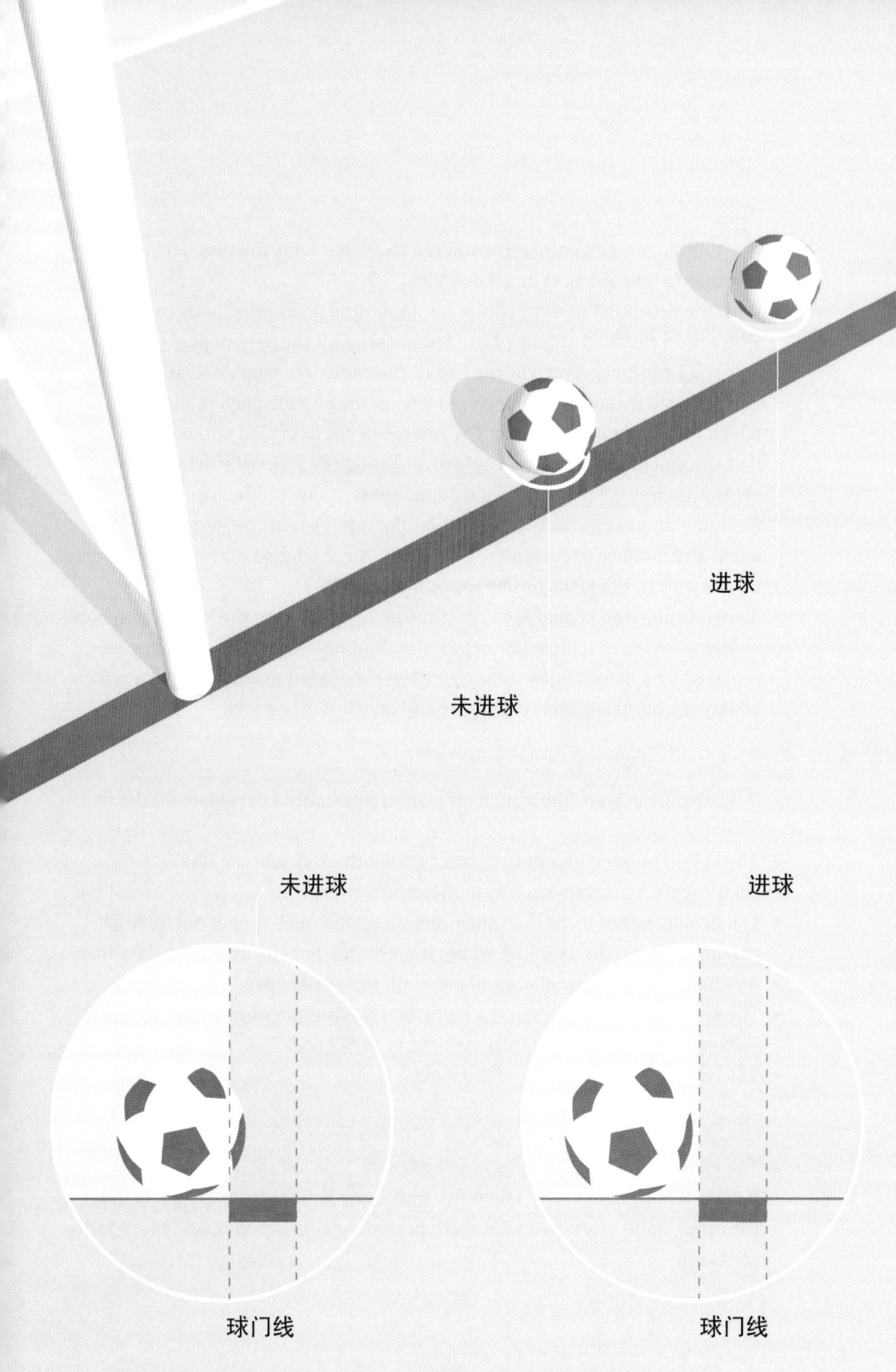

未进球

未进球

进球

球门线

球门线

- The referee tosses a coin again and the team that wins the toss decides whether to take the first or second kick
- With the exception of a substitute for an injured goalkeeper, only players who are on the field of play or are temporarily off the field of play (injury, adjusting equipment etc.) at the end of the match are eligible to take kicks
- Each team is responsible for selecting from the eligible players the order in which they will take the kicks. The referee is not informed of the order
- If at the end of the match and before or during the kicks one team has a greater number of players than its opponents, it must reduce its numbers to the same number as its opponents and the referee must be informed of the name and number of each player excluded. Any excluded player is not eligible to take part in the kicks (except as outlined below)
- A goalkeeper who is unable to continue before or during the kicks and whose team has not used its maximum permitted number of substitutes, may be replaced by a named substitute, or a player excluded to equalise the number of players, but takes no further part and may not take a kick

During kicks from the penalty mark

- Only eligible players and match officials are permitted to remain on the field of play
- All eligible players, except the player taking the kick and the two goalkeepers, must remain within the centre circle
- The goalkeeper of the kicker must remain on the field of play, outside the penalty area, on the goal line where it meets the penalty area boundary line
- An eligible player may change places with the goalkeeper
- The kick is completed when the ball stops moving, goes out of play or the referee stops play for any infringement of the Laws
- The referee keeps a record of the kicks

Subject to the conditions explained below, both teams take five kicks

- The kicks are taken alternately by the teams
- If, before both teams have taken five kicks, one has scored more goals than the other could score, even if it were to complete its five kicks, no more kicks are taken

- 裁判员再次掷硬币，猜中的一队决定先踢或后踢。
- 除替补队员替换受伤守门员的情况外，只有在比赛结束时在比赛场地内，或暂时离场（受伤、调整装备等）的场上队员有资格参加球点球决胜。
- 各队负责安排有资格的场上队员踢球点球的顺序，罚球队员顺序不必告知裁判员。
- 如果在比赛结束时、球点球决胜开始前或进行中，一队场上队员人数多于另一队，则必须削减队员人数与对方保持一致，且必须告知裁判员被排除的队员姓名及号码。被排除的队员不得参加球点球决胜（除下述情况外）。
- 在球点球决胜开始前或进行中，如果一队守门员无法继续比赛且该队替换名额还未用完，则守门员可由一名提名的替补队员，或为保持人数一致而被排除的场上队员替换，但其不得再次参加球点球决胜或踢球点球。

球点球决胜进行中

- 只有符合资格的场上队员和比赛官员可以留在比赛场地内。
- 除踢球点球的队员和两名守门员外，所有符合资格的场上队员必须留在中圈内。
- 踢球队员一方的守门员必须留在比赛场地内、在罚球区外球门线与罚球区线交汇的位置。
- 符合资格的场上队员可与守门员互换位置。
- 当球停止移动、离开比赛场地，或因发生任何违反规则的情况而裁判员停止比赛时，即为本次踢球点球结束。
- 裁判员记录球点球决胜情况。

双方球队各踢5轮球点球，并遵循如下规定：

- 双方球队轮流踢球。
- 在双方球队各踢完5次球点球前，如果一队进球数已经超过另一队罚满5次可能的进球数，则不再继续执行球点球决胜程序。

- If, after both teams have taken five kicks, the scores are level kicks continue until one team has scored a goal more than the other from the same number of kicks
- Each kick is taken by a different player and all eligible players must take a kick before any player can take a second kick
- The above principle continues for any subsequent sequence of kicks but a team may change the order of kickers
- Kicks from the penalty mark must not be delayed for a player who leaves the field of play. The player's kick will be forfeited (not scored) if the player does not return in time to take a kick

Substitutions and send offs during kicks from the penalty mark

- A player, substitute or substituted player may be cautioned or sent off
- A goalkeeper who is sent off must be replaced by an eligible player
- A player other than the goalkeeper who is unable to continue may not be replaced
- The referee must not abandon the match if a team is reduced to fewer than seven players

- 在双方球队踢完5轮球点球后，如果进球数相同，则继续踢球，直到出现踢完相同次数时，一队比另一队多进一球的情况为止。
- 每次踢球由不同的场上队员执行，直至双方符合资格的队员均踢过一次后，同一名队员才可踢第二次。
- 在全部队员踢完之后接下来的踢球中都应遵从上述条款，但球队可以更换踢球队员顺序。
- 不得因一名场上队员离场而拖延球点球决胜。如果队员未及时返场踢球点球，则视为丧失本次踢球资格（射失）。

球点球决胜阶段的队员替换与罚令出场

- 场上队员、替补队员或已替换下场的队员均可被警告或罚令出场。
- 被罚令出场的守门员必须由一名符合资格的场上队员替换。
- 除守门员外的其他无法继续参加球点球决胜的场上队员不可被替换。
- 如果一队场上队员人数少于7人，裁判员不必中止比赛。

11. Offside

1. **Offside position**

   It is not an offence to be in an offside position.

   A player is in an offside position if:

   - any part of the head, body or feet is in the opponents' half (excluding the halfway line) and
   - any part of the head, body or feet is nearer to the opponents' goal line than both the ball and the second-last opponent

   The hands and arms of all players, including the goalkeepers, are not considered.

   A player is not in an offside position if level with the:

   - second-last opponent or
   - last two opponents

2. **Offside offence**

   A player in an offside position at the moment the ball is played or touched by a team-mate is only penalised on becoming involved in active play by:

   - interfering with play by playing or touching a ball passed or touched by a team-mate or
   - interfering with an opponent by:

第十一章　越位

1. 越位位置
处于越位位置并不意味着构成越位犯规。

队员处于越位位置，如果其：
- 头、躯干或脚的任何部分处在对方半场（不包含中线），且
- 头、躯干或脚的任何部分较球和对方倒数第二名队员更接近于对方球门线。

所有队员包括守门员的手和臂部不在越位位置判定范围内。

队员不处于越位位置，如果其：
- 与对方倒数第二名队员齐平或
- 与对方最后两名队员齐平。

2. 越位犯规
一名队员在同队队员传球或触球的一瞬间处于越位位置，该队员随后以如下方式参与了实际比赛，才被判罚越位犯规：
- 在同队队员传球或触球后得球或触及球，从而干扰了比赛，或
- 干扰对方队员，包括：

- preventing an opponent from playing or being able to play the ball by clearly obstructing the opponent's line of vision or
- challenging an opponent for the ball or
- clearly attempting to play a ball which is close to him when this action impacts on an opponent or
- making an obvious action which clearly impacts on the ability of an opponent to play the ball

or

- gaining an advantage by playing the ball or interfering with an opponent when it has:

  - rebounded or been deflected off the goalpost, crossbar or an opponent
  - been deliberately saved by any opponent

A player in an offside position receiving the ball from an opponent who deliberately plays the ball (except from a deliberate save by any opponent) is not considered to have gained an advantage.

A 'save' is when a player stops a ball which is going into or very close to the goal with any part of the body except the hands (unless the goalkeeper within the penalty area).

3. **No offence**

There is no offside offence if a player receives the ball directly from:

- a goal kick
- a throw-in
- a corner kick

- 通过明显阻碍对方队员视线，以妨碍对方队员处理球，或影响其处理球的能力，或
- 与对方队员争抢球，或
- 有明显的试图触及离自己位置较近的来球的举动，且该举动影响了对方队员，或
- 做出影响对方队员处理球能力的明显举动。

或

- 在如下情况发生后触球，从而获得利益或干扰对方队员：
  - 球从球门柱、横梁、对方队员处反弹或折射过来。
  - 球从任一对方队员有意救球后而来。

处于越位位置的队员在对方队员有意触球（任一对方队员救球除外）后得球，不被视为获得利益。

"救球"是指队员用除手臂以外（守门员在本方罚球区内除外）的身体任何部位，阻止将要进入球门或极为接近球门的球。

3. 不存在越位犯规

如果队员直接从下列情况得球，不存在越位犯规：
- 球门球。
- 掷界外球。
- 角球。

4. Infringements and sanctions

If an offside offence occurs, the referee awards an indirect free kick where the offence occurred, including if it is in the player's own half of the field of play.

A defending player who leaves the field of play without the referee's permission shall be considered to be on the goal line or touchline for the purposes of offside until the next stoppage in play or until the defending team has played the ball towards the halfway line and it is outside their penalty area. If the player left the field of play deliberately, the player must be cautioned when the ball is next out of play.

An attacking player may step or stay off the field of play not to be involved in active play. If the player re-enters from the goal line and becomes involved in play before the next stoppage in play, or the defending team has played the ball towards the halfway line and it is outside their penalty area, the player shall be considered to be positioned on the goal line for the purposes of offside. A player who deliberately leaves the field of play and re-enters without the referee's permission and is not penalised for offside and gains an advantage, must be cautioned.

If an attacking player remains stationary between the goalposts and inside the goal as the ball enters the goal, a goal must be awarded unless the player commits an offside offence or Law 12 offence in which case play is restarted with an indirect or direct free kick.

4.违规与处罚

如果出现越位犯规，裁判员在越位发生的地点判罚间接任意球，这包括发生在越位队员的本方半场。

就越位而言，未经裁判员许可离开比赛场地的防守队员，应视为处于球门线或边线上，直到比赛停止，或防守方已将球向中线方向处理且球已在防守方罚球区外。如果一名队员故意离开比赛场地，在比赛停止时，裁判员必须警告该名队员。

攻方队员为了不卷入实际比赛可以移步至比赛场地外或留在比赛场地外。就越位而言，如果该攻方队员在随后比赛停止，或防守方已将球向中线方向处理且球已在防守方罚球区外之前，从球门线重新进入比赛场地内，并卷入实际比赛，应视其处于球门线上。未经裁判员许可故意离开比赛场地又重新回场的攻方队员，虽不被判罚越位，但从其位置获得了利益，裁判员必须警告该名队员。

如果球进门时，一名攻方队员在球门柱之间的球门内保持不动，进球必须视为有效，除非该名队员越位或违反规则第十二章条文，这种情况下，裁判员以间接或直接任意球恢复比赛。

12. Fouls and Misconduct

Direct and indirect free kicks and penalty kicks can only be awarded for offences and infringements committed when the ball is in play.

1. Direct free kick

A direct free kick is awarded if a player commits any of the following offences against an opponent in a manner considered by the referee to be careless, reckless or using excessive force:

- charges
- jumps at
- kicks or attempts to kick
- pushes
- strikes or attempts to strike (including head-butt)
- tackles or challenges
- trips or attempts to trip

If an offence involves contact it is penalised by a direct free kick or penalty kick.

- Careless is when a player shows a lack of attention or consideration when making a challenge or acts without precaution. No disciplinary sanction is needed
- Reckless is when a player acts with disregard to the danger to, or consequences for, an opponent and must be cautioned
- Using excessive force is when a player exceeds the necessary use of force and endangers the safety of an opponent and must be sent off

58

第十二章　犯规与不正当行为

只有在比赛进行中犯规或违规，才可判罚直接或间接任意球，以及球点球。

1. 直接任意球

如果裁判员认为，一名场上队员草率地、鲁莽地或使用过分力量对对方队员实施如下犯规，则判罚直接任意球：

- 冲撞。
- 跳向。
- 踢或企图踢。
- 推搡。
- 打或企图打（包括用头顶撞）。
- 用脚或其他部位抢截。
- 绊或企图绊。

如果是有身体接触的犯规，则判罚直接任意球或球点球。

- 草率是指队员在争抢时没有预防措施，缺乏注意力或考虑。这种情况不必给予纪律处罚。
- 鲁莽是指队员的行为没有顾及到可能对对方造成的危险或后果。这种情况下必须对队员予以警告。
- 使用过分力量是指队员使用了超出自身所需要的力量，危及了对方的安全。这种情况必须将队员罚令出场。

A direct free kick is awarded if a player commits any of the following offences:

- handles the ball deliberately (except for the goalkeeper within their penalty area)
- holds an opponent
- impedes an opponent with contact
- spits at an opponent

See also offences in Law 3

Handling the ball

Handling the ball involves a deliberate act of a player making contact with the ball with the hand or arm.

The following must be considered:

- the movement of the hand towards the ball (not the ball towards the hand)
- the distance between the opponent and the ball (unexpected ball)
- the position of the hand does not necessarily mean that there is an infringement
- touching the ball with an object held in the hand (clothing, shinguard, etc.) is an infringement
- hitting the ball with a thrown object (boot, shinguard, etc.) is an infringement

The goalkeeper has the same restrictions on handling the ball as any other player outside the penalty area. Inside their penalty area, the goalkeeper cannot be guilty of a handling offence incurring a direct free kick or any related sanction but can be guilty of handling offences that incur an indirect free kick.

2. Indirect free kick

An indirect free kick is awarded if a player:

- plays in a dangerous manner
- impedes the progress of an opponent without any contact being made
- prevents the goalkeeper from releasing the ball from the hands or kicks or attempts to kick the ball when the goalkeeper is in the process of releasing it
- commits any other offence, not mentioned in the Laws, for which play is stopped to caution or send off a player

如果场上队员实施如下犯规时，判罚直接任意球：
- 故意手球（守门员在本方罚球区内除外）。
- 使用手臂等部位拉扯、阻止对方队员行动。
- 在身体接触的情况下阻碍对方队员移动。
- 向对方队员吐口水。

以及规则第三章涉及到的其他犯规行为。

手球

手球是指队员用手或臂部故意触球的行为。

在判断是否故意手球时应考虑：
- 手向球的移动（不是球向手）。
- 对方队员和球之间的距离（意外来球）。
- 手的位置并不意味着犯规。
- 用手中的物品（衣物、护腿板等）触球视为犯规。
- 用掷出的物品（鞋、护腿板等）击球视为犯规。

在本方罚球区外，守门员和所有其他场上队员在手球上具有同等限制。不得因守门员在本方罚球区内的手球而判罚直接任意球，或执行任何相关的纪律处罚，但可能因手球犯规判罚间接任意球。

2. 间接任意球

如果一名场上队员犯有如下行为时，则判罚间接任意球：
- 以危险方式进行比赛。
- 在没有身体接触的情况下阻碍对方行进。
- 在守门员发球过程中，阻止守门员从手中发球、踢或准备踢球。
- 犯有规则中没有提及的，又需裁判员停止比赛予以警告或罚令出场的任何其他犯规。

An indirect free kick is awarded if a goalkeeper, inside their penalty area, commits any of the following offences:

- controls the ball with the hands for more than six seconds before releasing it
- touches the ball with the hands after:
  - releasing it and before it has touched another player
  - it has been deliberately kicked to the goalkeeper by a team-mate
  - receiving it directly from a throw-in taken by a team-mate

A goalkeeper is considered to be in control of the ball when:

- the ball is between the hands or between the hand and any surface (e.g. ground, own body) or by touching it with any part of the hands or arms except if the ball rebounds accidentally from the goalkeeper or the goalkeeper has made a save
- holding the ball in the outstretched open hand
- bouncing it on the ground or throwing it in the air

A goalkeeper cannot be challenged by an opponent when in control of the ball with the hands.

Playing in a dangerous manner

Playing in a dangerous manner is any action that, while trying to play the ball, threatens injury to someone (including the player themself) and includes preventing a nearby opponent from playing the ball for fear of injury.

A scissors or bicycle kick is permissible provided that it is not dangerous to an opponent.

Impeding the progress of an opponent without contact

Impeding the progress of an opponent means moving into the opponent's path to obstruct, block, slow down or force a change of direction when the ball is not within playing distance of either player.

All players have a right to their position on the field of play; being in the way of an opponent is not the same as moving into the way of an opponent.

如果守门员在本方罚球区内犯有如下行为时，则判罚间接任意球：
- 在发出球前，用手控制球超过6秒。
- 在下列情况下用手触球：
    - 发出球后，任一场上队员触球前。
    - 同队队员故意将球踢给守门员。
    - 接同队队员直接掷来的界外球。

当出现下列情况时，视为守门员控制球：
- 球在双手之间，或手与任何表面（如地面、自己的身体）之间，以及用手或臂部的任何部分触球，除非球从守门员身上意外反弹，或守门员做出扑救的情况。
- 用伸展开的手持球。
- 向地面拍球或向空中抛球。

守门员在用手控制球的情况下，对方不得与其争抢球。

以危险方式进行比赛

　　以危险方式进行比赛是指在尝试争球的过程中做出的任何动作，存在对对方（包括自己）造成伤害的危险，包括使附近的对方队员因为害怕受伤而不敢争抢球。
　　剪刀脚和倒钩动作如果不会对对方造成危险，则允许使用。

在没有身体接触的情况下阻碍对方行进

　　阻碍对方行进是指当球不在双方的合理争抢范围时，移动至对方的行进路线上以阻碍、阻挡、减缓或迫使对方改变行进方向。

　　所有队员有权在比赛场地内选择自己的位置。已处在对方行进路线上和移动至对方行进路线上是不同的概念。

A player may shield the ball by taking a position between an opponent and the ball if the ball is within playing distance and the opponent is not held off with the arms or body. If the ball is within playing distance, the player may be fairly charged by an opponent.

3. Disciplinary action

The referee has the authority to take disciplinary action from entering the field of play for the pre-match inspection until leaving the field of play after the match ends (including kicks from the penalty mark).

If, before entering the field of play at the start of the match, a player commits a sending-off offence, the referee has the authority to prevent the player taking part in the match (see Law 3.6); the referee will report any other misconduct.

A player who commits a cautionable or sending-off offence, either on or off the field of play, against an opponent, a team-mate, a match official or any other person or the Laws of the Game, is disciplined according to the offence.

The yellow card communicates a caution and the red card communicates a sending-off.

Only a player, substitute or substituted player may be shown the red or yellow card.

Delaying the restart of play to show a card
Once the referee has decided to caution or send off a player, play must not be restarted until the sanction has been administered.

Advantage
If the referee plays the advantage for an offence for which a caution / send off would have been issued had play been stopped, this caution / send off must be issued when the ball is next out of play, except when the denial of an obvious goal-scoring opportunity results in a goal the player is cautioned for unsporting behaviour.

Advantage should not be applied in situations involving serious foul play, violent conduct or a second cautionable offence unless there is a clear opportunity to score a goal. The referee must send off the player when the ball is next out of play but if the player plays the ball or challenges/interferes with an opponent, the referee will stop play, send off the player and restart with an indirect free kick.

如果球在一名队员的合理争抢范围内，且其没有用臂部或身体阻拦对方队员争球，则该名队员可以在对方队员和球之间选好位置护球。如果球在双方的合理争抢范围内，队员可用合理冲撞的方式与对方争抢球。

3. 纪律措施

裁判员从进入比赛场地进行赛前检查开始，至比赛结束（包括球点球决胜）离开比赛场地，均有权执行纪律措施。

如果上场队员在开赛进入比赛场地前，犯有可被罚令出场的犯规，裁判员有权阻止该名队员参加比赛（参见第三章第6条），裁判员将就任何其他不正当行为提交报告。

一名队员无论是在场内还是场外，对对方队员、同队队员、比赛官员或其他任何人，以及竞赛规则规定的犯有可被警告或罚令出场的犯规，均应对其做出符合其犯规行为的处罚。

黄牌代表警告，红牌代表罚令出场。

只可对场上队员、替补队员、已替换下场的队员出示红黄牌。

因拖延比赛恢复而出示红黄牌

一旦裁判员决定对队员予以警告或罚令出场，在处罚程序执行完成前，不得恢复比赛。

有利

如果裁判员在出现可警告或罚令出场的犯规时，没有停止比赛而掌握有利，则必须在随后比赛停止时出示红黄牌。除非是破坏明显进球得分机会后形成进球，这种情况下，以非体育行为警告相关队员。

在出现严重犯规、暴力行为或可被第二次警告的犯规时不应掌握有利，除非有明显的进球机会。裁判员必须在随后比赛停止时将相关队员罚令出场，但如果该队员触球或与对方队员争抢或干扰对方队员，裁判员则停止比赛，将该队员罚令出场，并以间接任意球恢复比赛。

If a defender starts holding an attacker outside the penalty area and continues holding inside the penalty area, the referee must award a penalty kick.

Cautionable offences

A player is cautioned if guilty of:

- delaying the restart of play
- dissent by word or action
- entering, re-entering or deliberately leaving the field of play without the referee's permission
- failing to respect the required distance when play is restarted with a corner kick, free kick or throw-in
- persistent infringement of the Laws of the Game (no specific number or pattern of infringements constitutes "persistent")
- unsporting behaviour

A substitute or substituted player is cautioned if guilty of:

- delaying the restart of play
- dissent by word or action
- entering or re-entering the field of play without the referee's permission
- unsporting behaviour

Cautions for unsporting behaviour

There are different circumstances when a player must be cautioned for unsporting behaviour including if a player:

- attempts to deceive the referee e.g. by feigning injury or pretending to have been fouled (simulation)
- changes places with the goalkeeper during play or without the referee's permission
- commits in a reckless manner a direct free kick offence
- commits a foul <u>or handles</u> the ball to interfere with or stop a promising attack

如果防守队员在罚球区外就开始使用手臂等部位拉扯、阻止对方队员行动，并持续至罚球区内，裁判员必须判罚球点球。

可警告的犯规

场上队员犯有如下行为时，应被警告：
- 延误比赛恢复。
- 以语言或行动表示不满。
- 未经裁判员许可进入、重新进入或故意离开比赛场地。
- 当比赛以角球、任意球或掷界外球恢复时，未退出规定距离。
- 持续违反规则（对"持续"的定义并没有明确的次数和犯规类型）。
- 非体育行为。

替补队员或已替换下场的队员犯有如下行为时，应被警告：
- 延误比赛恢复。
- 以语言或行动表示不满。
- 未经裁判员许可进入、重新进入比赛场地。
- 非体育行为。

对非体育行为的警告

在一些情况下必须以非体育行为警告相关队员，例如：
- 试图用假装受伤或假装被犯规（佯装）欺骗裁判员。
- 在比赛进行中，未经裁判员许可与守门员互换位置。
- 以鲁莽的方式犯有可判直接任意球的犯规。
- 通过犯规或手球的方式干扰或阻止有希望的进攻。

- handles the ball in an attempt to score a goal (whether or not the attempt is successful) <u>or in an unsuccessful attempt to prevent a goal</u>
- makes unauthorised marks on the field of play
- plays the ball when leaving the field of play after being given permission to leave
- shows a lack of respect for the game
- uses a deliberate trick to pass the ball (including from a free kick) to the goalkeeper with the head, chest, knee etc. to circumvent the Law, whether or not the goalkeeper touches the ball with the hands
- verbally distracts an opponent during play or at a restart

Celebration of a goal

Players can celebrate when a goal is scored, but the celebration must not be excessive; choreographed celebrations are not encouraged and must not cause excessive time-wasting.

Leaving the field of play to celebrate a goal is not a cautionable offence but players should return as soon as possible.

A player must be cautioned for:

- climbing onto a perimeter fence
- gesturing in a provocative, derisory or inflammatory way
- covering the head or face with a mask or other similar item
- removing the shirt or covering the head with the shirt

Delaying the restart of play

Referees must caution players who delay the restart of play by:

- appearing to take a throw-in but suddenly leaving it to a team-mate to take
- delaying leaving the field of play when being substituted
- excessively delaying a restart
- kicking or carrying the ball away, or provoking a confrontation by deliberately touching the ball after the referee has stopped play
- taking a free kick from the wrong position to force a retake

Sending-off offences

A player, substitute or substituted player who commits any of the following offences is sent off:

- 用手球的方式试图得分（无论进球与否）或阻止进球未果。
- 在比赛场地上制造未经许可的标记。
- 在经许可离场的过程中触球。
- 表现出对比赛缺乏尊重。
- 故意施诡计用头、胸、膝盖等部位将球传给守门员（包括任意球情况）以逃避规则相关处罚条款，无论守门员是否用手触球。
- 在比赛进行中或比赛恢复时，用语言干扰对方队员。

庆祝进球

队员可以在进球得分后进行庆祝，但庆祝活动不得过度。不鼓励在庆祝进球时表演自编舞蹈，这种庆祝不得过度浪费时间。

离开场地庆祝进球无需予以警告，但场上队员应尽快返场。

队员必须被警告的行为：
- 攀爬上周边的围栏。
- 做出挑衅、嘲讽或煽动性质的动作或姿态。
- 用面具或类似器物遮住头部或面部。
- 脱去上衣或用上衣遮住头部。

延误比赛恢复

裁判员必须警告以下列方式延误比赛恢复的队员：
- 看似要掷界外球，但突然将球交给同队队员掷球。
- 在被替换下场时延误离场时间。
- 过度地拖延比赛恢复。
- 在裁判员停止比赛后，故意将球踢走或拿走，引发冲突。
- 在错误的地点踢任意球以造成重踢。

罚令出场的犯规

场上队员、替补队员或已替换下场的队员犯有如下行为时，应被罚令出场：

- denying the opposing team a goal or an obvious goal-scoring opportunity by deliberately handling the ball (except a goalkeeper within their penalty area)
- denying an obvious goal-scoring opportunity to an opponent moving towards the opponents' goal by an offence punishable by a free kick (unless as outlined below)
- serious foul play
- spitting at an opponent or any other person
- violent conduct
- using offensive, insulting or abusive language and/or gestures
- receiving a second caution in the same match

A player, substitute or substituted player who has been sent off must leave the vicinity of the field of play and the technical area.

Denying a goal or an obvious goal-scoring opportunity
Where a player denies the opposing team a goal or an obvious goal-scoring opportunity by a deliberate handball offence the player is sent off wherever the offence occurs.

Where a player commits an offence against an opponent within their own penalty area which denies an opponent an obvious goal-scoring opportunity and the referee awards a penalty kick, the offending player is cautioned unless:

- The offence is holding, pulling or pushing or
- The offending player does not attempt to play the ball or there is no possibility for the player making the challenge to play the ball or
- The offence is one which is punishable by a red card wherever it occurs on the field of play (e.g. serious foul play, violent conduct etc.)

In all the above circumstances the player is sent off.

The following must be considered:

- distance between the offence and the goal
- general direction of the play
- likelihood of keeping or gaining control of the ball
- location and number of defenders

- 通过故意手球破坏对方球队进球或明显的进球得分机会（守门员在本方罚球区内除外）。
- 通过可判罚任意球的犯规，破坏对方朝本方球门移动着的明显的进球得分机会（本章下述"破坏进球或明显进球得分机会"中说明的相关情况除外）。
- 严重犯规。
- 向对方队员或其他任何人吐口水。
- 暴力行为。
- 使用攻击性、侮辱性或辱骂性的语言和/或动作。
- 在同一场比赛中得到第二次警告。

被罚令出场的场上队员、替补队员或已替换下场的队员，必须离开比赛场地周边区域及技术区域。

破坏进球或明显进球得分机会

无论发生在何处，当队员用故意手球的犯规破坏对方进球或明显进球得分机会时应被罚令出场。

当队员在本方罚球区内对对方犯规，且破坏了对方明显的进球得分机会时，裁判员判罚球点球，对犯规队员予以警告，除非：

- 使用手臂等部位拉扯、阻止对方队员行动，或推搡性质的犯规，或
- 犯规队员的目的不是争抢球或争抢球时没有触球的可能性，或
- 无论发生在比赛场地何处均应被罚令出场的犯规（如严重犯规、暴力行为等）。

发生上述情况，均应将犯规队员罚令出场。

必须考虑如下情况：

- 犯规发生地点与球门间的距离。
- 比赛发展的大致方向。
- 控制球或得到控球权的可能性。
- 防守队员的位置和人数。

Serious foul play
A tackle or challenge that endangers the safety of an opponent or uses excessive force or brutality must be sanctioned as serious foul play.

Any player who lunges at an opponent in challenging for the ball from the front, from the side or from behind using one or both legs, with excessive force or endangers the safety of an opponent is guilty of serious foul play.

Violent conduct
Violent conduct is when a player uses or attempts to use excessive force or brutality against an opponent when not challenging for the ball, or against a team-mate, team official, match official, spectator or any other person, regardless of whether contact is made.

In addition, a player who, when not challenging for the ball, deliberately strikes an opponent or any other person on the head or face with the hand or arm, is guilty of violent conduct unless the force used was negligible.

Offences where an object (or the ball) is thrown
If while the ball is in play, a player, substitute or substituted player throws an object (including the ball) at an opponent or any other person the referee must stop play and if the offence was:

- reckless – caution the offender for unsporting behaviour
- using excessive force – send off the offender for violent conduct.

4. **Restart of play after fouls and misconduct**
   - If the ball is out of play, play is restarted according to the previous decision
   - If the ball is in play and a player commits an offence inside the field of play against:
     - an opponent – indirect or direct free kick or penalty kick
     - a team-mate, substitute, substituted player, team official or a match official — a direct free kick or penalty kick
     - any other person – a dropped ball

严重犯规

危及到对方队员安全或使用过分力量、野蛮方式的抢截，必须视为严重犯规加以处罚。

任何队员用单腿或双腿从对方身前、侧向或后方，使用过分力量或危及对方安全的蹬踹动作，应视为严重犯规。

暴力行为

暴力行为是指队员的目的不是争抢球，而是对对方队员或同队队员、球队官员、比赛官员、观众或任何其他人，使用或企图使用过分力量或野蛮动作，无论是否与他人发生身体接触。

除此之外，队员的目的不是争抢球，而是故意用手或臂部击打对方队员，以及任何其他人的头或面部时，应视为暴力行为，除非他使用的力量非常轻微，足以忽略。

投掷物品（或比赛用球）的犯规

在比赛进行中，如果场上队员、替补队员或已替换下场的队员向对方队员或任何其他人扔掷物品（包括比赛用球），裁判员必须停止比赛，如果该犯规属于：

- 鲁莽的——以非体育行为警告犯规队员。
- 使用过分力量的——以暴力行为将犯规队员罚令出场。

4. 犯规与不正当行为出现后的比赛恢复方式

- 如果比赛此前已经停止，则以之前的决定恢复比赛。
- 如果比赛进行中，场上队员在比赛场地内对如下人员犯规：
  - 对方场上队员——以间接或直接任意球、球点球恢复比赛。
  - 对同队队员、替补队员、已替换下场的队员、球队官员或比赛官员——以直接任意球或球点球恢复比赛。
  - 对任何其他人——以坠球恢复比赛。

- If the ball is in play and a player commits an offence outside the field of play:
    - if the player is already off the field of play, play is restarted with a dropped ball

    if the player leaves the field of play to commit the offence, play is restarted with an indirect free kick from the position of the ball when play was stopped. However, if a player leaves the field of play as part of play and commits an offence against another player, play is restarted with a free kick taken on the boundary line nearest to where the offence occurred; for direct free kick offences a penalty kick is awarded if this is within the offender's penalty area
- If a player standing on or off the field of play throws an object at an opponent on the field of play, play is restarted with a direct free kick or penalty kick from the position where the object struck or would have struck the opponent
- Play is restarted with an indirect free kick if a:
    - player standing inside the field of play throws an object at any person outside the field of play
    - substitute or substituted player throws an object at an opponent standing inside the field of play

- 如果比赛进行中，一名场上队员在比赛场地外犯规：
  - 如果该队员此前已在比赛场地外，则以坠球恢复比赛。
  - 如果该队员离开比赛场地实施犯规，则在比赛停止时球所在地点以间接任意球恢复比赛。然而，如果场上队员在正常比赛的移动中离开比赛场地，随后对其他队员犯规，则在离犯规地点最近的边界线上以任意球恢复比赛。如果该地点位于犯规方罚球区内且该犯规可被判直接任意球，则判罚球点球。

- 如果站在比赛场地内或比赛场地外的场上队员，向比赛场地内的对方队员扔掷物品，则在对方队员被物品击中或可能被击中的地点以直接任意球或球点球恢复比赛。

- 如果出现下列情况，则以间接任意球恢复比赛：
  - 站在比赛场地内的场上队员向比赛场地外的任何人扔掷物品。
  - 替补队员或已被替换下场的队员向站在比赛场地内的对方队员扔掷物品。

13. Free Kicks

1. **Types of free kick**

   Direct and indirect free kicks are awarded to the opposing team of a player guilty of an offence or infringement.

   Indirect free kick signal
   The referee indicates an indirect free kick by raising the arm above the head; this signal is maintained until the kick has been taken and the ball touches another player or goes out of play.

   An indirect free kick must be retaken if the referee fails to signal that the kick is indirect and the ball is kicked directly into the goal.

   Ball enters the goal
   - if a direct free kick is kicked directly into the opponents' goal, a goal is awarded
   - if an indirect free kick is kicked directly into the opponents' goal, a goal kick is awarded
   - if a direct or indirect free kick is kicked directly into the team's own goal, a corner kick is awarded

2. **Procedure**

   All free kicks are taken from the place where the infringement occurred, except:

   - indirect free kicks to the attacking team for an offence inside the opponents' goal area are taken from the nearest point on the goal area line which runs parallel to the goal line
   - free kicks to the defending team in their goal area may be taken from anywhere in that area

第十三章　任意球

1. 任意球的种类

场上队员犯规或违规时，判由对方球队罚直接或间接任意球。

间接任意球示意信号

裁判员单臂上举过头，示意间接任意球，并保持这种姿势直到球踢出后被其他队员触及或比赛停止时为止。

如果裁判员未正确示意间接任意球，而球被直接射入球门，则必须重罚间接任意球。

球进门

- 如果直接任意球直接踢入对方球门，则判为进球得分。
- 如果间接任意球直接踢入对方球门，则判为球门球。
- 如果直接或间接任意球直接踢入本方球门，则判为角球。

2. 程序

所有任意球均应在犯规或违规的地点罚球，但下列情况除外：

- 攻方球队在对方球门区内获得的间接任意球，应在与球门线平行的，离犯规地点最近的球门区线上执行罚间接任意球。
- 守方球队在本方球门区内获得的任意球可在球门区内的任意地点罚球。

- free kicks for offences involving a player entering, re-entering or leaving the field of play without permission are taken from the position of the ball when play was stopped. However, if a player leaves the field of play as part of play and commits an offence against another player, play is restarted with a free kick taken on the boundary line nearest to where the offence occurred; for direct free kick offences a penalty kick is awarded if this is within the offender's penalty area
- the Law designates another position (see Laws 3, 11, 12)

The ball:

- must be stationary and the kicker must not touch the ball again until it has touched another player
- is in play when it is kicked and clearly moves except for a free kick to the defending team in their penalty area where the ball is in play when it is kicked directly out of the penalty area

Until the ball is in play all opponents must remain:

- at least 9.15 m (10 yds) from the ball, unless they are on their own goal line between the goalposts
- outside the penalty area for free kicks inside the opponents' penalty area

A free kick can be taken by lifting the ball with a foot or both feet simultaneously.

Feinting to take a free kick to confuse opponents is permitted as part of football.

If a player, while correctly taking a free kick, intentionally kicks the ball at an opponent in order to play the ball again but not in a careless or reckless manner or using excessive force, the referee allows play to continue.

- 场上队员未经裁判员允许进入、重新进入或离开比赛场地而被判罚的任意球，应在比赛停止时球所在地点罚球。然而，如果一名场上队员在正常比赛的移动中离开比赛场地，随后他对对方队员犯规，则应在距犯规发生地点最近的边界线上以任意球恢复比赛。如果该地点位于犯规方罚球区内，且该犯规可被判罚直接任意球，则判罚球点球。
- 规则规定的其他地点（详见第三章、第十一章、第十二章）。

球：
- 必须放定，且罚球队员不得在其他队员触及球前再次触球。
- 当球被踢且明显移动，则为比赛恢复。除非守方队员在本方罚球区内获得任意球，此时当球被直接踢出罚球区后，比赛才视为恢复。

在比赛恢复前，所有对方队员必须：
- 距球至少9.15米（10码），除非他们已经处在本方球门柱之间的球门线上。
- 守方队员在本方罚球区内罚任意球时，处在罚球区外。

任意球可以用单脚或双脚同时挑起的方式罚出。

作为比赛的一部分，允许用假动作罚任意球迷惑对方。

如果一名队员在以正确方式罚任意球的过程中，故意将球踢向对方以再次获得球权，但并未使用草率的、鲁莽的方式或过分的力量，裁判员允许比赛继续。

3. **Infringements and sanctions**

If, when a free kick is taken, an opponent is closer to the ball than the required distance, the kick is retaken unless the advantage can be applied; but if a player takes a free kick quickly and an opponent who is less than 9.15 m (10 yds) from the ball intercepts it, the referee allows play to continue. However, an opponent who deliberately prevents a free kick being taken quickly must be cautioned for delaying the restart of play.

If, when a free kick is taken quickly by the defending team from inside its penalty area, any opponents are inside the penalty area because they did not have time to leave, the referee allows play to continue.

If, when a free kick is taken by the defending team inside its penalty area, the ball is not kicked directly out of the penalty area the kick is retaken.

If, after the ball is in play, the kicker touches the ball again before it has touched another player an indirect free kick is awarded, if the kicker deliberately handles the ball:

- a direct free kick is awarded
- a penalty kick is awarded if the infringement occurred inside the kicker's penalty area unless the kicker was the goalkeeper in which case an indirect free kick is awarded

3. 违规与处罚

罚任意球时，如果对方队员距离球不足规定的距离，除非可掌握有利，否则应重罚任意球。如果队员快速罚出任意球，随后距球不足9.15米（10码）的对方队员将球截获，裁判员允许比赛继续。然而，故意阻止对方快速发球的队员必须以延误比赛恢复为由予以警告。

守方队员在本方罚球区内快速罚出任意球时，如果对方队员未来得及离开罚球区，裁判员允许比赛继续。

守方队员在本方罚球区内罚任意球时，如果没有将球直接踢出罚球区，则应重罚。

如果比赛已经恢复，罚球队员在其他队员触及球前再次触球，则判罚间接任意球。如果罚球队员故意用手触球：
- 判罚直接任意球。
- 如果违规情况发生在罚球队员本方罚球区内，则判罚球点球。除非罚球队员为守门员，这种情况下判罚间接任意球。

14. The Penalty Kick

A penalty kick is awarded if a player commits a direct free kick offence inside their penalty area <u>or off the field as part of play as outlined in Laws 12 and 13</u>.

A goal may be scored directly from a penalty kick.

1. Procedure

The ball must be <u>stationary</u> on the penalty mark.

The player taking the penalty kick must be properly identified.

The defending goalkeeper must remain on the goal line, facing the kicker, between the goalposts until the ball has been kicked.

The players other than the kicker and goalkeeper must be:

- at least 9.15 m (10 yds) from the penalty mark
- behind the penalty mark
- inside the field of play
- outside the penalty area

After the players have taken positions in accordance with this Law, the referee signals for the penalty kick to be taken.

The player taking the penalty kick must kick the ball forward; backheeling is permitted provided the ball moves forward.

The ball is in play when it is kicked <u>and clearly moves</u>.

The kicker must not play the ball again until it has touched another player.

<u>The penalty kick is completed when the ball stops moving, goes out of play or the referee stops play for any infringement of the Laws.</u>

Additional time is allowed for a penalty kick to be taken and completed at the end of each half of the match or extra time.

第十四章　罚球点球

队员在本方罚球区内，或如第十二章、第十三章已明确的正常比赛移动中离开比赛场地后，犯有可判罚直接任意球的犯规，则判罚球点球。

罚球点球可直接射入球门得分。

1. 程序

球必须放定在罚球点上。

必须明确主罚的队员。

守方守门员必须停留在球门柱之间的球门线上，面向主罚队员直至球被踢出。

主罚队员和守门员以外的其他场上队员必须：

- 距离罚球点至少9.15米（10码）。
- 在罚球点后。
- 在比赛场地内。
- 在罚球区外。

场上队员的位置符合规则规定后，裁判员示意执行罚球点球。

主罚队员必须向前踢球。允许使用脚后跟踢球，只要球向前移动。

当球被踢且明显移动，即为比赛恢复。

主罚队员在其他队员触及球前不得再次触球。

当球停止移动、离开比赛场地，或因发生任何违反规则的情况而裁判员停止比赛时，即为罚球完成。

在上下半场或加时赛上下半场结束时，允许补足时间以完成罚球点球程序。

2. Infringements and sanctions

Once the referee has signalled for a penalty kick to be taken, the kick must be taken. If, before the ball is in play, one of the following occurs:

the player taking the penalty kick or a team-mate infringes the Laws of the Game:

- if the ball enters the goal, the kick is retaken
- if the ball does not enter the goal, the referee stops play and restarts with an indirect free kick

except for the following when play will be stopped and restarted with an indirect free kick, regardless of whether or not a goal is scored:

- a penalty kick is kicked backwards
- a team-mate of the identified kicker takes the kick; the referee cautions the player who took the kick
- feinting to kick the ball once the kicker has completed the run-up (feinting in the run-up is permitted); the referee cautions the kicker

the goalkeeper or a team-mate infringes the Laws of the Game:

- if the ball enters the goal, a goal is awarded
- if the ball does not enter the goal, the kick is retaken; the goalkeeper is cautioned if responsible for the infringement

a player of both teams infringes the Laws of the Game, the kick is retaken unless a player commits a more serious offence (e.g. illegal feinting)

If, after the penalty kick has been taken:

the kicker touches the ball again before it has touched another player:

- an indirect free kick (or direct free kick for deliberate hand ball) is awarded

the ball is touched by an outside agent as it moves forward:

- the kick is retaken

2.违规与处罚

一旦裁判员示意执行罚球点球,球必须罚出。如果在比赛恢复前,出现如下任一情况:

主罚队员或同队队员违犯规则:
- 如果球进门,则重罚球点球。
- 如果球未进门,则裁判员停止比赛,以间接任意球恢复比赛。

如下情况,无论进球与否裁判员将停止比赛,以间接任意球恢复比赛:
- 向后踢球点球。
- 已确认的主罚队员的同队队员罚球点球,裁判员警告该名罚球队员。
- 罚球队员完成助跑后用假动作踢球(在助跑过程中使用假动作是允许的),裁判员警告该名队员。

守门员或同队队员违犯规则:
- 如果球进门,进球得分有效。
- 如果球未进门,应重罚球点球。如果守门员违犯规则,则对其予以警告。

双方队员违犯规则,应重罚球点球。除非某一队员违犯规则的程度更重(如使用不合法的假动作)。

球点球被罚出后,如果:
主罚队员在其他队员触及球前再次触球:
- 应判罚间接任意球(或因故意用手触球而判罚直接任意球)。

球在向前移动过程中被场外因素触及。
- 应重罚球点球。

the ball rebounds into the field of play from the goalkeeper, the crossbar or the goalposts and is then touched by an outside agent:

- the referee stops play
- play is restarted with a dropped ball at the position where it touched the outside agent

3. Summary table

	Outcome of the penalty kick	
	Goal	**No Goal**
Encroachment by attacking player	Penalty is retaken	Indirect free kick
Encroachment by defending player	Goal	Penalty is retaken
Offence by goalkeeper	Goal	Penalty is retaken and caution for goalkeeper
Ball kicked backwards	Indirect free kick	Indirect free kick
Illegal feinting	Indirect free kick and caution for kicker	Indirect free kick and caution for kicker
Wrong kicker	Indirect free kick and caution for wrong kicker	Indirect free kick and caution for wrong kicker

球从守门员身体、横梁或球门柱弹回比赛场地内，随后被场外因素触及：
- 裁判员停止比赛。
- 在被场外因素触及的地点以坠球恢复比赛。

3. 概要

	罚球点球的结果	
	进球	未进球
攻方队员违犯规则	重罚球点球	间接任意球
守方队员违犯规则	进球有效	重罚球点球
守门员违犯规则	进球有效	重罚球点球并警告守门员
向后踢球点球	间接任意球	间接任意球
不合法的假动作	间接任意球并警告罚球队员	间接任意球并警告罚球队员
非确认主罚的队员罚球	间接任意球并警告该名队员	间接任意球并警告该名队员

15. The Throw-in

A throw-in is awarded to the opponents of the player who last touched the ball when the whole of the ball passes over the touchline, on the ground or in the air.

A goal cannot be scored directly from a throw-in:

- if the ball enters the opponents' goal – a goal kick is awarded
- if the ball enters the thrower's goal – a corner kick is awarded

1. Procedure

At the moment of delivering the ball, the thrower must:

- face the field of play
- have part of each foot on the touchline or on the ground outside the touchline
- throw the ball with both hands from behind and over the head from the point where it left the field of play

All opponents must stand at least 2 m (2 yds) from the point at which the throw-in is taken.

The ball is in play when it enters the field of play. If the ball touches the ground before entering, the throw-in is retaken by the same team from the same position. If the throw-in is not taken correctly it is retaken by the opposing team.

If a player, while correctly taking a throw-in, intentionally throws the ball at an opponent in order to play the ball again but neither in a careless nor a reckless manner nor using excessive force, the referee allows play to continue.

The thrower must not touch the ball again until it has touched another player.

第十五章　掷界外球

当球的整体从地面或空中越过边线时，由最后触球队员的对方掷界外球。

界外球不能直接掷进球门得分：
- 如果球直接掷入对方球门——判踢球门球。
- 如果球直接掷入本方球——判踢角球。

1. 程序

在掷出球的瞬间，掷球队员必须：
- 面向比赛场地。
- 任何一只脚的一部分在边线上或在边线外的地面上。
- 在球离开比赛场地的地点，<u>用双手将球从头后经头顶掷出</u>。

所有对方队员必须站在距离掷球地点至少2米（2码）的位置。

当球掷入比赛场地内，即为比赛恢复。在球进入比赛场地之前，如果球接触地面，则由同一队在相同地点重新掷界外球。如果未依照正确程序掷界外球，则由对方掷界外球。

如果一名队员以正确的方式，故意将球掷向对方队员以再次触球，但并未使用草率的、鲁莽的方式或过分的力量，裁判员允许比赛继续。

掷球队员在其他队员触及球前不得再次触球。

2. Infringements and sanctions

If, after the ball is in play, the thrower touches the ball again before it has touched another player an indirect free kick is awarded; if the thrower deliberately handles the ball:

- a direct free kick is awarded
- a penalty kick is awarded if the infringement occurred inside the thrower's penalty area unless the ball was handled by the defending team's goalkeeper in which case an indirect free kick is awarded

An opponent who unfairly distracts or impedes the thrower (including moving closer than 2 m (2 yds) to the place where the throw-in is to be taken) is cautioned for unsporting behaviour and if the throw-in has been taken an indirect free kick is awarded.

For any other infringement of this Law the throw-in is taken by a player of the opposing team.

2.违规与处罚

如果比赛已经恢复，掷球队员在其他队员触及球前再次触球，则判罚间接任意球。如果掷球队员故意用手触球：

- 判罚直接任意球。
- 如果违规情况出现在掷球队员本方罚球区内，则判罚球点球。除非掷球队员为守门员，这种情况下判罚间接任意球。

对方队员通过不正当的方式干扰或阻碍掷球队员（包括移动至距掷球位置少于2米（2码）的地点）应以非体育行为予以警告，如果界外球已被掷出，则判罚间接任意球。

对于其他任何违反本章条文的情况，应由对方队员掷界外球。

16. The Goal Kick

A goal kick is awarded when the whole of the ball passes over the goal line, on the ground or in the air, having last touched a player of the attacking team, and a goal is not scored.

A goal may be scored directly from a goal kick, but only against the opposing team; <u>if the ball directly enters the kicker's goal a corner kick is awarded to the opponents if the ball left the penalty area.</u>

1. **Procedure**
    - The ball <u>must be stationary and</u> is kicked from any point within the goal area by a player of the defending team
    - The ball is in play when it leaves the penalty area
    - Opponents must be outside the penalty area until the ball is in play

2. **Infringements and sanctions**

    If the ball does not leave the penalty area or is touched by a player before it leaves the penalty area the kick is retaken.

    If, after the ball is in play, the kicker touches the ball again before it has touched another player an indirect free kick is awarded; if the kicker deliberately handles the ball:

    - a direct free kick is awarded
    - a penalty kick is awarded if the infringement occurred inside the kicker's penalty area unless the kicker was the goalkeeper in which case an indirect free kick is awarded

第十六章　球门球

当球的整体从地面或空中越过球门线，而最后由攻方队员触及，且并未出现进球，则判为球门球。

球门球可以直接射入对方球门而得分。如果球离开罚球区后直接进入踢球队员本方球门，则判给对方角球。

1. 程序
- 球必须放定，由守方球队中的一名场上队员在球门区内任意位置踢球。
- 当球被踢并离开罚球区，即为比赛恢复。
- 对方队员必须处在罚球区外直到比赛恢复。

2. 违规与处罚
如果球未离开罚球区或在离开罚球区前被队员触及，则重踢球门球。

如果比赛已经恢复，踢球队员在其他队员触及球前再次触球，则判罚间接任意球。如果踢球队员故意用手触球：
- 判罚直接任意球。
- 如果违规情况出现在踢球队员本方罚球区内，则判罚球点球。除非踢球队员为守门员，这种情况下判罚间接任意球。

If an opponent who is in the penalty area when the goal kick is taken touches or challenges for the ball before it has touched another player, the goal kick is retaken.

If a player enters the penalty area before the ball is in play and fouls or is fouled by an opponent, the goal kick is retaken and the offender may be cautioned or sent off depending on the offence.

For any other infringement of this Law the kick is retaken.

在踢球门球时处在罚球区内的对方队员，在其他队员触及球前触球或争抢球，应重踢球门球。

在比赛恢复前，如果队员进入罚球区内，对对方队员或被对方队员犯规，应重踢球门球。依据犯规情况，犯规队员可被警告或罚令出场。

对于其他任何违反本章条文的情况，应重踢球门球。

17. The Corner Kick

A corner kick is awarded when the whole of the ball passes over the goal line, on the ground or in the air, having last touched a player of the defending team, and a goal is not scored.

A goal may be scored directly from a corner kick, but only against the opposing team; if the ball directly enters the kicker's goal a corner kick is awarded to the opponents.

1. **Procedure**
   - The ball must be placed in the corner area nearest to the point where the ball passed over the goal line
   - The ball must be stationary and is kicked by a player of the attacking team
   - The ball is in play when it is kicked and clearly moves; it does not need to leave the corner area
   - The corner flagpost must not be moved
   - Opponents must remain at least 9.15 m (10 yds) from the corner arc until the ball is in play

2. **Infringements and sanctions**

   If, after the ball is in play, the kicker touches the ball again before it has touched another player an indirect free kick is awarded; if the kicker deliberately handles the ball:

   - a direct free kick is awarded
   - a penalty kick is awarded if the infringement occurred inside the kicker's penalty area unless the kicker was the goalkeeper in which case an indirect free kick is awarded

第十七章　角球

当球的整体从地面或空中越过球门线，而最后由守方队员触及，且并未出现进球，则判为角球。

角球可以直接射入对方球门而得分。如果角球直接射入踢球队员本方球门，则判给对方角球。

1. 程序
- 球必须放在球越过球门线时最接近的角球区内。
- 球必须放定，由攻方球队中的一名场上队员踢球。
- 当球被踢且明显移动时，即为比赛恢复。无须将球踢出角球区。
- 不得移动角旗杆。
- 对方队员必须距角球弧至少9.15米（10码），直到比赛恢复。

2. 违规与处罚
如果比赛已经恢复，踢球队员在其他队员触球前再次触球，则判罚间接任意球。如果发球队员故意用手触球：
- 判罚直接任意球。
- 如果违规情况出现在踢球队员本方罚球区内，则判罚球点球。除非踢球队员为守门员，这种情况下判罚间接任意球。

If a player, while correctly taking a corner kick, intentionally kicks the ball at an opponent in order to play the ball again but not in a careless or reckless manner or using excessive force, the referee allows play to continue.

For any other infringement of this Law the kick is retaken.

如果一名队员在以正确方式踢角球的过程中,故意将球踢向对方队员以再次获得球权,但并未使用草率的、鲁莽的方式或过分的力量,裁判员允许比赛继续。

对于其他任何违反本章条文的情况,应重踢角球。

Law changes
2016/2017

竞赛规则变更内容
2016/2017

Outline summary of Law changes

Herewith a simple outline of the main changes/clarifications.

Law 01 – The Field of Play
- Artificial and natural surfaces may not be combined on the field
- Competitions may determine field size for their competitions (within Law)
- All commercial advertising on the ground must be at least 1 m (1 yd) from boundary lines
- Logos/emblems of FAs, competitions etc... allowed on corner flags (no advertising)

Law 02 – The Ball
None

Law 03 – The Players (new title)
- A match may not start/continue if a team has fewer than 7 players
- Substitutes may take a restart but must first step onto the field
- Clarifies situation when a player is sent off before/after kick-off
- Direct FK (or penalty) if a substitute/team official interferes with play
- If something/someone (other than a player) touches a ball as it goes into the goal the referee can award the goal if the touch had no impact on the defenders
- If a goal is scored with an extra person on the field and referee has restarted play the goal stands and match continues

规则变更概要

本部分简要列出新规则所进行变更或明确的主要内容。

第一章 比赛场地

- 人造和天然草皮不可拼接使用。
- 竞赛方可以决定比赛场地的尺寸（在规则限定范围内）。
- 所有地面上的商业广告必须距场地边界线至少1米（1码）。
- 足球协会、竞赛方等机构的标志和标识允许出现在角旗上（不允许广告出现）。

第二章 球

无变更。

第三章 队员（新标题）

- 如果某队场上队员不足7人，比赛不能开始或者继续进行。
- 替补队员可以执行恢复比赛的程序，但其必须先步入比赛场地。
- 明确了在比赛开始前和开始后将队员罚令出场的情形。
- 如果替补队员或球队官员干扰了比赛，则判罚任意球（或球点球）。
- 如果某个因素或某人（非场上队员）触球，然后球进入了球门，如果这种接触没有阻碍防守队员，可判进球有效。
- 如果进球发生在比赛场地内有多出的人员时，且裁判员已经恢复比赛，则进球有效，比赛继续进行。

Law 04 – The Players' Equipment
- Any tape or other material on/covering socks must be same colour as the sock
- Player losing footwear/shinguard accidentally can play on until next stoppage
- Undershorts must be colour of shorts or hem; team must all wear same colour
- Electronic communication with substitutes is forbidden
- Player can return during play after changing/correcting equipment, once equipment has been checked (by referee, fourth official or AR) and referee signals

Law 05 – The Referee
- Decision can not be changed if play restarted or referee has left the field (HT+FT)
- If several offences occur at the same time the most serious is punished
- Referee can send a player off from pre-match pitch inspection onwards
- Referee can only use RC + YC after entering the field at start of the match
- Player injured by RC/YC foul can be quickly assessed/ treated and stay on field
- The equipment a referee can or may be allowed to use
- Diagrams of referee signals included (from Guidelines section)

Law 06 – The Other Match Officials (new title)
- More details about the duties of the assistants, AARs, fourth official
- Diagrams of assistant referee signals included (from Guidelines section)

Law 07 – The Duration of the Match
- More reasons for additional time (e.g. medical drinks breaks)

Law 08 – The Start and Restart of Play
- All restarts included (previously only kick-off and dropped ball)
- Ball must clearly move to be in play for all kicked restarts
- Ball can be kicked in any direction at kick-off (previously had to go forward)
- Referee can not 'manufacture' outcome of a dropped ball

第四章 队员装备

- 护袜上附着/包裹的胶带/材料必须与护袜同色。
- 意外脱落鞋子/护腿板的队员可以继续比赛直至比赛停止。
- 内衬裤颜色必须与短裤主色或短裤边缘颜色相同。
- 替补队员的电子通讯被禁止。
- 离开场地调整或更换装备的队员,在由比赛官员(裁判员、第四官员或助理裁判员)检查后,经裁判员给出信号,可以在比赛进行中返回场地比赛。

第五章 裁判员

- 如果比赛已经恢复,或者比赛结束(半场或全场)裁判员已经离开场地,则判罚决定不能更改。
- 多种犯规同时出现时,判罚最严重的犯规。
- 赛前检查场地时,裁判员可以将队员罚令出场。
- 赛前进入比赛场地后,裁判员才可以出示红牌或黄牌。
- 因对方可被出示黄牌/红牌的犯规而受伤的队员,可以在场内接受快速伤情评估/治疗,并且可以留在场内(不必出场)。
- 允许裁判员使用的装备。
- 包含了裁判员示意信号的图示。

第六章 其他比赛官员(新标题)

- 更多关于助理裁判员、附加助理裁判员,以及第四官员职责的细节。
- 包含了助理裁判员示意信号的图示(实践指南部分)。

第七章 比赛时间

- 更多需予以补时的情况(例如补水暂停等)。

第八章 比赛开始与恢复

- 包含了所有恢复比赛的方式(之前只包含了开球和坠球)。
- 在所有以踢球方式恢复比赛时,球必须明显移动,比赛才视为开始。
- 开球时球可以踢向任何方向(之前只允许向前踢)。
- 裁判员不能"制造"坠球的情形(例如决定球权归属等)。

Law 09 – The Ball in and out of Play
- If a ball rebounds off a match official it is in play unless it has wholly passed over a boundary line

Law 10 – Determining the Outcome of a Match (new title)
Kicks from the penalty mark:
- Referee will toss a coin to choose the goal (unless weather, safety, etc.)
- Player temporarily off the field (e.g. injured) at final whistle can take part
- Both teams must have same number of players before and during the kicks
- Clear statement of when a kick is over
- Kicks not delayed if player leaves the field; if not back in time kick is forfeited

Law 11 – Offside
- Halfway line 'neutral' for offside; player must be in opponents' half
- Players' arms not considered when judging offside position (including goalkeeper)
- Offside FK always taken where offence occurs (even in own half)
- Defender off the field only 'active' until defending team clear ball or play stops
- As above for attacker returning; before that re-entry point is the offside position

Law 12 – Fouls and Misconduct
- Foul with contact is a direct FK
- Advantage for a RC – indirect FK if offender then gets involved in play
- Change of wording for handball so that not every handball is a YC
- Some DOGSO offences in the penalty area are punished with a YC
- Attempted violent conduct is a RC, even if no contact
- Striking on head/face when not challenging an opponent is a RC (unless negligible)
- Offence against substitutes, team officials, match officials etc. is now a direct FK
- Foul off the field penalised with a direct FK on boundary line (penalty in own penalty area)

第九章 比赛进行与停止

- 球从比赛官员身上弹回时，比赛处于进行中，除非球的整体已经越过了场地边界线。

第十章 确定比赛结果（新标题）

罚球点球决胜：
- 裁判员通过掷硬币的方式决定所使用的球门（除非天气、安全等原因）。
- 在比赛结束时处于暂时离场状态（如受伤等）的队员，可以参加踢球点球决胜。
- 在踢球点球决胜开始前和进行中，双方队员人数必须相同。
- 明确表述了一次罚球何时视为结束。
- 不得因队员离场而拖延罚球，如果队员未按时返回，则视为罚失。

第十一章 越位

- 中线对于越位而言是"中立"的，队员必须处在对方半场才是越位位置。
- 队员的手和臂部不在越位位置判定范围内（包括守门员）。
- 因越位犯规而判罚的间接任意球，须在犯规发生地点罚球（即使在越位方本方半场）。
- 处于场外的防守队员处于"活跃状态"，至防守方将球解围或比赛停止为止。
- 上条原则对于从场外返回的进攻队员同样适用，在此之前重返场地的地点作为越位位置的判定点。

第十二章 犯规与不正当行为

- 有身体接触的犯规，均判罚直接任意球。
- 对需出示红牌的犯规掌握有利——如果该犯规队员随后参与了比赛，则判罚间接任意球。
- 对于手球的条文有所调整，故不是所有的手球犯规都出示黄牌。
- 有些在本方罚球区内破坏对方明显进球得分机会的犯规，将被出示黄牌。
- 试图实施暴力行为，也将被出示红牌，即使未发生身体接触。
- 在不以争抢球为目的的情况下，击打对方头部/面部将被出示红牌（除非力量微不足道）。
- 对替补队员、球队官员、比赛官员等人员实施的犯规，现在将被判罚直接任意球。
- 在比赛场地外发生的犯规，将在场地边界线上判罚直接任意球（如果在罚球区内则判罚球点球）。

Law 13 – Free Kicks
- Difference between 'stopping' a FK and 'intercepting' the ball after FK taken

Law 14 – The Penalty Kick
- Indirect FK + YC if wrong player deliberately takes the penalty
- Indirect FK if ball kicked backwards
- If 'illegal' feinting occurs it is always an indirect FK (and YC)
- Goalkeeper YC if infringes and PK is retaken

Law 15 – The Throw-in
- New wording makes it clear that ball must be thrown with both hands

Law 16 – The Goal Kick
- If GK kicked into own goal it is a corner kick to opponents
- An opponent in the penalty area when the goal kick is taken can not play the ball first

Law 17 – The Corner Kick
- If CK kicked into own goal it is a corner kick to opponents

第十三章 任意球
- "阻止"任意球踢出与"截得"已经踢出的任意球的区别。

第十四章 罚球点球
- 已确认的主罚队员以外的队员执行罚球点球,将被出示黄牌,并判给对方罚间接任意球。
- 向后踢球点球,将判给对方罚间接任意球。
- 只要"不合规的"假动作发生,即判给对方罚间接任意球(并且黄牌警告犯规队员)。
- 当守门员违规,球点球将被重踢时,向守门员出示黄牌。

第十五章 掷界外球
- 新条文明确了界外球必须用双手掷出。

第十六章 球门球
- 如果球门球被踢入本方球门,则由对方罚角球。
- 球门球踢出时位于罚球区内的对方队员不能先触球。

第十七章 角球
- 如果角球踢入本方球门,则由对方踢角球。

Details of all Law changes (in Law order)

The following are the main changes to the Laws of the Game which are not related to English/phraseology. For each change the old wording (where appropriate) and the new/changed wording are given followed by an explanation for the change.

The text shown in the 'old text' boxes may be the exact previous text or a more general outline of the meaning of the previous text.

Law 01 – The Field of Play

01.1 Artificial and natural surfaces may not be combined

Old text	New text
Matches may be played on natural or artificial surfaces, according to competition rules.	The field of play must be a wholly natural or, if competition rules permit, a wholly artificial playing surface, except where competition rules permit an integrated combination of artificial and natural materials (hybrid system).

Explanation

Clarifies that for safety reasons mixing natural and artificial surfaces is not permitted on the field of play. A different surface is permitted on the surrounding areas e.g. artificial turf for the assistant referees' patrol area. An integrated mix of natural and artificial material is permitted.

规则变更详解（按规则章节排序）

本部分为《足球竞赛规则》的主要变更内容，这些变更内容均有含义的改变而不仅仅是调整了语言措辞。每处变更，旧条文与相对应的新的/调整后的条文内容对照列出，并有相应的解析。

在"旧条文"一栏中使用的文字可能与上一版本的规则完全一致，也可能是对上一版本文字意义的大致概括。

第一章　比赛场地

01.1 人造和天然草皮不可拼接使用

旧条文	新条文
根据竞赛规程规定，比赛可以在天然或人造草坪场地上进行。	比赛场地必须为全天然草皮。若竞赛规程允许，可使用全人造草皮。此外，如果竞赛规程允许，可使用人造和天然结合材料制成的整体草皮（混合系统）。

解析

出于安全考虑，不允许将天然和人造草皮拼接混用于比赛场地。可在场地周边区域使用不同材质的草皮，如在助理裁判员"巡逻"区域使用人造草皮等。比赛场地仅允许使用人造和天然整体混合材质的草皮。

01.2 Competitions may determine length of boundary lines (within Law 1 parameters)
Additional text
Competitions may determine the length of the goal line and touchline within the above dimensions.
Explanation
Clarifies that competitions have the authority to determine the length of the touchlines and goal lines for their matches within the dimensions of Law 1.

01.3 The technical area
Explanation
Technical area information moved from end of Laws section

01.4 Goal Line Technology (GTL)
Explanation
Goal Line Technology (GLT) moved from Law 10

01.5 Commercial advertising on the ground	
Old text	**New text**
No form of commercial advertising, whether real or virtual, is permitted on the field of play, on the ground within the area enclosed by the goal nets or the technical area, or within 1 m (1 yd) of the touchline from the time the teams enter the field of play…	No form of commercial advertising, whether real or virtual, is permitted on the field of play, on the ground within the area enclosed by the goal nets or the technical area, or on the ground within 1 m (1 yd) of the boundary lines from the time the teams enter the field of play…

Explanation

Clarifies that restrictions on commercial advertising on the ground relate to the area behind the goal lines as well as the touchlines.

01.2 竞赛方可以决定边界线的长度（在规则第一章的限定范围内）

新增条文

竞赛方可以在上述尺寸范围内规定球门线和边线的长度。

解析

明确了竞赛组织方有权在第一章限定的尺寸范围内，决定比赛场地边线和球门线的长度。

01.3 技术区域

解析

技术区域的内容从规则第十七章之后移至本章。

01.4 球门线技术

解析

球门线技术（GLT）内容从第十章移至本章。

01.5 地面上的商业广告

旧条文	新条文
从球队进入比赛场地至上半场结束离开，下半场重新进入比赛场地至比赛结束，任何商业广告，不管是实物的还是图文的，都不允许出现在比赛场地和场地设备上，包括球门网和球门网内的地面或技术区域，以及距离边线1米（1码）以内距离。	从球队进入比赛场地起至上半场结束离开，下半场重新进入比赛场地至比赛结束，任何形式的商业广告，无论是实体的还是虚拟的，都不允许出现在比赛场地内、球门网围合区域内的地面上，以及技术区域，或在场地边界线外1米以内的地面上。

解析

明确了对球门线后相关区域地面上商业广告的限制与在边线外一致。

01.6 Logos and emblems on corner flags	
Old text	**New text**
The reproduction, whether real or virtual, of representative logos or emblems of FIFA, confederations, member associations, leagues, clubs or other bodies is forbidden on the field of play, the goal nets and the areas they enclose, the goals, the flagposts and their flags during playing time.	The reproduction, whether real or virtual, of representative logos or emblems of FIFA, confederations, <u>national football</u> associations, <u>competitions</u>, clubs or other bodies is forbidden on the field of play, the goal nets and the areas they enclose, the goals, and the flagposts during playing time. <u>They are permitted on the flags on the flagposts</u>.

Explanation

- **National football associations** replaces **member associations**
- **competitions** replaces **leagues** as cup competitions are not covered by the current wording.

- These logos are already widely used and allowing them on the flags is consistent with Law 2 which permits them on the ball.

Law 02 – The Ball
None

Law 03 – The Players

03.1 Title change

Old title	**New title**
The Number of Players	<u>The Players</u>

Explanation

New title reflects that the content includes reference to substitutes etc.

01.6 角旗旗帜上的标志和图案

旧条文	新条文
在比赛期间，国际足球联合会、洲际联合会、会员协会、联盟、俱乐部或其他团体的代表性标识或图案的复制品，不管是实物还是图文形式，都禁止出现在比赛场地、球门网和附属区域、球门柱和角旗上。	在比赛进行期间，国际足联、洲际足球联合会、国家足球协会、竞赛方、俱乐部，以及其他机构的代表性标志或图案的复制品，无论是实体还是虚拟形式，都禁止出现在比赛场地内、球门网及其围合区域、球门和旗杆上，但可出现在旗杆的旗帜上。

解析

- 国家足球协会取代了会员协会。
- 竞赛方取代联盟，否则杯赛未被包含在内。
- 这些标志已经广泛使用，允许其出现在角旗旗帜上与第二章中允许其出现在比赛用球上是一致的。

第二章　球

无变更。

第三章　队员

03.1 章节标题变更

旧章节标题	新章节标题
队员人数。	队员。

解析

新标题反映了本章内容还涉及替补队员等人员。

03.2 Minimum number of players

Old text	New text
A match may not start if either team consists of fewer than seven players. (...) although a match may not START if either team consists of fewer than seven players, the minimum number of players in a team required for a match to CONTINUE is left to the discretion of member associations. However, it is the opinion of the International F.A. Board that a match should not continue if there are fewer than seven players in either team.	A match may not start <u>or continue</u> if either team has fewer than seven players.

Explanation

The IFAB recommendation of the minimum number of players for a match to continue becomes Law. This is consistent with the minimum to start the match.

03.3 Restarts by substitutes

Old text	New text
A substitute who has not completed the substitution procedure by entering the field of play cannot restart play by taking a throw-in or corner kick.	<u>Substitutes can take any restart provided they first enter</u> the field of play.

Explanation

Clarifies that a substitute who steps onto the field of play can then take any restart, including a corner kick or throw-in; some wrongly interpreted the 'old' wording as requiring play to be restarted before a substitute can take a restart.

03.2 最少场上队员人数

旧条文	新条文
如果任何一队少于7人则比赛不能开始……尽管一个队需要继续比赛的最少人数由会员协会来定，但无论如何，国际足球理事会认为，如果任何一队少于7人，则不能继续比赛。	如果任何一队场上队员人数少于7人，则比赛不得开始或继续。

解析

国际足球理事会对于可继续比赛的最少人数建议成为正式规则条文。这与开始比赛的人数要求是一致的。

03.3 由替补队员恢复比赛

旧条文	新条文
一名替补队员在没有将脚踏入比赛场内而未完全履行替补程序，不能由其执行掷界外球或角球重新开始比赛。	如果由替换上场的队员执行任一恢复比赛的程序，他必须先进入比赛场地。

解析

明确了进入比赛场地内的替补队员可以执行任一恢复比赛的任务，包括踢角球和掷界外球。另外，有些对于旧条文的误解认为，在恢复比赛后，替补队员才能执行恢复比赛的任务。

03.4 Named substitute starts instead of named player	
Old text	**New text**
If a named substitute enters the field of play instead of a named player at the start of the match and the referee is not informed of this change: • the referee allows the named substitute to continue the match (...)	If a named substitute starts the match instead of a named player and the referee is not informed of this change: • the referee allows the named substitute to continue the match (...)

Explanation

Clarifies that if a named player is 'replaced' by a substitute before the match, the player can be a substitute on arrival. More logical that this takes effect when the match kicks off rather than when the substitute enters the field.

03.5 Extra persons on the field of play – status of sent off player	
Old text	**New text**
Anyone not indicated on the team list as a player, substitute or team official is deemed to be an outside agent, as is a player who has been sent off.	Anyone not named on the team list as a player, substitute or team official is deemed to be an outside agent.

Explanation

It is more logical to treat a sent off player like a substitute so that a player who returns to the field (having been sent off) is penalised with a free kick.

03.6 Infringements by substitutes and team officials	
Old text	**New text**
If a substitute or substituted player enters the field of play without the referee's permission: • if the referee has stopped play, it is restarted with an indirect free kick (...).	If play is stopped and the interference was by: • a team official, substitute, substituted or sent off player, play restarts with a direct free kick or penalty kick

03.4 被提名的替补队员代替已提名的上场队员开始比赛

旧条文	新条文
在比赛开始时，如果一名被提名的替补队员进入比赛场地代替已提名的上场队员，并且未通知裁判员： • 裁判员允许被提名的替补队员继续参赛。 ……	如果一名被提名的替补队员在未告知裁判员的情况下，取代被提名的上场队员开始比赛： • 裁判员允许该名替补队员继续比赛。 ……

解析

明确了如果一名提名的上场队员在比赛开始前被一名提名的替补队员取代，原上场队员可以在到达比赛场地后作为替补队员。较之在比赛开始时或替补队员进入比赛场地时生效更符合逻辑。

03.5 比赛场地内多出的人员——被罚令出场的队员身份

旧条文	新条文
没有列入比赛名单的队员、替补队员或球队官员被视为场外因素，其等同于被罚出场的队员。	除球队名单内的上场队员、替补队员以及球队官员外，其他任何人员视为场外因素。

解析

将被罚令出场的队员视为替补队员更符合逻辑，这样如果其返回比赛场地（已被罚令出场的情况下），将被判罚任意球。

03.6 替补队员和球队官员的违规行为

旧条文	新条文
如果替补队员或被替换下场的队员未经允许进入比赛场地： • 如果裁判员暂停比赛，则以间接任意球恢复比赛……	如果比赛停止是由如下情况干扰造成： • 球队官员、替补队员、已替换下场或被罚令出场的队员，则以直接任意球或球点球恢复比赛。

If a team official enters the field of play:
- if the referee stops the match, he must restart play with a dropped ball(...).

Explanation

There is a growing problem of substitutes/team officials entering the field to interfere with play or an opponent, e.g. stopping a goal. This is clearly 'unfair' and a direct free kick (or penalty kick if in own penalty area) is more appropriate.

03.7 Player who is sent off before or after kick-off

Additional text

A player who is sent off:
- before submission of the team list can not be named on the team list in any capacity
- after being named on the team list and before kick-off may be replaced by a named substitute (who can not be replaced)
- after the kick-off can not be replaced

Explanation

Clarifies whether a sent off player can be replaced.

03.8 Impact of substitute/team official/outside agent touching a ball which is going into the goal

Old text	New text
In the situations outlined in 3.6 above the referee must stop play if the 'intruder' interferes with play or touches the ball. If an outside agent enters the field of play: • the referee must stop play (although not immediately if the outside agent does not interfere with play)	If a ball is going into the goal and the interference does not prevent a defending player playing the ball, the goal is awarded if the ball enters the goal (even if contact was made with the ball) unless the ball enters the opponents' goal.

如果替补队员或被替换下场的队员未经允许进入比赛场地：
- 如果裁判员暂停比赛，则以间接任意球恢复比赛……

解析

替补队员/球队官员进入比赛场地干扰比赛或对方队员的现象日渐增多，例如阻止进球，这显然"不公平"。而判罚直接任意球（或在其本方罚球区内判罚球点球）的方法更加合理。

03.7 由替补队员恢复比赛

新增条文

上场队员被罚令出场：
- 在球队名单提交前被罚令出场，不得以任何身份列入球队名单内。
- 在提交球队名单后，比赛开始前被罚令出场，可由被提名的替补队员取代，替补队员名单不得增补，球队的替换人数不做削减。
- 在比赛开始后被罚令出场，不得被替换。

解析

明确了被罚令出场的队员能否被替换。

03.8 替补队员/球队官员/场外因素影响将要进门的球

旧条文	新条文
在上述3.6描述的情形下，如果"侵入场内的因素"干扰了比赛或触及到了球，裁判员必须暂停比赛。 如果一个场外因素进入比赛场内： • 裁判员必须停止比赛（如果场外因素没有干扰比赛，不必立即停止比赛）。	如果球将要进门时，干扰因素没有阻止防守队员处理球，随后球进门，则进球有效（即便干扰因素与球发生接触），除非球进入对方球门。

Explanation

This **'fair play'** change means the referee can apply the advantage principle so that if the attempt to stop a goal is unsuccessful the referee can award the goal (See 3.9)

03.9 Goal scored with an extra person on the field of play

Old text	New text

If, after a goal is scored, the referee realises, before play restarts, that there was an extra person on the field of play when the goal was scored:
• the referee must disallow the goal if:
  – the extra person was an outside agent and he interfered with play
  – the extra person was a player, substitute, substituted player or team official associated with the team that scored the goal
	If, after a goal is scored, the referee realises, before play restarts, that there was an extra person(s) on the field of play when the goal was scored:
	• the referee must disallow the goal if the extra person was:
	  – a player, substitute, substituted player, sent off player or team official of the team that scored the goal
	  – an outside agent who interfered with play <u>unless a goal results as outlined above in 'extra persons on the field of play;</u>
	Play is restarted with a goal kick or a corner kick.
	<u>If, after a goal is scored and play has restarted, the referee realises an extra person was on the field of play when the goal was scored, the goal can not be disallowed.</u> If the extra person is still on the field the referee must:
	• stop play
	• have the extra person removed
	• restart with a dropped ball or indirect free kick as appropriate
	The referee must report the incident to the appropriate authorities.

解析

这条有关"公平竞赛"的变动意味着裁判员可以掌握有利原则,如果干扰因素的尝试没能阻止球进门,裁判员应判罚进球有效(详见03.9)。

03.9 比赛场地内有多出的人员时出现进球

旧条文	新条文
如果在进球后、重新开始比赛前,裁判员意识到发生进球时场上多出一人: • 裁判员必须判进球无效,如果: 　– 多出的人是场外因素并且干扰了比赛。 　– 多出的人是进球队一方的队员、替补队员、被替换的队员或球队的官员。	如果裁判员在进球后、比赛恢复前意识到进球时比赛场地内有多出的人员: • 如果多出的人员是如下人员,裁判员必须判定进球无效: 　– 进球队一方的场上队员、替补队员、已替换下场或被罚令出场的队员及球队官员。 　– 干扰了比赛的场外因素,除非进球符合本章第7条"比赛场地内多出的人员"的说明。 以球门球、角球或坠球恢复比赛。 …… 如果裁判员在出现进球,且已经恢复比赛后意识到发生进球时比赛场地内有多出的人员,则不得取消进球。如果多出的人员仍在比赛场地内,裁判员必须: • 停止比赛。 • 责令多出的人员离开比赛场地。 • 以坠球或相应的任意球方式恢复比赛。裁判员必须向相关机构报告此事件。

Explanation

- Incorporates principle outlined in 3.8 (above)
- Clarifies how to restart if a goal is scored when there is an extra person on the field and play has not restarted.
- Clarifies that if a goal was scored when there was an extra person on the field and play has restarted the referee has to allow the game to continue; the referee can not disallow the goal or 'nullify' the period between the goal and the discovery of the extra person.

03.10 Reference to team captain (from Law 12)

Additional text

The team captain has no special status or privileges but has a degree of responsibility for the behaviour of the team.

Explanation

More logical to have this statement in Law 3 rather than Law 12.

Law 04 – The Players' Equipment

04.1 Tape/material on/covering socks

Old text	New text
The compulsory equipment of a player comprises the following (...) • stockings – if tape or similar material is applied externally it must be the same colour as that part of the sock it is applied to	• socks – tape or <u>any material applied or worn externally</u> must be the same colour as that part of the sock it is applied to <u>or covers</u>

Explanation

Clarifies that non-tape material must be the same colour as the sock it covers as some players wear ankle socks (or similar) which are a different colour to the sock.

解析

- 与上述03.8的原则相呼应。
- 明确了当比赛场地内有多出的人时出现进球，且比赛还未重新恢复时，以何种方式恢复比赛。
- 明确了当比赛场地内有多出的人时出现进球，且比赛已经重新恢复时，裁判员必须使比赛继续进行，不得取消进球，或将进球与发现多出人之间的这段时间作为"无效"阶段。

03.10 关于球队队长（自规则第十二章移至本章）

新增条文

球队队长并不享有特殊身份或权力，但他对球队的行为需承担一定责任。

解析

将此部分放在第三章较之第十二章更符合逻辑。

第四章 队员装备

04.1 护袜上附着/包裹的胶带/材料

旧条文	新条文
队员必需的基本装备： …… • 护袜——如果使用绷带或相似材料在外面包裹，则必须与所包裹部分的护袜颜色一致。	• 护袜——<u>胶带或任何附着、外套的材料</u>，其颜色必须与所附着或包裹部分的护袜颜色一致。

解析

明确了非胶带的材料颜色也必须与附着部分护袜颜色一致，因为有些队员穿着及踝短袜（或类似物件）的颜色与护袜不同。

04.2 Loss of footwear and shinguard

Old text	New text
If a player loses his footwear accidentally and immediately plays the ball and/or scores a goal, (…) (…) the goal is awarded.	A player whose footwear or shinguard is accidentally lost must replace it as soon as possible and no later than when the ball next goes out of play; if, before doing so, the player plays the ball and/or scores a goal, the goal is awarded.

Explanation

It is clearer to specify that footwear must be replaced quickly and no later than when the ball next goes out of play. It is logical to apply the principle to shinguards.

04.3 Colour of undergarments

Old text	New text
The basic compulsory equipment of a player comprises the following separate items: • a jersey or shirt with sleeves – if undergarments are worn, the colour of the sleeve must be the same main colour as the sleeve of the jersey or shirt • shorts – if undershorts or tights are worn, they must be of the same main colour as the shorts	The compulsory equipment of a player comprises the following separate items: • a shirt with sleeves • shorts Undershirts must be the same colour as the main colour of the shirt sleeve; undershorts/tights must be the same colour as the main colour of the shorts or the lowest part of the shorts – players of the same team must wear the same colour.

Explanation

- **Undershirts** replaces **undergarments**.
- Manufacturers now make shorts with a different coloured lower part (hem). Law change gives the choice of the undershorts/tights being the same colour as the shorts or the 'hem' but the team must all wear the same colour.

04.2 脱落鞋子和护腿板

旧条文	新条文
如果一名队员的球鞋偶然脱落，紧接着其触球并进球，……，则进球有效。	意外脱落鞋子或护腿板的场上队员，必须在随后比赛停止前尽快整理好装备，如果该名队员在整理好装备前触球且/或射门得分，则进球有效。

解析

明确了球鞋脱落后必须在随后比赛停止前更换好。将此条款运用到护腿板上也更加符合逻辑。

04.3 运动内衣裤的颜色

旧条文	新条文
队员必需的基本装备： • 有袖子的运动上衣—如果穿内衣，其袖子的颜色必须与运动上衣袖子的主色相同。 • 短裤—如果穿着紧身短裤或紧身长裤，它们必须与短裤的主色相同。	场上队员的必要装备包括如下单独分开的物件： • 有袖上衣。 • 短裤。 上衣内衣颜色必须与衣袖主色一致；内衬裤/紧身裤颜色必须与短裤主色或短裤底部颜色一致——同队场上队员必须颜色统一。

解析

- 内衣用词改变（undergarments变更为undershirts）。
- 现在的制造商生产的短裤底部（裤边）有时会有不同颜色。规则的变更允许内衬裤/紧身裤的颜色与"裤边"颜色一致，但同一球队必须要颜色统一。

04.4 Caps

Old text	New text
Non-dangerous protective equipment (...) is permitted as are sports spectacles.	Non-dangerous protective equipment (...) is permitted as are goalkeepers' caps and sports spectacles.

Explanation

Reference to goalkeepers' caps included so their use is permitted within the Laws.

04.5 Electronic communication with players (including substitutes)

Old text	New text
The use of any form of electronic communication systems between players and/or technical staff is not permitted.	The use of any form of electronic communication between players (including substitutes/substituted players) and/or technical staff is not permitted.

Explanation

Clarifies that electronic communication with substitutes is not permitted.

04.6 Player returning after changing/correcting equipment

Old text	New text
In the event of any infringement of this Law (...): • any player required to leave the field of play to correct his equipment must not re-enter without the referee's permission • the referee checks that the player's equipment is correct before allowing him to re-enter the field of play • the player is only allowed to re-enter the field of play when the ball is out of play	A player who leaves the field of play to correct or change equipment must: • have the equipment checked by a match official before being allowed to re-enter • only re-enter with the referee's permission (which may be given during play)

04.4 球帽	
旧条文	新条文
不危险的保护装备，……不应视为危险品并应允许使用。	可允许佩戴不具危险性的保护器具，……，类似的还包括<u>守门员球帽</u>和运动眼镜等。

解析

将守门员球帽列入，成为规则允许使用的装备。

04.5 队员使用的电子通讯系统（包括替补队员）	
旧条文	新条文
不允许队员和/或技术人员使用电子通讯系统。	不允许队员（<u>包括替补队员/已替换下场和被罚令出场队员</u>）和/或技术人员使用任何形式的电子通讯设备。

解析

明确了不允许替补队员使用电子通讯设备。

04.6 队员更换/调整装备后重新加入比赛	
旧条文	新条文
对于任何违反本章规定的： …… • 离开比赛场地调整装备的队员在未得到裁判员许可前不得重新进场。 • 裁判员在允许队员回场前需检查队员装备。 • 队员只有在比赛停止时方可重新进入比赛场地。	<u>离开比赛场地调整或更换装备的队员必须</u>： • <u>由一名比赛官员在其被许可重新进入比赛场地前检查好装备。</u> • 只可在裁判员许可后重新进入比赛场地（<u>可在比赛进行中</u>）。

Explanation

Law was unclear about whether a player who chooses to leave the field of play (e.g. to change boots) can return during play. New wording allows the fourth official/assistant referee to check the equipment and, regardless of the reason for leaving the field, the player is treated the same as if returning after an injury. This is better for the game and reduces conflict/irritation.

Law 05 – The Referee

05.1 Decisions of the referee – opinion and discretion

Additional text

Decisions will be made to the best of the referee's ability according to the Laws of the Game and the 'spirit of the game' and will be based on the opinion of the referee who has the discretion to take appropriate action within the framework of the Laws of the Game.

Explanation

Throughout the Laws, there is reference to 'in the opinion of the referee' and 'at the discretion of the referee' so this statement removes the need to use 'in the opinion of/at the discretion of' regularly. The concept of the 'spirit of the game' now appears in the Laws.

05.2 Decisions of the referee – when decisions can not be changed

Old text	New text
The referee may only change a decision on realising that it is incorrect or, at his discretion, on the advice of an assistant referee or the fourth official, provided that he has not restarted play or terminated the match.	The referee may not change a decision on realising that it is incorrect or on the advice of another match official if play has restarted or the referee has signalled the end of the first or second half (including extra time when played) and left the field or terminated the match.

Explanation

Clarifies that once the referee signals the end of a half and leaves the field a decision can not be changed even if information then comes to light e.g. during the half-time interval.

解析

先前的规则没有明确离开比赛场地（如更换球鞋）的场上队员能否在比赛进行中重新加入比赛。新条文明确了无论场上队员因何种原因离开场地，和受伤后返回比赛场地一样，若在第四官员/助理裁判员检查装备后可及时返场。这有利于比赛，减少争议和不满情绪。

第五章　裁判员

05.1 裁判员的决定——认为和酌情

新增条文

裁判员依据《足球竞赛规则》和"足球运动精神"，尽自身最大能力,在规则框架内酌情考量，做出自己认为最合适的决定。

解析

"裁判员认为"和"酌情考量"成为贯彻规则始终的原则。在其他条文陈述时不必再次重复。"足球运动精神"的概念也正式出现在规则正文中。

05.2 裁判员的决定——何时不能更改判罚决定

旧条文	新条文
裁判员如果意识到其决定错误，或经助理裁判员、第四官员建议后，可以改变决定，但必须在比赛未重新开始且未终止前作出。	如果裁判员本人，或经其他比赛官员建议后意识到自己决定错误，而比赛已经恢复，或裁判员已经示意上下半场结束（包括加时赛）并离开比赛场地，或已经中止了比赛，则不可更改判罚决定。

解析

明确了一旦裁判员示意某一半场结束，且已离开比赛场地，即使随后得到确切信息，也不得更改此前的判罚决定（如在中场休息期间）。

05.3 Several offences committed at the same time	
Old text	**New text**
• punishes the more serious offence when a player (or players from the same team) commits more than one offence at the same time • Offences committed by players from different teams: the referee must stop play and restart it with a dropped ball.	• punishes the more serious offence, in terms of sanction, restart, physical severity and tactical impact, when more than one offence occurs at the same time.

Explanation

It should not matter if it is one or several players or from which team(s) as the most serious offence should be penalised. Same change included in Law 14.

05.4 Authority to take disciplinary action from pre-match inspection of the field (see 12.8)	
Old text	**New text**
The referee has the authority to take disciplinary sanctions from the moment he enters the field of play until he leaves the field of play after the final whistle	• has the authority to take disciplinary action from entering the field of play for the pre-match inspection until leaving the field of play after the match ends (including kicks from the penalty mark). If, before entering the field of play at the start of the match, a player commits a sending-off offence, the referee has the authority to prevent the player taking part in the match (see Law 3.6); the referee will report any other misconduct.

05.3 多个犯规同时出现

旧条文	新条文
• 当一名队员同时犯有一种以上的犯规时，则对较严重的犯规进行判罚。 • 犯规由不同的队员造成：裁判员必须停止比赛，以坠球方式重新开始比赛	• 当多种犯规同时发生时，从纪律处罚、比赛恢复方式、身体接触程度和战术影响等方面考量，判罚相对严重的犯规。

解析

应当判罚程度最为严重的犯规，无论实施犯规的队员人数有多少、是否属于同一支球队。在第十四章中也有相应的变更。

05.4 从比赛开始前检查场地起就拥有执行纪律处罚的权力（详见12.8）

旧条文	新条文
裁判员从进入比赛场地起，直至终场哨响，离开比赛场地，都有权执行纪律处罚。	• 从进入比赛场地开始赛前检查直至比赛结束（包括球点球决胜）离开比赛场地，裁判员均有权执行纪律处罚。如果在开赛进入场地前，一名上场队员犯有可被罚令出场的犯规，裁判员有权阻止其参加该场比赛（详见第三章第6条），并将任何其他不正当行为上报。

95

Explanation

New wording identifies exactly when the referee's authority to take action starts. The current Law 12 wording relates to when there was no pre-match warming up, teams did not enter the field together etc. It is logical that if, for example, two players have a fight in the tunnel, or in the pre-match warm up, they can not be allowed to play as this would risk match control and not be good for the image of the game.

During the inspection of the field of play the referee can have the markings changed etc., so it is logical that this is when the authority to 'send off' a player starts. Non-sending-off offences will be reported so YCs cannot be issued prior to the match or carried into the match (See also 12.8).

05.5 Authority to show red and yellow cards

Old text	New text
The referee has the power to show yellow or red cards during the half-time interval and after the match has finished as well as during extra time and kicks from the penalty mark, since the match remains under his jurisdiction at these times.	• has the power to show yellow or red cards <u>from entering the field of play at the start of the match until after the match has ended, including during the half-time interval, extra time and kicks from the penalty mark</u>

Explanation

Clarifies (in light of 5.4) that the referee may only use red and yellow cards from entering the field of play at the start of the match.

05.6 Player may have quick on-field assessment/treatment after YC/RC offence

Old text

The referee... ...stops the match if, in his opinion, a player is seriously injured and ensures that the player is removed from the field of play. An injured player may not be treated on the field and may only return after the match has restarted (...)

Exceptions to the requirement to leave the field are only when:
• a goalkeeper is injured

解析

新条文明确了裁判员从何时开始行使职责。原有第十二章的措辞并没有涉及到赛前热身、球队没有同时入场等。符合逻辑的是，例如，两名队员在球员通道内，或在赛前热身时斗殴，则不得让其参加比赛，因为这不利于控制比赛，也有损于比赛的良好形象。

例如，在赛前检查场地时，裁判员可以要求调整场地内的标记等，所以在这时开始行使将队员"罚令出场"的职责是符合逻辑的。非罚令出场的纪律处罚应上报有关机构，因此在赛前不应出示黄牌，或将黄牌带入比赛（详见12.8）。

05.5 出示红黄牌的权力

旧条文	新条文
裁判员在半场休息、比赛刚结束，以及在加时赛和执行踢球点球决胜时有权出示黄牌或红牌，因为在上述时间，比赛仍然属于裁判员可控制阶段。	从开赛前进入比赛场地直至比赛结束，包括中场休息、加时赛和球点球决胜期间，裁判员都有权出示红黄牌。

解析

明确了（依据05.4）裁判员自赛前进入比赛场地才可使用红黄牌。

05.6 队员在受到应出示红黄牌的犯规后，可在场地内接受快速诊断和治疗

旧条文

裁判员⋯如果他认为队员受伤严重则停止比赛，并确保将其移出比赛场地。受伤的队员只有在比赛重新开始后才能进场参加比赛。当裁判员决定对一名已经受伤并准备离开比赛场地接受治疗的队员出牌时，应在该队员未离开场地前出示。⋯⋯

当发生以下情况时，可以不遵循以上的规定：

- 当守门员受伤时。

- a goalkeeper and an outfield player have collided and need immediate attention
- players from the same team have collided and need immediate attention
- a severe injury has occurred

Additional text

- a player is injured as the result of a physical offence for which the opponent is cautioned or sent off (e.g. reckless or serious foul challenge), if the assessment/treatment is completed quickly

Explanation

It is widely seen as unfair that a player who is injured by a serious foul and the trainer/doctor comes on, the player has to leave the field giving the offending team a numerical benefit (see Practical Guidelines).

05.7 Impact of an outside agent touching a ball which is going into the goal

Old text	New text
An extra ball, other object or animal enters the field of play during the match, the referee must: • stop play only if it interferes with play. Play must be restarted with a dropped ball	an extra ball, other object or animal enters the field of play during the match, the referee must: • stop play (and restart with a dropped ball) only if it interferes with play unless the ball is going into the goal and the interference does not prevent a defending player playing the ball, the goal is awarded if the ball enters the goal (even if contact was made with the ball) unless the ball enters the opponents' goal.

Explanation

This makes Law 5 consistent with the change in Law 3 (see 3.8).

- 当守门员和其他队员发生碰撞需要立即引起关注时。
- 当同队队员发生碰撞需要立即引起关注时。
- 当发生严重受伤时。

附加条文

- 场上队员因遭受对方队员有身体接触，且可被警告或罚令出场的犯规（如鲁莽或严重犯规性质的抢截）而受伤，其伤情能够在短时间完成评估/得到治疗时。

解析

经常见到这样的不公平情况：队员受到严重犯规而受伤，医生入场后，该队员必须离场，给了犯规队人数上的优势（详见实践指南）。

05.7 场外人员触及球并影响球进门

旧条文	新条文
如果在比赛中多余的球、其他物品或动物进入场内，裁判员必须： • 只要其干扰了比赛，即停止比赛，并以坠球形式重新开始比赛。	比赛进行中，多余的球、其他物品或动物出现在场内，裁判员必须： • 只有当其干扰了比赛，裁判员才停止比赛（随后以坠球恢复比赛），除非球将要进门，干扰因素没有阻止防守队员处理球，且随后球进门，则视为进球有效（即便干扰因素与球发生接触），除非球进入另一方球门。

解析

这使得第五章与第三章中的变动达到了统一（详见03.8）。

05.8 Referee's equipment

Additional text

Compulsory equipment
- Whistle(s)
- Watch(es)
- Red and yellow cards
- Notebook (or other means of keeping a record of the match)

Other equipment

Referees may be permitted to use:
- Equipment for communicating with other match officials – buzzer/beep flags, headsets etc (...)
- EPTS or other fitness monitoring equipment

Referees and other match officials are prohibited from wearing jewellery or any other electronic equipment.

Explanation

Moved from Law 4; wording clarifies what equipment a match official is or may be permitted to use.

Law 06 – The Other Match Officials

06.1 Title change

Old title	New title
The Assistant Referee	The Other Match Officials

Explanation

The duties of all the other match officials (assistant referees, fourth official, additional assistant referees and reserve assistant referee) are now included in this Law.

06.2 Referee's authority over other match officials

Additional text

The match officials operate under the direction of the referee.

05.8 裁判员装备

新增条文

必要装备：

- 一个或多个口哨。
- 一块或多块手表。
- 红黄牌。
- 记录簿（或其他可记录比赛情况的用具）。

其他装备

可允许裁判员使用：

- 与其他比赛官员进行交流的设备——振动/蜂鸣信号旗、耳麦等。
- 表现跟踪电子系统或其他体质监测设备。

禁止裁判员和其他比赛官员佩戴珠宝首饰或任何其他电子设备。

解析

从第四章移至本章，条款明确了比赛官员可被允许使用那些装备。

第六章　其他比赛官员

06.1 标题变动

旧标题	新标题
助理裁判员	其他比赛官员

解析

现将所有其他比赛官员（助理裁判员、第四官员、附加助理裁判员及替补助理裁判员）的职责全部包括在本章内。

06.2 裁判员的职权高于其他比赛官员

新增条文

比赛官员在裁判员的领导下履行各自职责。

Explanation

Emphasises the referee's leadership role.

06.3 Assistance given to the referee by other match officials

Additional text

The match officials assist the referee with inspecting the field of play, the balls and players' equipment (including if problems have been resolved) and maintaining records of time, goals, misconduct etc(...).

Explanation

Statement early in the Law of the usual assistance given to the referee avoids repetition in sections on each match official

06.4 Procedure if an official is unable to officiate

Old text	New text
Prior to the start of the competition, the organiser states clearly whether, if the referee is unable to continue, the fourth official takes over as the referee or whether the senior assistant referee or senior additional assistant referee takes over as referee with the fourth official becoming an assistant referee	Competition rules must state clearly who replaces a match official who is unable to start or continue and any associated changes. In particular, it must be clear whether, if the referee is unable to start or continue, the fourth official or the senior assistant referee or senior additional assistant referee takes over

Explanation

Wording simplified so each scenario does not need to be listed.

06.5 Duties of the fourth official

Additional text

A fourth official (...) assists the referee at all times:
- checking a player's/ substitute's equipment (...)
- indicating the minimum amount of additional time the referee intends to play at the end of each half (including extra time).

解析

强调了裁判员的领导角色。

06.3 其他比赛官员对裁判员的协助

新增条文

其他比赛官员协助裁判员检查比赛场地、比赛用球及队员装备（包括再次检查相关问题是否已被解决），以及记录比赛时间、进球、不正当行为等。

解析

提前在本章中提及对裁判员的协助内容，避免在随后关于各比赛官员的章节中不必要的重复。

06.4 当其中一名官员无法继续执法后的程序

旧条文	新条文
赛事开始前，组委会要明确在比赛中裁判员不能继续担任执法工作的情况下，应由第四官员担任比赛的裁判员，还是由第一助理裁判员担任裁判员，而第四官员担任助理裁判员	竞赛规程必须明确由谁替换不能开始或继续执法的比赛官员，以及任何相应产生的更替。尤其要明确，当裁判员不能继续执法时，是由第四官员、第一助理裁判员，还是第一附加助理裁判员替换。

解析

简化了文字，不必列出各种替换情形。

06.5 第四官员的职责

新增条文

第四官员的协助包括：

- 检查场上队员/替补队员的装备。（…）
- 在各半场（包括加时赛）结束时，展示裁判员将要补足的最短补时时间。

Explanation

Tasks usually performed by fourth officials have been added.

Law 07 – The Duration of the Match

07.1 Additional time

Additional text

Allowance is made by the referee in each half for all time lost in that half through:
- assessment and/or removal from the field of play of injured players (...)
- stoppages for drinks or other medical reasons permitted by competition rules

Explanation

These frequent causes of additional time have been added. In particular, approved 'drinks breaks' have been added so that they have validity within the Laws.

Law 08 – The Start and Restart of Play

08.1 Inclusion of reference to all restarts

Additional text

Free kicks (direct or indirect), penalty kicks, throw-ins, goal kicks and corner kicks are other restarts (see Laws 13 to 17)

Explanation

Illogical (especially to non-referees) that the Law about restarts only included the kick-off and dropped ball so reference to other restarts of play has been added.

08.2 Infringements when the ball is not in play

Additional text

If an infringement occurs when the ball is not in play this does not change how play is restarted.

Explanation

Clarifies that the restart is not changed for an incident when the ball is not in play e.g. holding before a corner kick; violent conduct after a FK is awarded etc.

解析

第四官员通常需要完成的任务已被列入。

第七章 比赛时间

07.1 补充时间

新增条文

裁判员对每半场所有因如下情况而损耗的时间予以补足：
- 对受伤队员的伤情评估和/或将其移出比赛场地。（…）
- 竞赛规程允许的因补水或其他医疗原因造成的暂停。

解析

列出了以上经常造成补时的情形，将"补水暂停"列入规则使其生效。

第八章 比赛开始与恢复

08.1 包含了所有恢复比赛的方式

新增条文

任意球（直接或间接任意球）、罚球点球、掷界外球、球门球和角球是其他恢复比赛的方式（详见规则第十三章至第十七章）。

解析

本章有关比赛恢复的方式仅包括开球和坠球是不符合逻辑的（尤其是对非裁判人群），所以现将其他恢复比赛的方式列在本章。

08.2 当比赛停止时，违反规则的行为

附加条文

比赛停止时发生的违规违例行为，不会改变随后恢复比赛的方式。

解析

明确了在比赛停止时发生的事件不应改变随后重新恢复比赛的方式，如在罚角球之前的拉扯、判罚任意球后发生的暴力行为等。

08.3 Kick-off: ball must clearly move to be in play; can be kicked in any direction

Old text	New text
The ball is in play when it is kicked and moves forward	The ball is in play when it is kicked and clearly moves

Explanation

Not requiring the ball to go forward at the kick-off means an attacker does not need to stand in the opponents' half (which is not permitted) to receive the ball. As with other Laws, the ball must clearly move to stop the practice of a player just touching the ball and then unsportingly pretending the kick has not been taken.

08.4 Dropped ball position

Additional text

The referee drops the ball at the position where it was when play was stopped, unless play was stopped inside the goal area in which case the ball is dropped on the goal area line which is parallel to the goal line at the point nearest to where the ball was when play was stopped.

Explanation

Clear statement here removes the many other times this appears in the current Laws.

08.5 Referee can not determine the drop ball contest

Old text	New text
The referee cannot decide who may or may not contest a dropped ball.	Any number of players may contest a dropped ball (including the goalkeepers); the referee cannot decide who may contest the dropped ball or its outcome.

Explanation

Clarifies that referees should not 'manufacture' dropped ball situations.

08.3 开球：球必须明显移动后才视为比赛开始，球可踢向任意方向

旧条文	新条文
• 当球被踢并向前移动比赛即为开始。	• 当球被踢且明显移动时，比赛即为开始。

解析

不再要求开球时向前踢球，意味着进攻队员不必站在对方半场（规则上是不允许的）接球。在其他章节中，球必须明显移动，以此来防止队员通过轻轻触球，假装球未被发出的非体育行为。

08.4 坠球的位置

新增条文

裁判员在比赛停止时球所在地点执行坠球，除非比赛停止时球在球门区内，在此情况下，应在与球门线平行的球门区线上、在比赛停止时距球最近的地点执行坠球。

解析

明确表述了坠球的位置，删除了规则其他章节中反复出现的上述描述。

08.5 裁判员不能决定坠球的结果

旧条文	新条文
裁判员不能决定谁可以或不可以参与坠球争抢。	所有场上队员均可参与坠球（包括守门员）。裁判员不得决定由谁参与坠球或坠球的结果。

解析

明确了裁判员不应"制造"坠球的情形。

08.6 Dropped ball kicked directly into the goal

Old text	New text
If the ball enters the goal (...) (...) directly (...).	If a dropped ball enters the goal without touching <u>at least two players</u> (...).

Explanation

Replacing 'directly' with 'without touching at least 2 players' is clearer and consistent with wording in other Laws.

Law 09 – The Ball In and Out of Play

09.1 Ball rebounding off a match official

Old text	New text
The ball is in play at all other times, including when: • it rebounds off a goalpost, crossbar or corner flagpost and remains in the field of play • it rebounds off the referee or an assistant referee when they are on the field of play	The ball is in play at all other times, including when: • it rebounds off <u>a match official</u>, goalpost, crossbar or corner flagpost and remains in the field of play

Explanation

Change confirms that the ball is still in play if it rebounds off an official who is just off the field of play (AR, AAR) and the ball does not wholly pass over the line.

Law 10 – Determining the Outcome of a Match

10.1 Title change

Old title	New title
The Method of Scoring	<u>Determining the Outcome of a Match</u>

Explanation

Kicks from the Penalty Mark, Away goals, etc. now included in this Law.

08.6 坠球直接踢入球门

旧条文	新条文
如果球进入球门（…）（…）直接（…）	如果坠球后，球未经至少两名场上队员触及而进入球门：……

解析

将"直接"用"未经至少两名场上队员触及"替换，更为清晰，且与其他章节的表述形成统一。

第九章 比赛进行与停止

09.1 球从比赛官员身上弹回

旧条文	新条文
其他所有时间均为比赛进行中，包括： • 球从球门柱、横梁或角旗杆弹回场内。 • 球从比赛场地上的裁判员或助理裁判员身上弹回场内。	所有其他时间，均为比赛进行中，包括球从比赛官员、球门柱、横梁或角旗杆弹回，且仍在比赛场地内。

解析

变动确定了当球从比赛场地外的比赛官员（助理裁判员、附加助理裁判员）身上弹回，且球的整体未完全越过线时，比赛仍在进行中。

第十章 确定比赛结果

10.1 标题变更

旧标题	新标题
计胜方法	确定比赛结果

解析

罚球点球决胜、客场进球等被归入本章。

10.2.1 Choosing the goal for the kicks from the penalty mark (KFPM)

Old text	New text
The referee chooses the goal at which the kicks will be taken. The penalty area where the kicks from the penalty marks are taking place may be changed only if the goal or the playing surface becomes unusable.	Unless there are other considerations (e.g. ground conditions, safety etc..) the referee tosses a coin to decide the goal at which the kicks will be taken which may only be changed for safety reasons or if the goal or playing surface becomes unusable.

Explanation

Referees find it difficult to decide which goal to use with home supporters at one end and away supporters at the other end. Subject to over-riding considerations (security, condition of the field etc...) the fairest method is to toss a coin.

10.2.2 Eligible players (including those temporarily off the field)

Old text	New text
With the exception of the foregoing case, only players who are on the field of play at the end of the match, which includes extra time where appropriate, are eligible to take kicks from the penalty mark.	With the exception of a substitute for an injured goalkeeper, only players who are on the field of play or are temporarily off the field (injury, adjusting equipment etc...) at the end of the match are eligible to take kicks from the penalty mark.

Explanation

Clarifies that a player temporarily off the field legitimately (injury, changing equipment etc...) can take part, as can a substitute who replaces a goalkeeper.

10.2.3 Naming and order of penalty taker

Old text	New text
Each team is responsible for selecting the players from those on the field of play at the end of the match and the order in which they will take the kicks.	Each team is responsible for selecting from the eligible players the order in which they will take the kicks. The referee is not informed of the order.

10.2.1 选择踢球点球决胜（KFPM）的球门

旧条文	新条文
裁判员选定用于踢球点球的球门。只有在球门或球场表面不能正常使用时才能更换罚球区。	裁判员通过掷硬币决定球点球决胜使用的球门，除非有其他考虑（如场地条件、安全性等）。只有因为安全原因或在球门、场地草皮无法正常使用的情况下，才可更换球点球决胜使用的球门。

解析

在主客队球迷各自处于两侧球门后面时，裁判员很难决定使用哪一个球门。除其他重要考虑因素（如安全、场地条件等）之外，掷硬币是最为公平的方式。

10.2.2 符合资格的队员（包括暂时离场的队员）

旧条文	新条文
除上一条所述情况外，只有比赛结束时，包括在规定的加时赛比赛结束时，在场上的队员方可参加踢球点球。	除替补队员替换受伤守门员的情况外，只有在比赛结束时在比赛场地内，或暂时离场（受伤、调整装备等）的场上队员有资格参加球点球决胜。

解析

明确了暂时离场的场上队员（受伤、更换装备等）可参加踢点球决胜比赛，就像替换受伤的守门员一样。

10.2.3 罚球队员的提名和顺序

旧条文	新条文
每个队负责挑选、安排在比赛最后阶段的场上队员踢球点球及其顺序。	各队负责安排有资格的场上队员踢球点球的顺序，罚球队员顺序不必告知裁判员。

Explanation

Clarifies that the names and/or the order of the kickers do not have to be given to the referee (some incorrectly ask for the names and stop the order being changed).

10.2.4 Same number of players

Old text	New text
If at the end of the match and before the kicks start to be taken from the penalty mark one team has a greater number of players than its opponents, it must reduce its numbers to equate with that of its opponents and the captain must inform the referee of the name and number of each player excluded. If a player is injured or sent off during the taking of kicks from the penalty mark and the team has one player fewer, the referee should not reduce the number of players taking kicks for the other team. An equal number of players from each team is required only at the start of the taking of kicks from the penalty mark.	If at the end of the match <u>and before or during</u> the kicks one team has a greater number of players than its opponents, it must reduce its numbers to the same number as its opponents <u>and the referee must be informed</u> of the name and number of each player excluded.

Explanation

This applies the 'fair play' principle at the start of KFPM i.e. one team should not benefit from having fewer kickers than their opponents as this could mean their 'best' kicker taking a 2nd kick against the opponents' last/worst kicker.

解析

明确了不必将罚球队员的姓名/或顺序告知裁判员（询问罚球队员姓名和禁止改变罚球顺序是不合理的）。

10.2.3 罚球队员的提名和顺序

旧条文	新条文
如果在比赛结束踢球点球之前，某队的场上队员人数多于另一队，该队必须减去多出的人数与对方人数一致，并且该队的队长必须通知裁判员每一名离场队员的姓名和号码。任何离场的队员不允许参加踢球点球决胜。 如果在球点球决胜阶段一名上场队员受伤或被罚令出场使他的队比对方队少一人，裁判员不必让多出一名队员的队减去一人。两队人数要求相同仅仅是在踢球点球决胜之前。	如果在比赛结束时、球点球决胜开始前或进行中，一队场上队员人数多于另一队，则必须削减队员人数与对方保持一致，且必须告知裁判员被排除的队员姓名及号码。

解析

这体现了踢点球决胜开始时的"公平竞赛"原则，一队不应因为人数少于另一方，而在第二回合罚球时，用其最好的队员罚球，与对方相对差的队员对垒，从而获利。

10.2.5 Goalkeeper unable to continue

Old text	New text
A goalkeeper who is injured while kicks are being taken from the penalty mark and is unable to continue as goalkeeper may be replaced by a named substitute provided his team has not used the maximum number of substitutes permitted under the competition rules	A goalkeeper who is unable to continue <u>before or</u> during the kicks and whose team has not used its maximum permitted number of substitutes, may be replaced by a named substitute, <u>or a player excluded to equalise the number of players, but the goalkeeper takes no further part and may not take a kick.</u>

Explanation

Clarifies that a goalkeeper can be replaced at any time by a substitute (or by a player excluded to make the numbers equal) but may not take a kick.

10.2.6 When penalty is completed (see 14.3)

Additional text

<u>The kick is completed when the ball stops moving, goes out of play or the referee stops play for any infringement of the Laws.</u>

Explanation

Clarifies when a referee should decide a kick is over (see 14.3).

10.2.7 Sequence of kickers

Additional text

- Each kick is taken by a different player and all eligible players must take a kick before any player can take a second kick
- <u>The above principle continues for any subsequent sequence of kicks but a team may change the order of kickers</u>

Explanation

Clarifies that all team members must take the same number of kicks before a player can take another kick; the order can be changed for the new 'round' of kicks.

10.2.5 守门员无法继续比赛

旧条文	新条文
在踢球点球过程中，当一方守门员受伤不能继续比赛时，可由该队在竞赛规程规定的最大替补限额内，使用被提名而尚未使用过的替补队员进行替换。	在球点球决胜开始前或进行中，如果一队守门员无法继续比赛且该队替换名额还未用完，则守门员可由一名提名的替补队员，或为保持人数一致而被排除的场上队员替换，但其不得再次参加球点球决胜或踢球点球。

解析

明确了守门员可在任何时间被替补队员（或为保持人数一致而被减去的队员）替换，但不能踢球点球。

10.2.6 何时视为罚球完成（详见14.3）

新增条文

当球停止移动、离开比赛场地，或因发生任何违反规则的情况而裁判员停止比赛时，即为本次踢球点球结束。

解析

明确了裁判员如何判定罚球完成（详见14.3）

10.2.7 罚球队员的顺序

新增条文

- 每次踢球由不同的场上队员执行，直至双方符合资格的队员均踢过一次后，同一名队员才可踢第二次。
- 在全部队员踢完之后接下来的踢球中都应遵从上述条款，但球队可以更换踢球队员顺序。

解析

明确了场上队员在踢第二回合前，同队的所有场上队员必须踢完一轮；在新一回合时可调整踢球点球队员的顺序

10.2.8 Player leaving the field of play

Additional text

Kicks from the penalty mark must not be delayed for a player who leaves the field of play. The player's kick will be 'forfeited' (not scored) if the player does not return in time to take a kick.

Explanation

Clarifies that the referee must not delay KFPM if a player leaves the field of play; if the player is not back in time the kick is missed (forfeited). It is important to stop this potentially unfair conduct (instructions from the coach, deliberate delay, match fixing etc.).

Law 11 – Offside

11.1 Status of halfway line

Old text	New text
A player is not in an offside position if: • he is in his own half of the field of play or (…).	A player is in an offside position if: • any part of the head, body or feet is in the opponents' half (excluding the halfway line)

Explanation

Clarifies that the halfway line is 'neutral' for offside i.e. a player must have part of the body in the opponents' half to be in an offside position.

11.2 Status of players' arms

Additional text

A player is in an offside position if:
• any part of the head, body or feet is nearer to the opponents' goal line than both the ball and the second-last opponent. The hands and arms of all players, including the goalkeepers, are not included.

Explanation

Clarifies that the hands and arms of the defenders, attackers and goalkeepers are not included when judging offside.

10.2.8 队员离开比赛场地

新增条文

- 不得因一名场上队员离场而拖延球点球决胜。如果队员未及时返场踢球点球，则视为丧失本次踢球资格（射失）。

解析

明确了当场上队员离开比赛场地，裁判员不得拖延球点球决胜；如果该队员未及时返回，则视为球未罚进（弃权）。阻止这些潜在的不正当行为（如接受教练员的指导、蓄意延误时间、操控比赛等）非常重要。

第十一章 越位

11.1 中线的归属

旧条文	新条文
队员不处于越位位置： - 他在本方半场内。	队员处于越位位置，如果其： - 头、躯干或脚的任何部分处在对方半场（不包含中线）。

解析

明确了就越位而言，中线属于"中立"部分，队员身体的一部分必须处在对方的半场才能视为处在越位位置。

11.2 队员手臂位置的界定

新增条文

队员处于越位位置，如果其：

- 头、躯干或脚的任何部分较球和对方倒数第二名队员更接近于对方球门线。所有队员包括守门员的手和臂部不在越位位置判定范围内。

解析

明确了在判定越位位置时，防守队员、进攻队员和守门员的手和臂部不在考虑范围内。

11.3 Position not offence judged at the moment the ball is played

Old text	New text
A player in an offside position is only penalised if, at the moment the ball touches or is played by one of his team, he is, in the opinion of the referee, involved in active play by...	A player in an offside position at the moment the ball is played or touched by a team-mate is only penalised on becoming involved in active play by...

Explanation

Clarifies that it is the player's (offside) position which is judged when the ball is played. The offence occurs after the ball is played e.g. an offside player who scores after a save by the goalkeeper commits the offence after the ball was played.

11.4 Offence following a rebound or save

Old text	New text
gaining an advantage by being in that position by playing a ball: • that rebounds or is deflected to him off the goalpost, crossbar or an opponent • (...) from a deliberate save by any opponent	gaining an advantage by being in that position by playing the ball or interfering with an opponent when it has: • rebounded or been deflected off the goalpost, crossbar or an opponent • been deliberately saved by any opponent

Explanation

Clarifies that 'interfering with an opponent' after a rebound, deflection or save is an offside offence.

11.5 Position of free kick

Old text	New text
p. 36 In the event of an offside offence, the referee awards an indirect free kick to the opposing team to be taken from the place where the infringement occurred;.	If an offside offence occurs, the referee awards an indirect free kick where the offence occurred, including if it is in the player's own half of the field of play.

11.3 在传触球的瞬间，处于越位位置并不意味着越位犯规

旧条文	新条文
处于越位位置的队员，在同队队员踢或触及球的一瞬间，裁判员认为其参与了现实比赛时才被判为越位犯规…	一名队员在同队队员传球或触球的一瞬间处于越位位置，该队员随后以如下方式参与了实际比赛，才被判罚越位犯规…

解析

明确了队员的（越位）位置以传球或触球的一瞬间进行判断。而越位犯规发生在传触球之后，例如，处于越位位置的队员在守门员救球后将球打进，则被判为越位犯规。

11.4 接反弹球或救球后的越位犯规

旧条文	新条文
"在越位位置获得利益"是指处于越位位置的队员触及： 1. 从球门柱或横梁弹回的球，或从对方队员身上弹回或变向的球。 2. 从对方队员有意识救球而弹回或变向的球。	在如下情况发生后触球，从而获得利益或干扰对方队员： • 球从球门柱、横梁、对方队员处反弹或折射过来。 • 球从任一对方队员有意救球后而来。

解析

明确了反弹、折射或救球后"干扰对方队员"也是越位犯规。

11.5 罚任意球的位置

旧条文	新条文
对于任何越位犯规，裁判员应判给对方在犯规发生地点踢间接任意球	如果出现越位犯规，裁判员在越位发生的地点判罚间接任意球，这包括发生在越位队员的本方半场。

p. 111 When an offside offence occurs, the referee awards an indirect free kick to be taken from the position of the offending player when the ball was last played to him by one of his team-mates

Explanation

The Law and the interpretation were contradictory. Throughout the Laws, the general principle is that a FK is awarded where an offence occurs so this now applies to offside. A FK can be awarded in a player's own half if the player moves from an offside **position** in the opponents' half to commit an offside **offence** in the player's own half.

11.6 Defending player off the field

Old text	New text
Any defending player leaving the field of play for any reason without the referee's permission shall be considered to be on his own goal line or touch line for the purposes of offside until the next stoppage in play. If the player left the field of play deliberately, he must be cautioned when the ball is next out of play.	A defending player who leaves the field of play without the referee's permission shall be considered to be on the goal line or touchline for the purposes of offside until the next stoppage in play or until the defending team has played the ball towards the halfway line and it is outside their penalty area. If the player left the field of play deliberately, the player must be cautioned when the ball is next out of play.

Explanation

It is unfair that an injured defending player off the field 'plays everyone onside' until play stops. The new wording defines the end of the phase of play when the defender is no longer considered to be on the field for the purposes of offside.

当越位犯规发生时，裁判员判罚间接任意球，罚球地点在当球被同队队员最后触及时犯规队员所在的位置。

解析

原规则的正文和诠释部分是相互矛盾的。在规则的原则中，任意球应该在犯规发生的地点罚出，所以现将这一条运用于越位一章。如果队员从越位位置回到本方半场被判罚越位犯规，则在本方半场被判罚间接任意球。

11.6 处在比赛场外的防守队员

旧条文	新条文
就越位而言，任何防守队员无论何种原因未经裁判员允许离开比赛场地，应视其为处在本方球门线或边线上直到比赛停止。如果队员故意离开比赛场地，当比赛停止时，裁判员必须警告故意离场的队员。	就越位而言，未经裁判员许可离开比赛场地的防守队员，应视为处于球门线或边线上，直到比赛停止，<u>或防守方已将球向中线方向处理且球已在防守方罚球区外</u>。如果一名队员故意离开比赛场地，在比赛停止时，裁判员必须警告该名队员。

解析

在场外受伤未能返回场内的防守队员"使得所有人都不处在越位位置"一直到比赛停止，这是不公平的。新条文明确了，在比赛的这一片段结束后，就越位而言，在场外受伤的防守队员不再视为处在比赛场地内。

11.7 Attacking player off the field

Old text	New text
It is not an offence in itself for a player who is in an offside position to step off the field of play to show the referee that he is not involved in active play. However, if the referee considers that he has left the field of play for tactical reasons and has gained an unfair advantage by re-entering the field of play, the player must be cautioned for unsporting behaviour. The player needs to ask for the referee's permission to re-enter the field of play.	An attacking player may step or stay off the field of play not to be involved in active play. If the player re-enters from the goal line and becomes involved in play before the next stoppage in play or the defending team has played the ball towards the halfway line and it is outside their penalty area, the player shall be considered to be positioned on the goal line point for the purposes of offside. A player who deliberately leaves the field of play and re-enters without the referee's permission and is not penalised for offside and gains an advantage, must be cautioned.

Explanation

Clarifies how to deal with an attacking player who leaves or stays off the field of play and then returns.

11.8 Attacking player in the goal

Old text	New text
If an attacking player remains stationary between the goalposts and inside the goal net as the ball enters the goal, a goal must be awarded. However, if (…) (…) the attacking player distracts an opponent, the goal must be disallowed, the player cautioned for unsporting behaviour and play restarted with a dropped ball(…).	If an attacking player remains stationary between the goalposts and inside the goal as the ball enters the goal, a goal must be awarded unless the player commits an offside offence or Law 12 offence in which case play is restarted with an indirect or direct free kick.

11.7 处在比赛场外的进攻队员

旧条文	新条文
处在越位位置的队员离开比赛场地，以向裁判员表明其不在越位活动区域不是犯规，但无论如何，如果裁判员认为该队员离开场地是出于战术目的，并在重新进入场地时获得了不正当利益，该队员因非体育行为必须被裁判员警告。队员重新进入场内需要得到裁判员的允许。	攻方队员为了不卷入实际比赛可以移步至比赛场地外或留在比赛场地外。就越位而言，如果该攻方队员在随后比赛停止，或防守方已将球向中线方向处理且球已在防守方罚球区外之前，从球门线重新进入比赛场地内，并卷入实际比赛，应视其处于球门线上。未经裁判员许可故意离开比赛场地又重新回场的攻方队员，虽不被判罚越位，但从其位置获得了利益，裁判员必须警告该名队员。

解析

明确了如何认定离场或处在场外、随后返回比赛场内的进攻队员。

11.8 处在球门内的进攻队员

旧条文	新条文
在球被踢进球门过程中，如果一名攻方队员在球门柱之间的球门网内保持不动，则必须判进球有效。不过，如果攻方队员干扰了对方，必须判进球无效并警告属于非体育行为的队员，以坠球在当时球所在位置重新开始比赛。……	如果球进门时，一名攻方队员在球门柱之间的球门内保持不动，进球必须视为有效，除非该名队员越位或违反规则第十二章条文，这种情况下，裁判员以间接或直接任意球恢复比赛。

109

Explanation

Consistent with updated offside wording (i.e. removal of 'distracts') and the ability to penalise an offence off the field with a free kick when the ball is in play.

Law 12 – Fouls and Misconduct

12.1 Infringements when the ball is not in play

Additional text

Direct and indirect free kicks and penalty kicks can only be awarded for fouls and misconduct committed whilst the ball is in play.

Explanation

A definitive statement (from the interpretations section) that the ball must be in play for misconduct to be penalised with a free kick or penalty kick.

12.2 Direct free kick – add 'challenges'

Old text	New text
A direct free kick is awarded to the opposing team if a player commits any of the following seven offences in a manner considered by the referee to be careless, reckless or using excessive force • tackles an opponent	A direct free kick is awarded if a player commits any of the following offences in a manner considered by the referee to be careless, reckless or using excessive force • tackles or challenges an opponent.

Explanation

'tackles' implies a challenge with the foot but some challenges can be with other parts of the body (e.g. knee) and technically were not covered.

12.3 Contact means direct free kick

Additional text

If an offence involves contact it is penalised by a direct free kick or penalty kick.

Explanation

Clarifies that a direct free kick must be awarded if an offence involves contact.

解析

与更新后的越位条款，以及比赛进行中，对于场外的犯规应判罚任意球的条款保持一致性。

第十二章 犯规与不正当行为

12.1 比赛停止时发生的违规行为

新增条文

只有在比赛进行中犯规或违规，才可判罚直接或间接任意球，以及球点球。

解析

给出了确定的表述（从诠释部分移至本章）：必须是在比赛进行中，才可判罚任意球或球点球。

12.2 直接任意球——"抢截"的涵义

旧条文	新条文
裁判员认为，如果队员草率地、鲁莽地或使用过分的力量违反下列7种犯规中的任意一种，将判给对方踢直接任意球： • 抢截对方队员。	如果裁判员认为一名场上队员草率地、鲁莽地或使用过分力量对对方队员实施如下犯规，则判罚直接任意球： • 用脚或其他部位抢截。

解析

原条文的"抢截"（tackle）是指使用脚的抢截动作，但有些抢截动作是使用身体其他的部位（如膝关节），从技术上讲，之前未涉及到。

12.3 有身体接触–直接任意球

新增条文

如果是有身体接触的犯规，则判罚直接任意球或球点球。

解析

明确了只要是包含身体接触的犯规，必须判罚直接任意球。

12.4 Reckless – removal of 'complete' from definition

Old text	New text
Reckless means that the player has acted with complete disregard to the danger to, or consequences for, his opponen(...) (...) must be cautioned.	Reckless is when a player acts with disregard to the danger to, or consequences for, an opponent and must be cautioned.

Explanation

There were legal concerns about the meaning /relevance of 'complete'.

12.5 Serious foul play – removal of 'far' from definition

Old text	New text
Using excessive force means that the player has far exceeded the necessary use of force and is in danger of injuring his opponent(...) (...) must be sent off.	Using excessive force is when a player exceeds the necessary use of force and endangers the safety of an opponent and must be sent off.

Explanation

There were legal concerns about the meaning/relevance of 'far'.

12.6 Direct free kick – add 'impedes an opponent with contact'

Additional text

A direct free kick is awarded if a player commits any of the following offences:
- impedes an opponent with contact

Explanation

Confirmation that impeding an opponent with contact is a direct free kick.

12.7 Impeding without contact means indirect free kick

Old text	New text
An indirect free kick is also awarded to the opposing team if(...) (...) a player impedes the progress of an opponent.	An indirect free kick is awarded if(...) a player impedes the progress of an opponent without any contact being made.

111

12.4 鲁莽性质——将"完全"从定义中删除

旧条文	新条文
"鲁莽地"表示队员完全不顾及其行为可能对对方造成的危险或带来的后果，……必须给予警告。	鲁莽是指队员的行为没有顾及到可能对对方造成的危险或后果。这种情况下必须对队员予以警告。

解析

对于"完全"的认定与相关性存在法律上的困难。

12.5 严重犯规——将"远远"从定义中删除

旧条文	新条文
"使用过分的力量"表示队员使用远远超过其自身所需要的力量，并且使对方有受伤的危险……必须被罚出场地。	使用过分力量是指队员使用了超出自身所需要的力量，危及了对方的安全。这种情况必须将队员罚令出场。

解析

对于"远远"的认定与相关性存在法律上的困难。

12.6 直接任意球——新增"在有身体接触的情况下阻碍对方队员移动"

附加条文

如果场上队员实施如下犯规时，判罚直接任意球：
- 在身体接触的情况下阻碍对方队员移动。

解析

明确了队员在有身体接触的情况下阻碍对方队员移动，应判直接任意球。

12.7 没有身体接触的情况下阻碍对方移动，判罚间接任意球

旧条文	新条文
（……）队员在出现下列情况时，也将判给对方踢间接任意球： • 阻碍对方队员行进。	……则判罚间接任意球： • 在没有身体接触的情况下阻碍对方行进。

Explanation

Confirmation that impeding an opponent without contact is an indirect free kick.

12.8 Authority to take disciplinary action from pre-match inspection of the field (see 5.4)

Old text	New text
The referee has the authority to take disciplinary sanctions from the moment he enters the field of play until he leaves the field of play after the final whistle.	The referee has the authority to take disciplinary action from entering the field of play <u>for the pre-match inspection</u> until leaving the field of play after the <u>match ends (including kicks from the penalty mark)</u>. <u>If, before entering the field of play at the start of the match, a player commits a sending-off offence, the referee has the authority to prevent the player taking part in the match (see Law 3.6); the referee will report any other misconduct.</u>

Explanation

Same change as outlined and explained in Law 5 (see 5.4).

12.9 Advantage played for a red card offence and player then becomes involved

Additional text

Advantage should not be applied in situations involving serious foul play, violent conduct or a second cautionable offence <u>unless there is a clear opportunity to score a goal. The referee must send off the player when the ball is next out of play but if the player plays the ball or challenges/interferes with an opponent, the referee will stop play, send off the player and restart with an indirect free kick</u>.

解析

明确了队员在没有身体接触的情况下阻碍对方队员移动，应判间接任意球。

12.8 从赛前检查比赛场地起有权执行纪律处罚（详见05.4）

旧条文	新条文
裁判员从进入比赛场地开始直到比赛结束后离开场地前，均有权进行纪律处罚。	裁判员从进入比赛场地进行赛前检查开始，至比赛结束（包括球点球决胜）离开比赛场地，均有权执行纪律措施。 如果上场队员在开赛进入比赛场地前，犯有可被罚令出场的犯规，裁判员有权阻止该名队员参加比赛（参见第三章第6条），裁判员将就任何其他不正当行为提交报告。

解析

与第五章解析说明的内容一致（详见05.4）。

12.9 犯规队员需出示红牌的情况下，掌握有利后犯规队员参与比赛

新增条文

在出现严重犯规、暴力行为或可被第二次警告的犯规时不应掌握有利，除非有明显的进球机会。裁判员必须在随后比赛停止时将相关队员罚令出场，但如果该队员触球或与对方队员争抢或干扰对方队员，裁判员则停止比赛，将该队员罚令出场，并以间接任意球恢复比赛。

Explanation

Clarifies that on the rare occasion that a referee plays advantage for a RC offence (only if a goal-scoring opportunity is imminent) if the RC player then becomes involved in play, the game must be stopped as it would be against 'fair play' if the player scored, contributed to a goal or stopped the opponents scoring.

12.10 Cautions for handball

Old text	New text
There are different circumstances when a player must be cautioned for unsporting behaviour, e.g. if a player: • commits a foul for the tactical purpose of interfering with or breaking up a promising attack • holds an opponent for the tactical purpose of pulling the opponent away from the ball or preventing the opponent from getting to the ball • handles the ball to prevent an opponent gaining possession or developing an attack • handles the ball in an attempt to score a goal (irrespective of whether or not the attempt is successful)	There are different circumstances when a player must be cautioned for unsporting behaviour, e.g. if a player: • commits a foul <u>or handles</u> the ball to interfere with or stop a promising attack • handles the ball in an attempt to score a goal (whether or not the attempt is successful) <u>or in an unsuccessful attempt to prevent a</u> goal

Explanation

- 'Preventing an opponent gaining possession' is removed as a YC offence as it causes some referees to YC every handball.
- Handling is included as a YC offence when it 'stops/interferes with a promising attack' (as with other offences which have the same effect).
- Clarifies that a player who tries unsuccessfully to handle the ball to stop a goal being scored should receive a YC.

解析

明确了在不常见的情况下，当裁判员对应出示红牌的犯规掌握有利（仅在立即有进球机会发生的情形下），若本该罚令出场的队员参与比赛，则必须停止比赛。如果该队员进球、对进球做出贡献，或阻止了对方进球，这将违背"公平竞赛"原则。

12.10 警告手球犯规

旧条文	新条文
当一名队员因非体育行为必须被警告时有多种不同的情况，例如： • 为达到战术目的而干扰或破坏对方的有利进攻。 • 为达到战术目的而拉扯对方队员，将对方队员从球旁拽到一边或者阻止对方队员得到球。 • 用手球阻止对方队员得到球或阻止对方进攻。 • 用手击球试图得分（不管是否得分）。	在一些情况下必须以非体育行为警告相关队员，例如： • 通过犯规或<u>手球</u>的方式干扰或阻止有希望的进攻。 • 用手球的方式试图得分（无论进球与否）或<u>阻止</u>进球未果。

解析

- 将"阻止对方队员得到球"从应黄牌警告的条文中删除，这条描述造成了一些裁判员对每个手球犯规都出示黄牌。
- 在应黄牌警告的犯规中，将通过手球"干扰或阻止有希望的进攻"包含在内（正如其他造成同样后果的犯规一样）。
- 明确了用手球阻止进球未果的队员应得到黄牌。

12.11 Denial of an obvious goal-scoring opportunity in the penalty area

Additional text

Where a player denies the opposing team a goal or an obvious goal-scoring opportunity by a deliberate handball offence the player is sent off wherever the offence occurs.

Where a player commits an offence against an opponent within their own penalty area which denies an opponent an obvious goal-scoring opportunity and the referee awards a penalty kick, the offending player is cautioned unless:
- The offence is holding, pulling or pushing or
- The offending player does not attempt to play the ball or there is no possibility for the player making the challenge to play the ball or
- The offence is one which is punishable by a red card wherever it occurs on the field of play (e.g. serious foul play, violent conduct etc.)

In all the above circumstances the player is sent off.

Explanation

When a DOGSO offence is committed by a defender in the penalty area, the penalty kick effectively restores the goal-scoring opportunity so the punishment for the player should be less strong (a YC) than when the offence is committed outside the penalty area. However, where the offence is handball or clearly not a genuine attempt to play or challenge for the ball (as defined in the wording) the player will be sent off.

12.12 Serious foul play – inclusion of 'challenge'

Old text	New text
A tackle that endangers the safety of an opponent must be sanctioned as serious foul play.	A tackle or challenge that endangers the safety of an opponent must be sanctioned as serious foul play.

Explanation

Same change as in 12.2 – 'challenge' includes offences with the arms, elbows etc.

12.11 在罚球区内破坏明显进球得分机会

新增条文

无论发生在何处，当队员用故意手球的犯规破坏对方进球或明显进球得分机会时应被罚令出场。

当队员在本方罚球区内对对方犯规，且破坏了对方明显的进球得分机会时，裁判员判罚球点球，对犯规队员予以警告，除非：
- 使用手臂等部位拉扯、阻止对方队员行动，或推搡性质的犯规，或
- 犯规队员的目的不是争抢球或争抢球时没有触球的可能性，或
- 无论发生在比赛场地何处均应被罚令出场的犯规（如严重犯规、暴力行为等）。

发生上述情况，均应将犯规队员罚令出场。

解析

当防守队员在罚球区内实施了破坏明显进球得分机会（DOGSO）的犯规后，球点球的判罚已经有效地弥补了攻方的得分机会，所以相较轻（黄牌）于在罚球区外同样的犯规。不过，如果犯规类型是手球或明显不是真正企图去触及球或争抢球（如上述文字描述），那么该队员应被罚令出场。

12.12 严重犯规——扩充了"抢截行为"

旧条文	新条文
危及对方安全的抢截动作，必须视为严重犯规并予以判罚。	危及到对方队员安全或使用过分力量、野蛮方式的抢截，必须视为严重犯规加以处罚。

解析

与12.2变动一致——"抢截"包括了使用手臂、肘等部位的犯规。

12.13 Violent Conduct – no contact

Old text	New text
A player is guilty of violent conduct if he uses excessive force or brutality against an opponent when not challenging for the ball or excessive force or brutality against a team-mate, spectator, match official or any other person.	Violent conduct is when a player uses or attempts to use excessive force or brutality against an opponent when not challenging for the ball, or against a team-mate, team official, match official, spectator or any other person, regardless of whether contact is made.

Explanation

Clarifies that attempted violence is punished by a RC even if unsuccessful.

12.14 Violent Conduct – contact with the head/face

Additional text

In addition, a player who, when not challenging for the ball, deliberately strikes an opponent or any other person on the head or face with the hand or arm, is guilty of violent conduct unless the force used was negligible.

Explanation

Clarifies that a player who deliberately hits/strikes an opponent on the head/face (when not challenging for the ball) should be sent off (unless negligible force).

12.13 暴力行为——没有接触

旧条文	新条文
如果队员的行为目的不是对球，而是使用过分的力量或野蛮的方式与对方队员争抢，或者用过分的力量或野蛮的行为对待同队队员、观众、比赛官员或其他人，应视为暴力行为。	暴力行为是指队员的目的不是争抢球，而是对对方队员或同队队员、球队官员、比赛官员、观众或任何其他人，使用或企图使用过分力量或野蛮动作，无论是否与他人发生身体接触。

解析

明确了企图实施暴力行为，即使没有成功也应被罚令出场。

12.14 暴力行为——与头/面部的接触

新增条文

除此之外，队员的目的不是争抢球，而是故意用手或臂部击打对方队员，以及任何其他人的头或面部时，应视为暴力行为，除非他使用的力量非常轻微，足以忽略。

解析

明确了队员故意击打对方头部/面部（目的不是争抢球）应被罚令出场（除非是微不足道的）。

12.15 Offences against substitutes, team officials, match officials etc...

Old text	New text
If the ball is in play and a player commits an offence inside the field of play: • against an opponent, play is restarted with a direct free kick from the position where the offence occurred (see Law 13 – Position of free kick) or a penalty kick (if inside the offending player's own penalty area) • against a team-mate, play is restarted with an indirect free kick from the position where the offence occurred (see Law 13 – Position of free kick) • against a substitute or substituted player, play is restarted with an indirect free kick from the position of the ball when play was stopped (see Law 13 – Position of free kick) • against the referee or an assistant referee, play is restarted with an indirect free kick from the position where the offence occurred (see Law 13 – Position of free kick) • against another person, play is restarted with a dropped ball from the position of the ball when play was stopped, unless play was stopped inside the goal area, in which case the referee drops the ball on the goal area line parallel to the goal line at the point nearest to where the ball was located when play was stopped	If the ball is in play and a player commits an offence inside the field of play against: • an opponent - indirect or direct free kick or penalty kick • a team-mate, substitute, substituted player, team official or a match official – a direct free kick or penalty kick • any other person – a dropped ball

12.15 对替补队员、球队官员、比赛官员等人员实施的犯规

旧条文	新条文
假如球在比赛中而队员犯规发生在场内： • 对对方犯规，比赛应在犯规发生地点用直接任意球（参见第十三章—任意球的位置），或者罚球点球重新开始比赛（如果犯规发生在犯规队员罚球区内）。 • 对队友犯规，比赛应在犯规发生地点用间接任意球重新开始（参见第十三章—任意球的位置）。 • 对替补队员或替换下场的队员犯规，应在比赛暂停时球所在的位置用间接任意球重新开始比赛（参见第十三章—任意球的位置）。 • 对裁判员或助理裁判员犯规，比赛应在犯规发生地点用间接任意球重新开始比赛（参见第十三章—任意球的位置）。 • 对其他人犯规，应在比赛停止时球所在位置以坠球重新开始比赛。除非球在球门区内裁判员将比赛停止，遇到这种情况，裁判员应在与球门线平行的球门区线上，在比赛停止时距球最近的位置坠球。	如果比赛进行中，场上队员在比赛场地内对如下人员犯规： • 对方场上队员——以间接或直接任意球、球点球恢复比赛。 • 对同队队员、替补队员、已替换下场的队员、球队官员或比赛官员——以直接任意球或球点球恢复比赛。 • 对任何其他人——以坠球恢复比赛。

Explanation

The punishment for an offence against another participant reflects the seriousness of such an action e.g. football sends out a weak/poor message if an offence against a match official is only an indirect free kick.

12.16 Fouls off the field of play (see 13.3 + 14.1)

Old text	New text
If the ball is in play and the offence occurred outside the field of play... • if the player leaves the field of play to commit the offence, play is restarted with an indirect free kick from the position of the ball when play was stopped (see Law 13 –Position of free kick)	If the ball is in play and the offence occurred outside the field of play(...) However, if a player leaves the field of play as part of play and commits an offence against another player, play is restarted with a free kick taken on the boundary line nearest to where the offence occurred; for direct free kick offences a penalty kick is awarded if this is within the offender's penalty area.

Explanation

Law is changed as football would expect that if 2 players leave the field as part of normal action and one fouls the other off the field, a free kick should be awarded. No one would understand if the referee gave a RC/YC and then restarted with a dropped ball (or IDFK). The FK is awarded on the touchline/goal line nearest to where the foul occurred; if this is on the goal line in the offender's penalty area a penalty is awarded.

Law 13 – Free Kicks

13.1 Free kicks are awarded to the opposing team

Old text	New text
Free kicks are direct or indirect.	Direct and indirect free kicks are awarded to the opposing team of a player guilty of an offence or infringement.

解析

对比赛中的其他参与者实施犯规后的处罚，应体现出严重性。例如，对比赛官员实施犯规，仅判罚间接任意球，足球这项运动将会传达出软弱无能的信息。

12.16 比赛场地外的犯规（详见13.3+14.1）

旧条文	新条文
假如球在比赛中而犯规发生在场外… • 假如队员从场地内走到场外犯规，应该在比赛停止时球所在的位置以间接任意球重新开始比赛（参见第十三章—任意球的位置）。	如果比赛进行中，一名场上队员在比赛场地外犯规： …… 然而，如果场上队员在正常比赛的移动中离开比赛场地，随后对其他队员犯规，则在离犯规地点最近的边界线上以任意球恢复比赛。如果该地点位于犯规方罚球区内且该犯规可被判直接任意球，则判罚球点球。

解析

此条变动的目的在于：当两名场上队员在正常移动中离开比赛场地，一名队员对另一名队员在比赛场外实施了犯规，则应判罚任意球。如果裁判员出示了红黄牌后以坠球（或间接任意球）恢复比赛是无法让人理解的。而现在，将在距犯规发生地点最近的边线/球门线以任意球恢复比赛；如果该地点位于犯规方罚球区内，则判罚球点球。

第十三章 任意球

13.1 任意球判给对方球队

旧条文	新条文
任意球分为直接或间接任意球两种。	场上队员犯规或违规时，判由对方球队罚直接或间接任意球。

Explanation

Stating that a free kick is awarded to the opposing team at the start of the Law allows the removal of the many uses of the phrase 'to the opposing team'.

13.2 Position of free kicks

Addition text

All free kicks are taken from the place where the infringement occurred except:

Explanation

Clear statement at the start of this Law allows the removal of specific reference to the position of the free kick in many of the Laws.

13.3 Fouls off the field of play

Old text	New text
Free kicks awarded for offences involving a player entering, re-entering or leaving the field of play without permission are taken from the position of the ball when play was stopped.	Free kicks for offences involving a player entering, re-entering or leaving the field of play without permission are taken from the position of the ball when play was stopped. However, if a player leaves the field of play as part of play and commits an offence against another player, play is restarted with a free kick taken on the boundary line nearest to where the offence occurred; for direct free kick offences, a penalty kick is awarded, if this is within the offender's penalty area.

Explanation

Consistent with change outlined in 12.16 and 14.1.

解析

将任意球是判给对方球队的说明列在本章的开头，避免了频繁使用"判给对方球队"的说法。

13.2 任意球的位置

新增条文

所有任意球均应在犯规或违规的地点罚球，但下列情况除外：

解析

将此说明列在本章的开头，避免了在规则中反复说明任意球罚球的位置。

13.3 比赛场地外的犯规

旧条文	新条文
场上队员未经裁判员允许进入、重新进入或离开比赛场地而被判罚的任意球应在比赛停止时球所在的地点罚球。	场上队员未经裁判员允许进入、重新进入或离开比赛场地而被判罚的任意球，应在比赛停止时球所在地点罚球。然而，如果一名场上队员在正常比赛的移动中离开比赛场地，随后他对对方队员犯规，则应在距犯规发生地点最近的边界线上以任意球恢复比赛。如果该地点位于犯规方罚球区内，且该犯规可被判罚直接任意球，则判罚球点球。

解析

与12.16和14.1的内容保持一致

13.4 Ball must clearly move to be in play

Old text	New text
The ball is in play when it is kicked and moves.	The ball is in play when it is kicked and <u>clearly</u> moves...

Explanation

Change consistent with kick-off (8.3), penalty kick (14.2) and corner kick (17.2).

13.5 Stopping/intercepting free kicks

Old text	New text
If a player decides to take a free kick quickly and an opponent who is near the ball deliberately prevents him taking the kick, the referee must caution the player for delaying the restart of play. If a player decides to take a free kick quickly and an opponent who is less than 9.15 m (10 yds) from the ball intercepts it, the referee must allow play to continue.	If a player <u>takes</u> a free kick quickly and an opponent who is less than 9.15 m (10 yds) from the ball intercepts it, the referee allows play to continue. However, <u>an opponent who deliberately prevents</u> a free kick being taken must be cautioned for delaying the restart of play.

Explanation

Paragraphs reversed; clearer distinction between 'preventing' a free kick being taken and 'intercepting' a quick free kick after it has been taken.

Law 14 – The Penalty Kick

14.1 Penalty for foul off the field of play (see 12.16 + 13.3)

Old text	New text
A penalty kick is awarded against a team that commits one of ten offences for which a direct free kick is awarded inside his own penalty area.	A penalty kick is awarded if a player commits a direct free kick offence inside their penalty area <u>or off the field as part of play as outlined in Laws 12 and 13</u>.

13.4 球必须明显移动，比赛才视为进行

旧条文	新条文
当球被踢并移动时,比赛即为开始。	当球被踢且明显移动，则为比赛恢复。……

解析

与开球（08.3）、罚球点球（14.2）和角球（17.2）变更的内容一致。

13.5 阻止/截得任意球

旧条文	新条文
如果队员决定快速踢出任意球，而在距球很近的一名守方队员故意阻止其踢球，裁判员必须警告守方队员延误比赛重新开始。如果队员决定快速踢出任意球，而在距球不足9.15米的一名守方队员将球截获，裁判员必须允许比赛继续。	如果队员快速罚出任意球，随后距球不足9.15米（10码）的对方队员将球截获，裁判员允许比赛继续。然而，故意阻止对方快速发球的队员必须以延误比赛恢复为由予以警告。

解析

将本段内容颠倒，更加明确了"阻止"任意球发出和"截得"已经发出的任意球的区别。

第十四章 罚球点球

14.1 因比赛场地外发生的犯规判罚的球点球（详见12.16+13.3）

旧条文	新条文
某队在本方罚球区内犯有可判为直接任意球的10种犯规中的任意一种，应判罚球点球。	队员在本方罚球区内，或如第十二章、十三章已明确的正常比赛移动中离开比赛场地后，犯有可判罚直接任意球的犯规，则判罚球点球。

Explanation

Repeat of Law 12 and 13 changes that a penalty is awarded for an offence by a defender off the field of play with the ball in play if the nearest point to the offence is inside their own penalty area.

14.2 Stationary position and movement of the ball

Old text	New text
The ball: • must be placed on the penalty mark • The ball is in play when it is kicked and moves	The ball: • must be <u>stationary</u> on the penalty mark • The ball is in play when it is kicked <u>and clearly moves</u>

Explanation

Consistent with other changes.

14.3 When penalty is completed (see 10.2.6)

Additional text

<u>The penalty kick is completed when the ball stops moving, goes out of play or the referee stops play for any infringement of the Laws.</u>

Explanation

Clarifies when a penalty kick is over.

14.4 Some offences are always punished with an indirect free kick

Old text	New text
If the referee gives the signal for a penalty kick to be taken and, before the ball is in play, one of the following occurs: the player taking the penalty kick infringes the Laws of the Game:	Once the referee has signalled for a penalty kick to be taken, the kick must be taken. If, before the ball is in play, one of the following occurs: the player taking the penalty kick or a team-mate infringes the Laws of the Game:

解析

重复强调第十二章和第十三章的变动,即当比赛进行中,防守队员在比赛场地外犯规时,如果离犯规地点最近一点在其本方罚球区内时,则判罚球点球。

14.2 球的放定和移动

旧条文	新条文
球: • 必须放定在罚球点上。 • 当球被踢并向前移动时比赛即为进行。	球: • 球必须放定在罚球点上。 • 当球被踢且明显移动,即为比赛恢复。

解析

与其他章节变更保持一致。

14.3 何时视为罚球完成(详见10.2.6)

附加条文

当球停止移动、离开比赛场地,或因发生任何违反规则的情况而裁判员停止比赛时,即为罚球完成。

解析

明确了罚球过程何时结束。

14.4 有些违规行为必须判罚间接任意球

旧条文	新条文
如果裁判员发出执行罚球点球信号后,球进入比赛之前发生下列情况:主罚队员在踢球点球时违反竞赛规则:	一旦裁判员示意执行罚球点球,球必须罚出。如果在比赛恢复前,出现如下任一情况:主罚队员或同队队员违犯规则:

- the referee allows the kick to be taken
- if the ball enters the goal, the kick is retaken
- if the ball does not enter the goal, the referee stops play and the match is restarted with an indirect free kick to the defending team from the place where the infringement occurred

the goalkeeper infringes the Laws of the Game:
- the referee allows the kick to be taken
- if the ball enters the goal, a goal is awarded
- if the ball does not enter the goal, the kick is retaken

a team-mate of the player taking the kick infringes the Laws of the Game:
- the referee allows the kick to be taken
- if the ball enters the goal, the kick is retaken
- if the ball does not enter the goal, the referee stops play and the match is restarted with an indirect free kick to the defending team from the place where the infringement occurred

a team-mate of the goalkeeper infringes the Laws of the Game:
- the referee allows the kick to be taken
- if the ball enters the goal, a goal is awarded
- if the ball does not enter the goal, the kick is retaken

- if the ball enters the goal, the kick is retaken
- if the ball does not enter the goal, the referee stops play and restarts with an indirect free kick

except for the following offences/ infringements when play will be stopped and restarted with an indirect free kick regardless of whether or not a goal is scored:
- a team-mate of the identified kicker takes the kick; the referee cautions the player who took the kick
- a penalty kick is kicked backwards;
- feinting to kick the ball once the kicker has completed the run-up (feinting in the run-up is permitted); the referee cautions the kicker

- 裁判员允许踢出该球点球。
- 如果球进入球门，应重踢。
- 如果球未进入球门，裁判员应停止比赛，由守方在违规地点踢间接任意球重新开始比赛。

守门员违反竞赛规则：
- 裁判员允许踢出该球点球。
- 如果球进入球门，得分有效。
- 如果球未进入球门，应重踢。

主罚队员的同队队员违反竞赛规则：
- 裁判员允许踢出该球点球。
- 如果球进入球门，应重踢。
- 如果球未进入球门，裁判员应停止比赛，由守方在违规地点踢间接任意球重新开始比赛。

守门员的同队队员违反竞赛规则：
- 裁判员允许踢出该球点球。
- 如果球进入球门，得分有效。
- 如果球未进入球门，应重踢。

- 如果球进门，则重罚球点球。
- 如果球未进门，则裁判员停止比赛，以间接任意球恢复比赛。

如下情况，无论进球与否裁判员将停止比赛，以间接任意球恢复比赛：
- 向后踢球点球。
- 已确认的主罚队员的同队队员罚球点球，裁判员警告该名罚球队员。
- 罚球队员完成助跑后用假动作踢球（在助跑过程中使用假动作是允许的），裁判员警告该名队员。

Explanation

Emphasises that the standard re-take/goal/indirect free kick decision does not apply to these situations, especially the wrong player taking the kick or 'illegal' feinting which are 'deliberate' acts of unsporting behaviour

14.5 Offences by the goalkeeper

Additional text

If the ball does not enter the goal the kick is retaken; the goalkeeper is cautioned if responsible for the infringement

Explanation

As the Law has been changed to deal more strongly with a penalty kicker who 'illegally feints', it is consistent that a goalkeeper who infringes the Law causing a retake is cautioned. This should encourage goalkeepers not to infringe this Law.

14.6 Several offences committed at the same time

Old text	New text
a player of both the defending team and the attacking team infringes the Laws of the Game the kick is retaken	a player of both teams infringes the Laws of the Game the kick is retaken unless a player commits a more serious offence (e.g. illegal feinting)

Explanation

Repeat of change in Law 5 where the more serious is penalised (See 5.3).

解析

强调了重罚/判定进球有效/判罚间接任意球等决定不适用于这些情形，尤其是非主罚队员罚球或"不合规的"假动作，此类行为是"故意"的非体育道德行为。

14.5 守门员违反规则

新增条文

如果球未进门，应重罚球点球。如果守门员违犯规则，则对其予以警告。

解析

由于规则的变更对使用"不合规的佯装踢球"的罚球队员处罚更加严厉，守门员违规也应予以警告，已与对其他队员的处罚保持统一。此举也可以敦促守门员不出现违规。

14.6 多种违规行为同时发生

旧条文	新条文
攻守双方队员都违反竞赛规则： • 应重踢。	双方队员违犯规则，应重罚球点球。除非某一队员违犯规则的程度更重（如使用不合法的假动作）。

解析

重复了第五章的变更，处罚更为严重的犯规（详见05.3）。

Law 15 – The Throw-in

15.1 Ball is thrown with both hands

New text

At the moment of delivering the ball, the thrower must:
- face the field of play
- have part of each foot either on the touch line or on the ground outside the touch line
- throws the ball with both hands from behind and over the head from the point where it left the field of play

Explanation

- **throws** is a more logical word to use than **delivers**
- combining bullet points 3 and 4 emphasises that the 'one handed' foul throw (ball thrown with one hand and guided with the other) is not permitted.

15.2 Encroaching within 2m (2 yds)

Old text	New text
If an opponent unfairly distracts or impedes the thrower • he is cautioned for unsporting behaviour	An opponent who unfairly distracts or impedes the thrower (including moving closer than 2m (2 yds) from the place where the throw-in is to be taken) is cautioned for unsporting behaviour and if the throw-in has been taken an indirect free kick is awarded.

Explanation

Clarifies that not respecting the 2m (2 yds) distance is considered unfairly distracting or impeding and an IDFK is the restart if the throw-in has been taken.

第十五章　掷界外球

15.1 双手掷球

新条文

在掷出球的瞬间，掷球队员必须：

- 面向比赛场地。
- 任何一只脚的一部分在边线上或在边线外的地面上。
- 在球离开比赛场地的地点，用双手将球从头后经头顶掷出。

解析

- 掷（球）相较发（球）是更符合逻辑的用词。
- 将原规则此处的要点3和4合并，以此强调"单手"违规掷球（单手将球掷出，另一只手护球调整方向）是不允许的。

15.2 提前进入2米（2码）距离

旧条文	新条文
如果对方队员不正当地阻碍或干扰掷球队员： • 他将因非体育行为被警告。	对方队员通过不正当的方式干扰或阻碍掷球队员（包括移动至距掷球位置少于2米（2码）的地点）应以非体育行为予以警告，如果界外球已被掷出，则判罚间接任意球。

解析

明确了未遵循2米（2码）距离的行为会被视为以不正当的方式干扰或阻碍掷球队员，如果界外球已被掷出，则以间接任意球作为恢复比赛的方式。

Law 16 – The Goal Kick

16.1 Corner kick if kicked directly into own goal

Additional text

- A goal may be scored directly from a goal kick but only against the opposing team; if the ball directly enters the kicker's goal a corner kick is awarded to the opponents if the ball left the penalty area.

Explanation

Clarifies the correct restart if a player scores an 'own goal' directly from a goal kick (e.g. in strong wind).

16.2 Ball must be stationary

New text

- The ball must be stationary and is kicked from any point within the goal area by a player of the defending team

Explanation

Clarifies that the ball must be stationary as this was not in the 'old' wording.

16.3 Attacker in the penalty area

Additional text

- If an opponent who is in the penalty area when the goal kick is taken touches or challenges for the ball before it has touched another player, the goal kick is retaken.

Explanation

Clarifies that any opponent(s) in the penalty area when the goal kick is taken can not touch/challenge for the ball until another player has touched it so that the player does not gain an advantage from having not left the penalty area as required by Law.

第十六章 球门球

16.1 如果直接踢入本方球门，应判罚角球

新增条文

球门球可以直接射入对方球门而得分。如果球离开罚球区后直接进入踢球队员本方球门，则判给对方角球。

解析

明确了若队员踢球门球出现"乌龙球"后（例如遇到强风），正确的恢复比赛方式。

16.2 球必须放定

新增条文

- 球必须放定，由守方球队中的一名场上队员在球门区内任意位置踢球。

解析

明确了球必须放定，这在旧条文措辞中并未提及。

16.3 罚球区内的攻方队员

新增条文

在踢球门球时处在罚球区内的对方队员，在其他队员触及球前触球或争抢球，应重踢球门球。

解析

明确了踢球门球时，任何处在罚球区内的对方队员不得在其他队员触球前触及/争抢球，以此确保在规则规定的前提下，踢球门球时未离开罚球区的对方队员不能获利。

Law 17 – The Corner Kick

17.1 Corner kick if kicked directly into own goal

Additional text

- A goal may be scored directly from a corner kick but only against the opposing team; <u>if the ball directly enters the kicker's goal a corner kick is awarded to the opponents.</u>

Explanation

Clarifies correct restart if a player scores an 'own goal' directly from a corner kick.

17.2 Ball must be stationary and then clearly move to be in play

New text

- The ball must be placed in the corner <u>area</u>
- The ball <u>must be stationary</u> and is kicked by a player of the attacking team
- The ball is in play when it is kicked <u>and clearly moves</u> (...)

Explanation

- Area replaces 'arc'
- Clarifies that the ball must be stationary
- Reflects change to other Laws, but which is especially important for corner kicks to stop a player just touching the ball then unsportingly pretending that the corner has not been taken

第十七章　角球

17.1 如果直接踢入本方球门，应判罚角球。

新增条文

角球可以直接射入对方球门而得分。如果角球直接射入踢球队员本方球门，则判给对方角球。

解析

明确了若队员踢角球出现"乌龙球"后，正确的恢复比赛方式。

17.2 球必须放定，且明显移动后，方为比赛恢复

新条文

- 球必须放在角球区内。
- 球必须放定，由攻方球队中的一名场上队员踢球。
- 当球被踢且明显移动时，即为比赛恢复。……

解析

- "区"替换了"弧"。
- 明确了球必须放定。
- 与其他章节的变动相一致，但在发角球时显的尤为重要的是，队员轻轻触球，假装角球尚未踢出，要阻止这种非体育行为。

Glossary

术语汇编

The Glossary contains words/phrases which need clarification or explanation beyond the detail in the Laws and/or which are not always easily translated into other languages.

Football Bodies

The IFAB – The International Football Association Board
Body composed of the four British FAs and FIFA which is responsible for the Laws of the Game worldwide. In principle, changes to the Laws may only be approved at the Annual General Meeting usually held in February or March

FIFA – Fédération Internationale de Football Association
The governing body responsible for football throughout the world

Confederation
Body responsible for football in a continent. The six confederations are AFC (Asia), CAF (Africa), CONCACAF (North, Central America and Caribbean), CONMEBOL (South America), OFC (Oceania) and UEFA (Europe)

National Football Association
Body responsible for football in a country

术语汇编收纳了在规则正文中需要详细说明或解释的词语/词组，以及较难准确地翻译成其他语言的术语。

足球机构

IFAB——国际足球理事会
国际足球理事会由4个英联邦足球协会和国际足球联合会组成，是负责《足球竞赛规则》的全球机构。原则上，竞赛规则的修订只能由年度大会批准，该会议通常在每年二三月举行。

FIFA——国际足球联合会
国际足球联合会是世界足球运动的主管机构。

洲际联合会
洲际联合会负责本大洲足球运动，6个洲际联合会分别是亚洲足球联合会（AFC）、非洲足球联合会（CAF）、中北美洲及加勒比海足球联合会（CONCACAF）、南美洲足球联合会（CONMEBOL）、大洋洲足球联合会（OFC）和欧洲足球协会联盟（UEFA）。

国家足球协会
负责本国足球运动。

Football terms

A

Abandon
To end/terminate a match before the scheduled finish

Advantage
The referee allows play to continue when an offence has occurred if this benefits the non-offending team

Additional time
Time allowed at the end of each half for time 'lost' because of substitutions, injuries, disciplinary action, goal celebration etc.

Assessment of injured player
Quick examination of an injury, usually by a medical person, to see if the player requires treatment

Away goals rule
Method of deciding a match/tie when both teams have scored the same number of goals; goals scored away from home count double

足球术语

A

中止
在比赛程序尚未完成前,终止/取消该场比赛。

有利
当犯规发生,未犯规的一方能从中获得利益时,裁判员允许比赛继续进行。

补时
因队员替换、受伤、纪律处罚、庆祝进球等"损耗"的时间,在各半场结束时予以补足。

对受伤队员的伤情评估
通常由医护人员对场上受伤队员伤势进行的快速诊断,用以确定是否需要治疗。

客场进球规则
当两队进球数相同时,用来判定比赛胜负的方法。此时客场球队的进球将被双倍计算。

B

Brutality
An act which is savage, ruthless or deliberately violent

C

Caution
Official sanction which results in a report to a disciplinary authority; indicated by showing a yellow card; two cautions in a match result in a player being dismissed (sent off)

Charge (an opponent)
Physical challenge against an opponent, usually using the shoulder and upper arm (which is kept close to the body)

D

Deceive
Act to mislead/trick the referee into giving an incorrect decision/disciplinary sanction which benefits the deceiver and/or their team

Direct free kick
A free kick from which a goal can be scored by kicking the ball directly into the opponents' goal

Discretion
Judgment used by a referee or other match official when making a decision

B

野蛮行为

野蛮、粗暴的行为或故意使用暴力的行径。

C

警告

一种被记录和报告的正式纪律处罚，以出示黄牌作为表示。一名队员在一场比赛中得到两次警告将被驱逐出场（罚令出场）。

冲撞（对方队员）

用身体对对方队员使用的争抢动作，通常使用肩部或上臂（紧贴身体）。

D

欺骗

误导/使用诡计使裁判员做出错误的判罚/纪律处罚，以使该名队员自身和/或其球队获利。

直接任意球

可以直接射入对方球门得分的任意球。

酌情考虑

裁判员或其他比赛官员在做出判罚时的判断。

Dismissal
Another word for 'sending-off' (red card)

Dissent
Public disagreement (verbal and/or physical) with a match official's decision; punishable by a caution (yellow card)

Distract
Disturb, confuse or draw attention (usually unfairly)

Dropped ball
A 'neutral' method of restarting play – the referee drops the ball between players of both teams; the ball is in play when it touches the ground

E

Electronic player tracking system (EPTS)
System which records and analyses data about the physical and physiological performance of a player

Endanger the safety of an opponent
Put an opponent at danger or risk (of injury)

Excessive force
Using more force/energy than is necessary

Extra time
A method of trying to decide the outcome of a match involving two additional periods of play

驱逐出场

同"罚令出场"（红牌）。

异议

对裁判员的判罚以公开方式表示异议（用语言和/或肢体动作），需在公众视野下给予警告（黄牌）。

干扰

扰乱、迷惑或吸引注意力（通常是以不公平的方式）。

坠球

一种"中立"的恢复比赛方式——裁判员在双方队员之间执行坠球，当球接触地面时比赛即为恢复。

E

表现跟踪电子系统(EPTS)

记录、分析球员体能和生理活动数据的系统。

危及对方安全

使对方队员处在(受伤的)危险或风险中。

过分力量

使用超出必要的力量或力气。

加时赛

一种决定比赛结果的方式，分为两个不超过15分钟且相等时长的半场。

F

Feinting
An action which attempts to confuse an opponent. The Laws define permitted and 'illegal' feinting

Field of play (Pitch)
The playing area confined by the touchlines and goal lines and goal nets where used

G

Goal line technology (GLT)
Electronic system which immediately informs the referee when a goal has been scored i.e. the ball has wholly passed over the goal line in the goal
(See Law 1 for details)

H

Hybrid system
A combination of artificial and natural materials to create a playing surface which requires sunlight, water, air circulation and mowing

F

假动作
试图迷惑对方队员的行为。规则中已经定义了允许的和不合规的假动作。

比赛场地
由边线、球门线和球门网围成的比赛区域。

G

球门线技术（GLT）
可立即向裁判员传递进球与否，即球的整体是否越过球门线信息的电子系统（细节详见第一章）。

H

混和系统
人造和天然结合材料制成的草皮，同样需要阳光、水分、空气循环和剪草处理。

I

Indirect free kick
A free kick from which a goal can only be scored if another player (of any team) touches the ball after it has been kicked

Infringement
An action which is against/breaks/violates the Laws

Impede
To delay, block or prevent an opponent's action or movement

Intentional
A deliberate action (not an accident)

Intercept
To prevent a ball reaching its intended destination

K

Kicks from the penalty mark
Method of deciding the result of a match by each team alternately taking kicks until one team has scored one more goal and both teams have taken the same number of kicks (unless during the first 5 kicks for each team, one team could not equal the other team's score even if they scored from all their remaining kicks)

N

Negligible
Insignificant, minimal

I

间接任意球

在踢出后,由其他场上队员(任意一方)触球后才可进球得分的任意球。

违规违例

违背/破坏/违反规则的行为。

阻碍

延缓/阻挡或阻止对方队员的行动或移动。

故意

蓄意的行为(并非偶然)。

阻截

阻止球到达预定的地点。

K

踢球点球决胜

决定比赛胜负的方式。由双方球队轮流踢球点球,直至当双方罚球次数相同时,一队进球数比另一队多一球(除非在前5轮罚球时,一队罚完剩余所有轮次可能的进球数都无法追平另一队)。

N

微不足道

不明显地、轻微地。

O

Offence
An action which breaks/infringes/violates the Laws of the Game; sometimes relates particularly to illegal actions committed against a person, especially an opponent

Offensive, insulting or abusive language
Verbal or physical behaviour which is rude, hurtful, disrespectful; punishable by a sending-off (red card)

Outside agent
Any person who is not a match official or on the team list (players, substitutes and team officials)

P

Penalise
To punish, usually by stopping play and awarding a free kick or penalty kick to the opposing team *(see also Advantage)*

Played
Action by a player which makes contact with the ball

Playing distance
Distance to the ball which allows a player to touch the ball by extending the foot/leg or jumping or, for goalkeepers, jumping with arms extended. Distance depends on the physical size of the player

O

犯规违规

违背/破坏/违反规则的行为。有些情况下指对人，特别是对对方队员的不合规行为。

攻击性、侮辱性或辱骂性的语言

粗鲁的、伤害性的、无礼的语言或肢体行为，应罚令出场（红牌）。

场外因素

除比赛官员和球队名单（上场队员、替补队员、球队官员）以外的任何人。

P

判罚

一种惩罚。通常是以停止比赛并判给对方任意球或球点球的方式（同时可参考有利）。

处理球

队员做出的用身体接触球的动作。

合理争抢范围

队员可以通过伸脚/伸腿或起跳，以及守门员跳起后手臂展开而接触到球的距离范围。此距离取决于队员的体型。

Q

Quick free kick
A free kick taken (with the referee's permission) very quickly after play was stopped

R

Reckless
Any action (usually a tackle or challenge) by a player which disregards (ignores) the danger to, or consequences for, the opponent

Restart
Any method of resuming play after it has been stopped

S

Sanction
Disciplinary action taken by the referee

Save
An action by a player to stop the ball when it is going into or very close to the goal using any part of the body except the hands (unless a goalkeeper within their own penalty area)

Send off (Dismissal)
Disciplinary action when a player is required to leave the field for the remainder of the match having committed a sending-off offence (indicated by a red card); if the match has started the player can not be replaced

Q

快发任意球

在比赛停止后快速发出的任意球（经裁判员允许）。

R

鲁莽的

队员的行为动作（通常是在抢截或争抢时）不顾及（忽视）可能对对方造成的危险或后果。

比赛恢复

比赛停止后，以任何方式继续比赛。

S

纪律处罚

裁判员实施的纪律措施。

救球

是指队员用除手之外（守门员在本方罚球区内除外）的任何身体部位阻止即将进门或非常接近球门的球。

罚令出场（驱逐出场）

当队员犯有可被罚令出场的犯规（出示红牌作为表示），不得参加剩余时间的比赛，并要求离开比赛场地时实施的纪律处罚。如果比赛已经开始，则该名队员不得被替换。

Serious foul play
A tackle or challenge for the ball that endangers the safety of an opponent or uses excessive force or brutality; punishable by a sending-off (red card)

Signal
Physical indication from the referee or any match official; usually involves movement of the hand or arm or flag, or use of the whistle (referee only)

Simulation
An action which creates a wrong/false impression that something has occurred when it has not *(see also deceive)*; committed by a player to gain an unfair advantage

Spirit of the game
The main/essential principles/ethos of football

Suspend
To stop a match for a period of time with the intention of eventually restarting play e.g. fog, heavy rain, thunderstorm, serious injury

T

Tackle
A challenge for the ball with the foot (on the ground or in the air)

Team official
Any non-player listed on the official team list e.g. coach, physiotherapist, doctor *(see technical staff)*

Team list
Official team document usually listing the players, substitutes and team officials

Technical staff
Official non-playing team members listed on the official team list e.g. coach, physiotherapist, doctor *(see team official)*

严重犯规
当抢截或争抢球时，采用危及对方队员安全，使用过分的力量、野蛮的方式，应罚令出场（红牌）。

信号
裁判员或其他比赛官员使用的肢体示意，通常以手臂、手旗的动作或使用哨音（仅裁判员）的方式。

假摔（伪装）
队员制造出错误/虚假表象的动作行为，好像有情况发生而其实并没有，企图借此获得不正当的利益（参考欺骗）。

足球运动精神
足球运动主要/核心的原则/精神。

中断
将比赛暂停一段时间，试图最终能恢复继续比赛。例如，大雾、大雨、雷电、严重受伤等情况。

T

抢截
使用脚争抢球（在地面或空中）。

球队官员
任何列入球队正式名单中的非参赛人员，如教练员、理疗师、医生（见技术人员）。

球队名单
列出上场队员、替补队员和球队官员信息的正式文件。

技术官员
列入球队正式名单中的非参赛人员，如教练员、理疗师、医生（见球队官员）。

Technical area
Defined area (in stadia) for the team officials which includes seating
(See Law 1 for details)

U

Undue interference
Action/influence which is unnecessary

Unsporting behaviour
Unfair action/behaviour; punishable by a caution

V

Violent conduct
An action, which is not a challenge for the ball, which uses or attempts to use excessive force or brutality against an opponent or when a player deliberately strikes someone on the head or face unless the force used is negligible

技术区域

（体育场馆内）供球队官员和替补队员使用的有坐席的区域（详见第一章具体内容）。

U

不当干涉

不必要的举动/干扰。

非体育行为

有失公平的不当举动/行为，应予警告。

V

暴力行为

队员不以争抢球为目的，而对对方使用或企图使用过分力量或野蛮动作，或故意击打其他人的头部或面部的行为，除非使用的力量微不足道。

Referee terms

Match official(s)
General term for person or persons responsible for controlling a football match on behalf of a football association and/or competition under whose jurisdiction the match is played

Referee
The main match official for a match who operates on the field of play. Other match officials operate under the referee's control and direction. The referee is the final/ultimate decision-maker

Other match officials
Competitions may appoint other match officials to assist the referee:

- **Assistant referee**
  A match official with a flag positioned on one half of each touchline to assist the referee particularly with offside situations and goal kick/corner kick/throw-in decisions

- **Fourth official**
  A match official with responsibility for assisting the referee with both on-field and off-field matters, including overseeing the technical area, controlling substitutes etc.

- **Additional assistant referee (AAR)**
  A match official positioned on the goal line to assist the referee particularly with situations in/around the penalty area and goal/no-goal decisions

- **Reserve assistant referee**
  Assistant referee who will replace an assistant (and, if competition rules permit, a fourth official and/or AAR) who is unable to continue

裁判术语

比赛官员
指在足球协会和/或竞赛主办方管辖下进行的比赛中，代表足球协会和/或竞赛方履行执法比赛职责的个人或团队。

裁判员
在比赛场地内执法的主要比赛官员，其他比赛官员在裁判员的管理和领导下履行职责。裁判员的判罚决定为最终决定。

其他比赛官员
竞赛方可委派其他比赛官员协助裁判员：

• 助理裁判员
持旗的比赛官员，处在两个半场的边线位置协助裁判员做出判罚决定，尤其是涉及越位、球门球、角球、界外球的判罚。

• 第四官员
负责协助裁判员管理场上、场下事务的比赛官员，包括监管技术区域及替补队员等。

• 附加助理裁判员（AAR）
该比赛官员处在球门线位置协助裁判员做出判罚决定，尤其是涉及罚球区内/附近的情况，以及进球/未进球的判罚。

• 候补助理裁判员
应为一名助理裁判员。用于替换无法继续执法的助理裁判员（如果赛事规程许可，也可替换第四官员和/或附加助理裁判员）。

Practical Guidelines
for Match Officials

比赛官员
实践指南

Introduction

These guidelines contain practical advice for match officials which supplements the information in the Laws of the Game section.

Reference is made in Law 5 to referees operating within the framework of the Laws of the Game and the 'spirit of the game'. Referees are expected to use common sense and to apply the 'spirit of the game' when applying the Laws of the Game, especially when making decisions relating to whether a match takes place and/or continues.

This is especially true for the lower levels of football where it may not always be possible for the Law to be strictly applied. For example, unless there are safety issues, the referee should allow a game to start/continue if:

- one or more corner flags is missing
- there is a minor inaccuracy with the markings on the field of play such as the corner area, centre circle etc.
- the goal posts/crossbar are not white

In such cases, the referee should, with the agreement of the teams, play/continue the match and must submit a report to the appropriate authorities.

Key:

- AR = assistant referee
- AAR = additional assistant referee

引言

比赛官员实践指南包含的建议是对《足球竞赛规则》内容的补充。

在第五章中已提及,裁判员依据《足球竞赛规则》和"足球运动精神"尽自身最大能力,做出自己认为最合适的决定。希望裁判员在执行《足球竞赛规则》时,结合常识、领会"足球运动精神",尤其是在做是否开始和/或继续比赛的相关决定时。

这在低级别的足球比赛中尤为重要。因为在这些级别的比赛中,完全按照规则执行是有难度的。如果在如下情况中,只要不存在安全隐患,裁判员应该开始/继续比赛:
- 缺少一面或多面角旗。
- 比赛场地个别标线不够精确,例如角球区、中圈弧等。
- 球门柱/横梁颜色不是白色的。

在这些情况下,经由双方球队同意,裁判员应该开始/继续比赛,并向相关机构提交报告。

关键词:
- AR=助理裁判员
- AAR=附加助理裁判员

Positioning, Movement and Teamwork

1. **General positioning and movement**

   The best position is one from which the referee can make the correct decision. All recommendations about positioning must be adjusted using specific information about the teams, the players and events in the match.

   The positions recommended in the graphics are basic guidelines. The reference to a "zone" emphasises that a recommended position is an area within which the referee is likely to be most effective. The zone may be larger, smaller or differently shaped depending on the exact match circumstances.

   Recommendations:
   - The play should be between the referee and the lead AR
   - The lead AR should be in the referee's field of vision so the referee should usually use a wide diagonal system
   - Staying towards the outside of the play makes it easier to keep play and the lead AR in the referee's field of vision
   - The referee should be close enough to see play without interfering with play
   - "What needs to be seen" is not always in the vicinity of the ball. The referee should also pay attention to:
     - player confrontations off the ball
     - possible offences in the area towards which play is moving
     - offences occurring after the ball is played away

选位、移动与团队配合

1. 常规选位与移动

裁判员能够做出准确判断的位置就是最佳的位置。所有有关位置的建议，在比赛中都应根据双方球队、队员，以及场上发生的各种情况进行调整。

插图中所建议的裁判员位置是常规建议，是能够帮助裁判员作出最佳判断的区域。这些区域可大可小，也可有不同形状，全部由比赛的实际情况而定。

建议：
- 比赛应在裁判员和视线较好的助理裁判员注视下进行。
- 视线较好的助理裁判员应在裁判员的视线范围之内，因此裁判员应按对角线方法选位。
- 在比赛发展的区域外进行选位，便于观察比赛进程，同时也能将视线较好的助理裁判员纳入自己的视野范围内。
- 在不影响比赛进程的情况下，裁判员应尽量靠近比赛发展的区域。
- "需要留意的"区域并不总在球的附近。裁判员也应该注意：
    - 无球状态下的球员争端。
    - 比赛发展方向的区域内可能发生的犯规。
    - 球离开后的区域内发生的犯规。

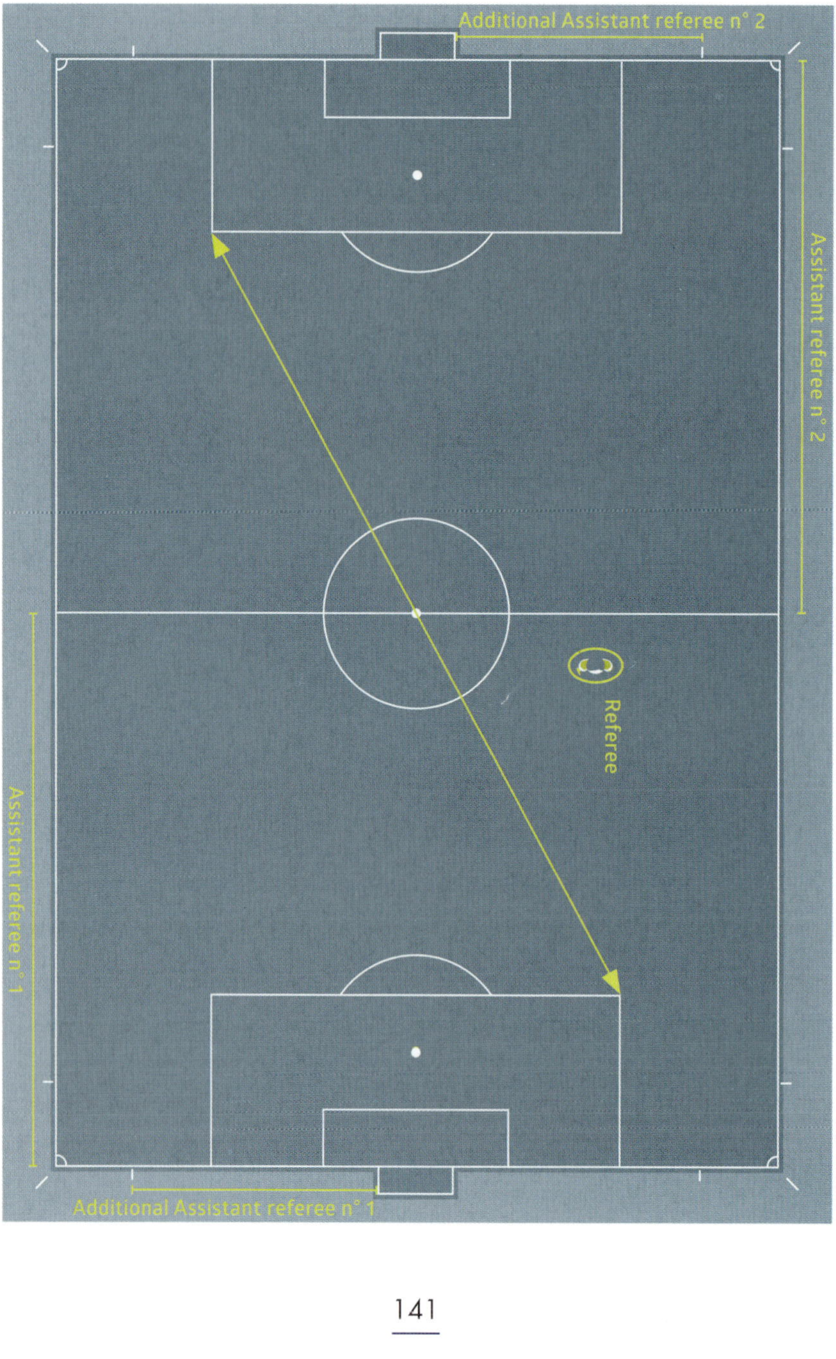
Additional Assistant referee n° 2
Assistant referee n° 2
Referee
Assistant referee n° 1
Additional Assistant referee n° 1

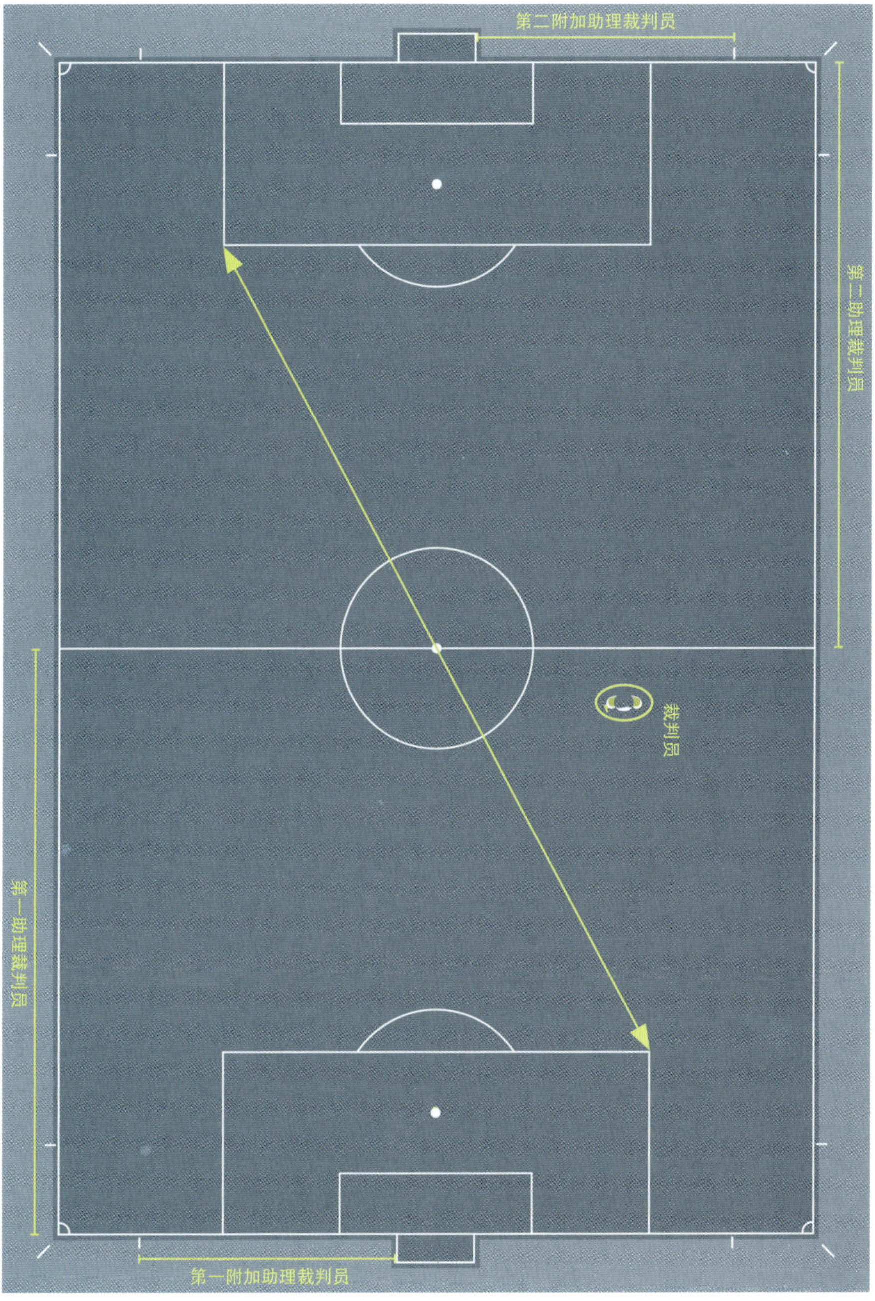
第二附加助理裁判员
第二助理裁判员
裁判员
第一助理裁判员
第一附加助理裁判员

Positioning of assistant referees and additional assistant referees

The AR must be in line with the second-last defender or the ball if it is nearer to the goal line than the second-last defender. The AR must always face the field of play, even when running. Side-to-side movement should be used for short distances. This is especially important when judging offside as it gives the AR a better line of vision.

The AAR position is behind the goal line except where it is necessary to move onto the goal line to judge a goal/no goal situation. The AAR is not allowed to enter the field of play unless there are exceptional circumstances.

Goalkeeper (GK)

Defender

Attacker

Referee

Assistant Referee

Additional Assistant Referee

助理裁判员与附加助理裁判员的选位

助理裁判员的位置必须与守方倒数第二名队员齐平，或当球较守方倒数第二名队员更接近于球门线时与球齐平。助理裁判员必须时刻面向比赛场地内，即使是在跑动中。侧滑步应用于短距离移动。这种移动对助理裁判员判断越位尤为重要，因为可以得到更好的观察角度。

附加助理裁判员的位置在球门线后，除非需要进行移动来判断球是否进门。除特殊情况外，不允许附加助理裁判员进入比赛场地内。

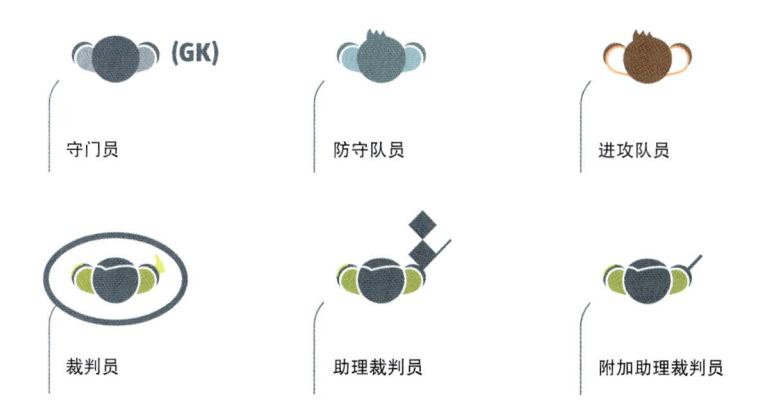

(GK) 守门员	防守队员	进攻队员
裁判员	助理裁判员	附加助理裁判员

2. Positioning and teamwork

Consultation

When dealing with disciplinary issues, eye contact and a basic discreet hand signal from the AR to the referee may be sufficient. When direct consultation is required, the AR may advance 2-3 metres onto the field of play if necessary. When talking, the referee and AR should both face the field of play to avoid being heard by others and to observe the players and field of play.

Corner kick

The AR's position for a corner kick is behind the corner flag in line with the goal line but the AR must not interfere with the player taking the corner kick and must check that the ball is properly placed in the corner area.

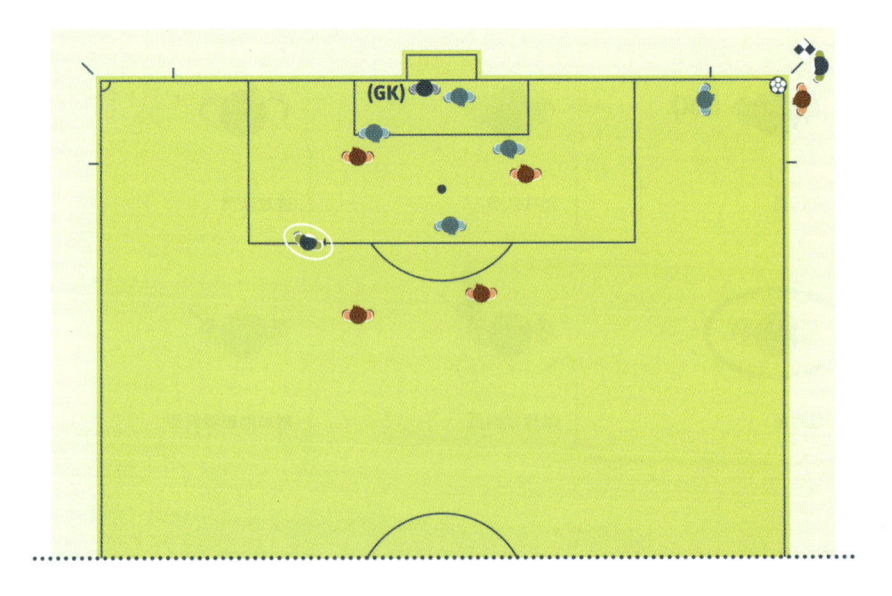

2. 选位与团队配合

（征询）商议

当涉及纪律处罚事宜时，在某些情况下用目光或赛前协商的手势信号与裁判员沟通即可。当需要直接商议时，助理裁判员可以进入场内2~3米。商议时裁判员和助理裁判员都要面向场内，以避免其他人听到商议内容，并利于观察场内的队员。

角球

助理裁判员在队员踢角球时应站在角旗后、球门线的延长线位置，不能影响踢角球的队员，且必须查看球是否正确摆放在角球区内。

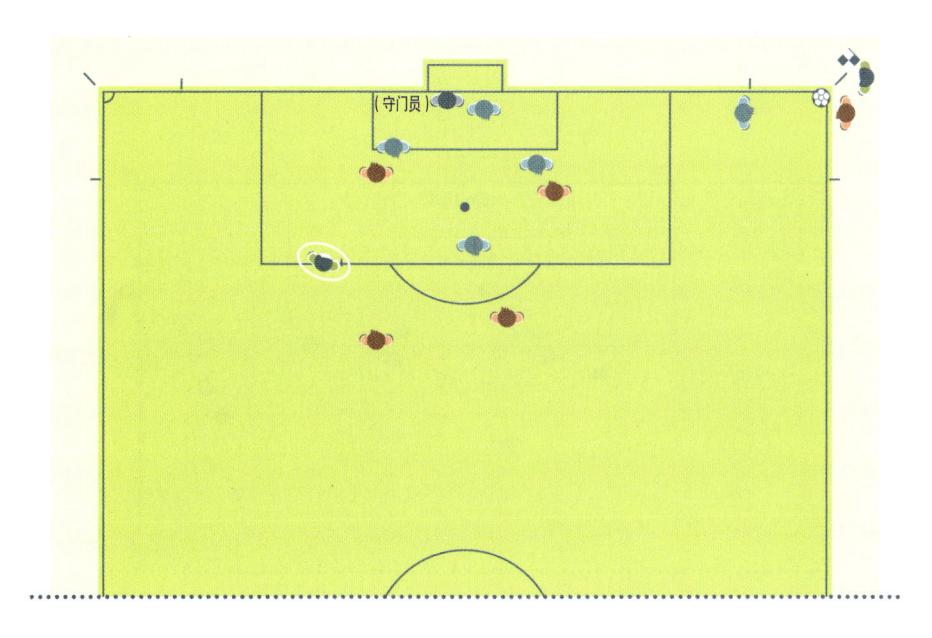

Free kick

The AR's position for a free kick must be in line with the second-last defender to check the offside line. However, the AR must be ready to follow the ball by moving down the touchline towards the corner flag if there is a direct shot on goal.

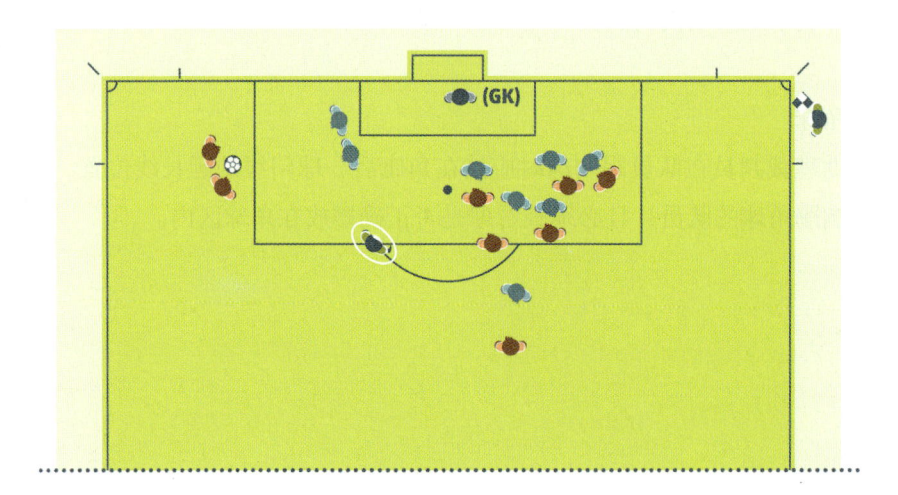

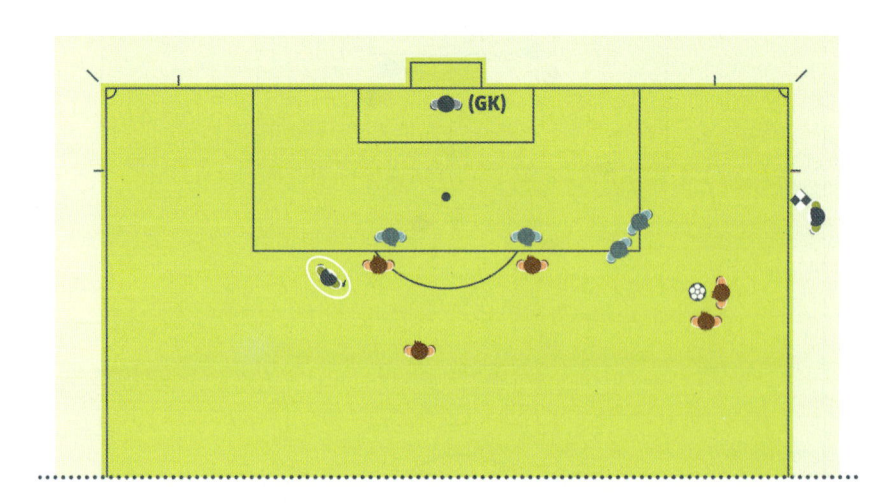

任意球

在踢任意球时，助理裁判员必须处在与守方倒数第二名队员齐平的位置以观察越位情况。无论如何，他还必须有所准备，即发生直接射门时要沿边线快速冲向角旗方向以跟随球。

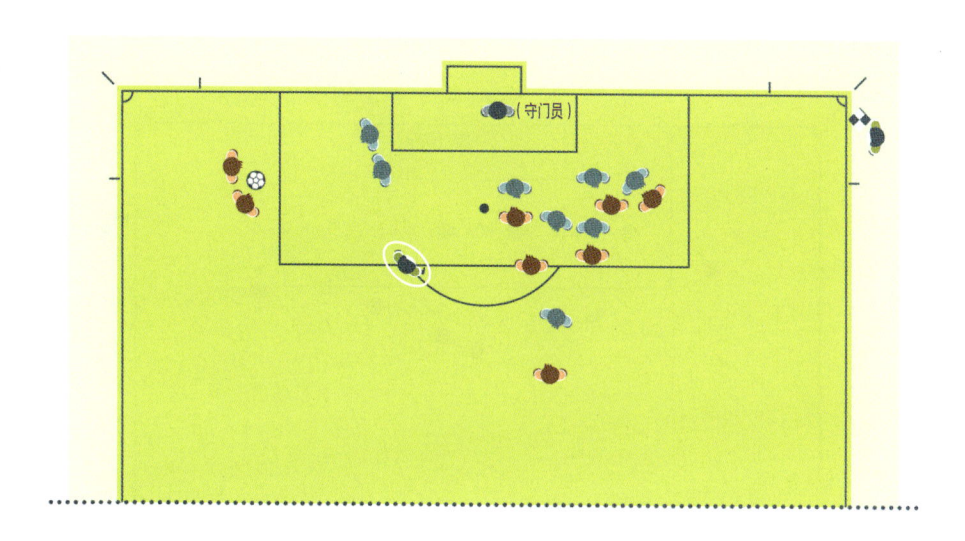

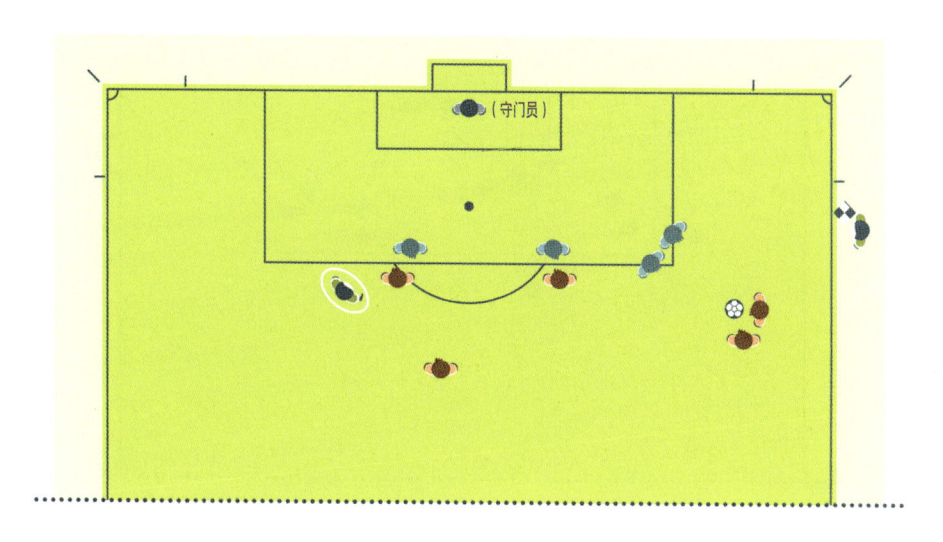

145

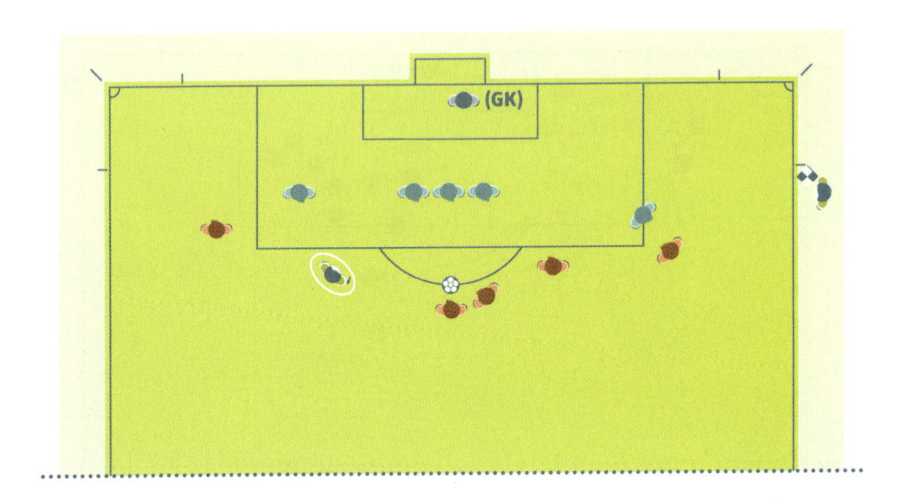

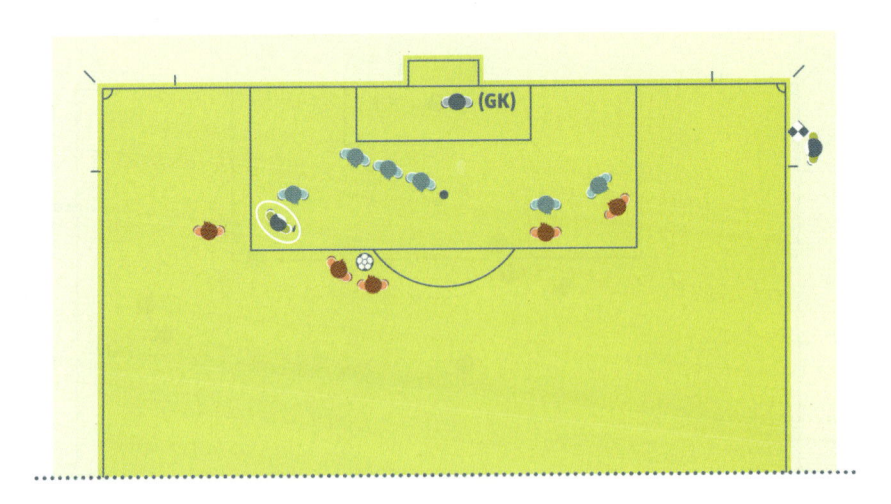

(守门员)

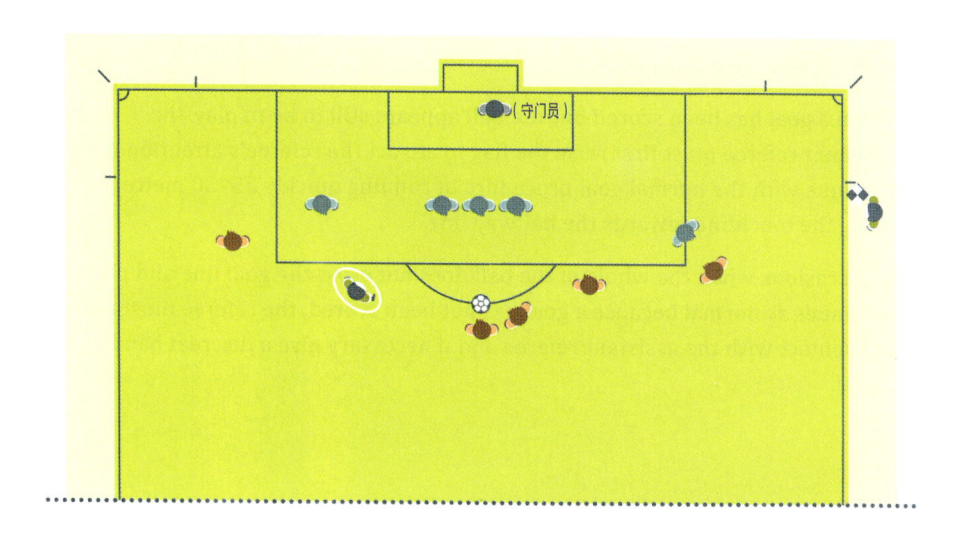

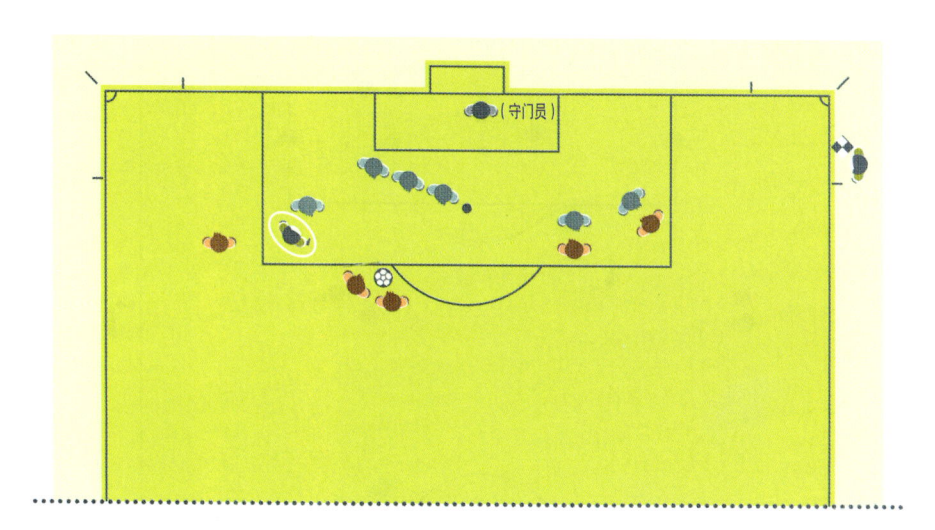

(守门员)

Goal/no goal

When a goal has been scored and there is no doubt about the decision, the referee and assistant referee must make eye contact and the assistant referee must then move quickly 25–30 metres along the touchline towards the halfway line without raising the flag.

When a goal has been scored but the ball appears still to be in play, the assistant referee must first raise the flag to attract the referee's attention then continue with the normal goal procedure of running quickly 25–30 metres along the touchline towards the halfway line.

On occasions when the whole of the ball does not cross the goal line and play continues as normal because a goal has not been scored, the referee must make eye contact with the assistant referee and if necessary give a discreet hand signal.

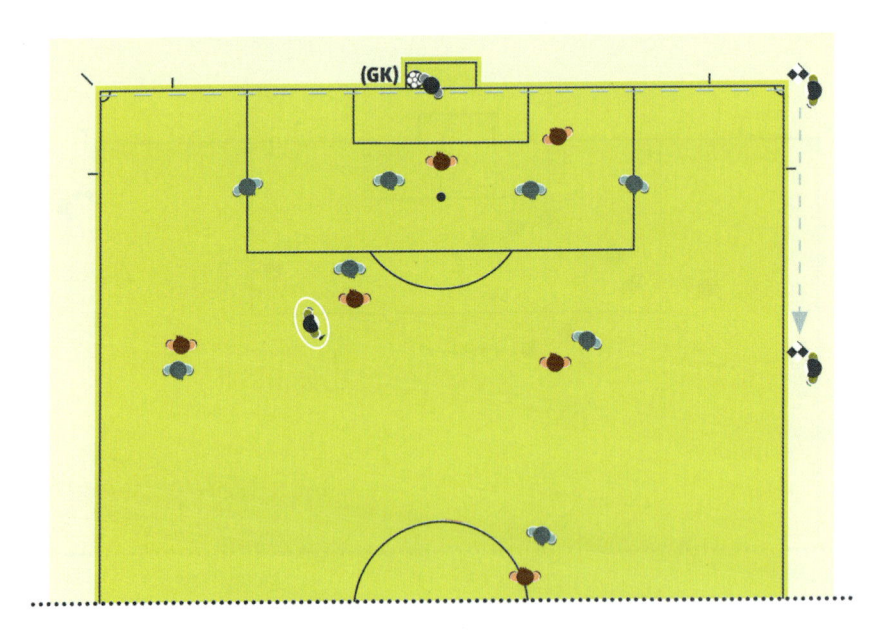

"进球/未进球"

当球已进球门并且没有任何疑问时，裁判员和助理裁判员必须用目光相互交流，然后助理裁判员不举旗沿边线快速向中线方向移动25～30米以表示进球。

当球已进球门而比赛仍在继续时，助理裁判员必须首先举旗向裁判员示意球已经进门，然后像正常的进球程序一样沿边线快速向中线方向跑25～30米以表示进球。

有时，球的整体没有越过球门线，比赛正常进行。此时，裁判员必须和助理裁判员进行目光交流，如果需要则用赛前准备好的手势信号相互配合。

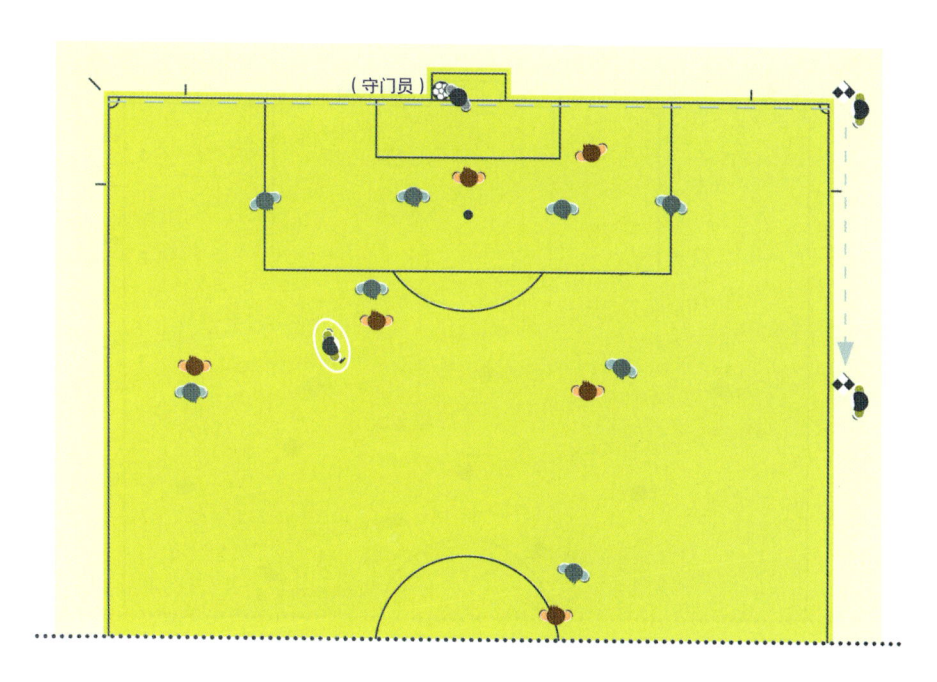

Goal kick

The AR must first check if the ball is inside the goal area. If the ball is not placed correctly, the AR must not move from the position, make eye contact with the referee and raise the flag. Once the ball is placed correctly inside the goal area, the AR must move to the edge of the penalty area to check that the ball leaves the penalty area (ball in play) and that the attackers are outside. Finally, the AR must take a position to check the offside line.

However, if there is an AAR, the AR should take up a position in line with the edge of the penalty area and then the offside line and the AAR must be positioned at the intersection of the goal line and the goal area, and check if the ball is placed inside the goal area. If the ball is not placed correctly, the AAR must communicate this to the referee.

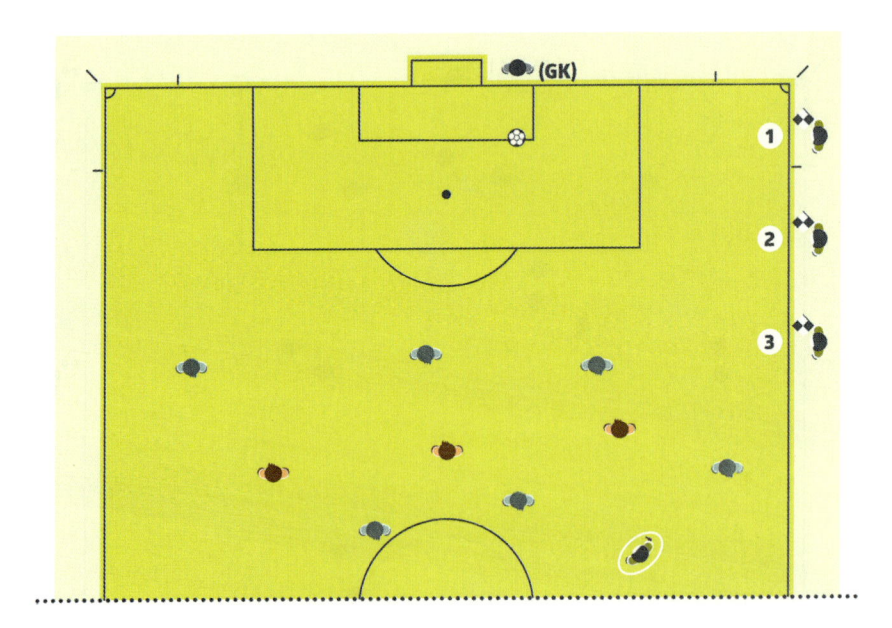

球门球

助理裁判员必须确认球是否放在球门区内。如果球没有放在正确的位置上，助理裁判员不得移动位置，用目光与裁判员交流并举旗示意。当球正确放在球门区内，助理裁判员必须移动到罚球区线延长位置确认球离开罚球区（比赛开始），以及攻方队员在罚球区外。最后，助理裁判员必须选择观察越位线的位置。

如果有附加助理裁判员，则助理裁判员应选择罚球区线延长线位置，以及随后的越位线位置。而附加助理裁判员选择球门线与球门区线相交的位置，检查球是否放在球门区内。如果球没有放在正确的位置上，附加助理裁判员必须与裁判员沟通。

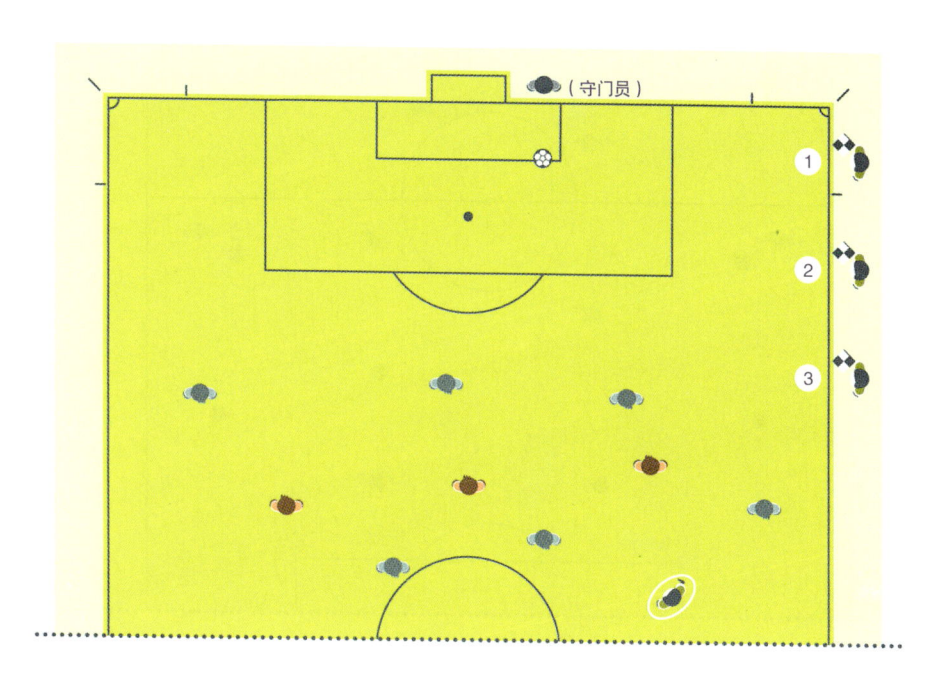

147

Goalkeeper releasing the ball

The AR must take a position in line with the edge of the penalty area and check that the goalkeeper does not handle the ball outside the penalty area. Once the goalkeeper has released the ball, the AR must take a position to check the offside line.

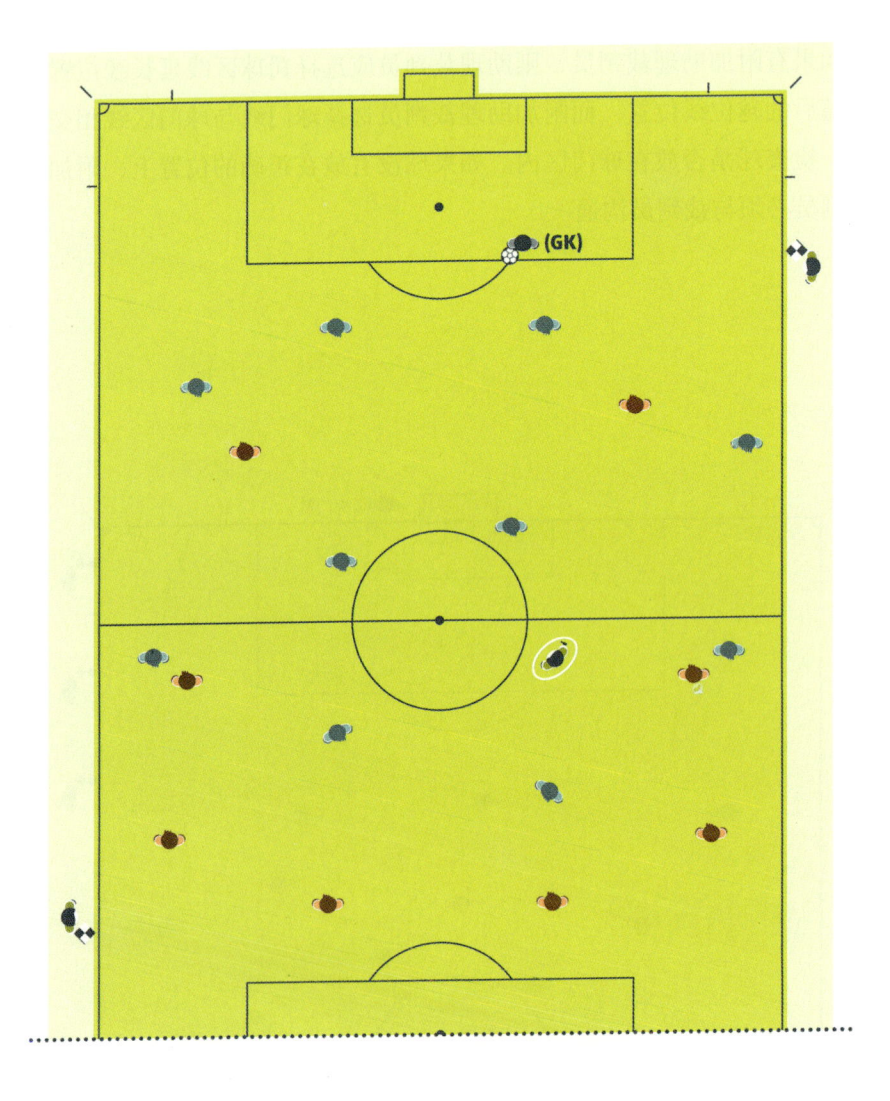

守门员发球

助理裁判员必须选择罚球区线的延长位置查看守门员是否在罚球区外手球。一旦守门员发出球后，助理裁判员必须选择观察越位线的位置。

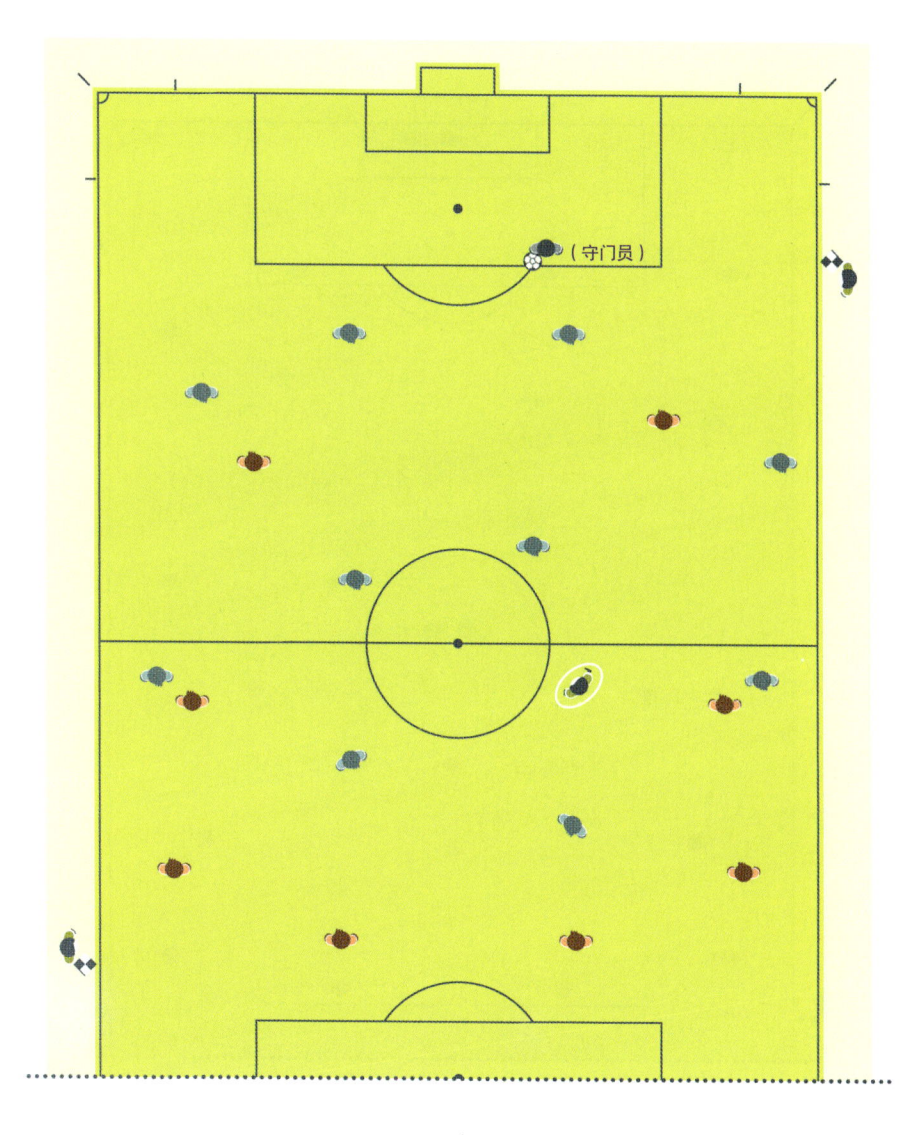

Kick-off
The ARs must be in line with the second-last defender.

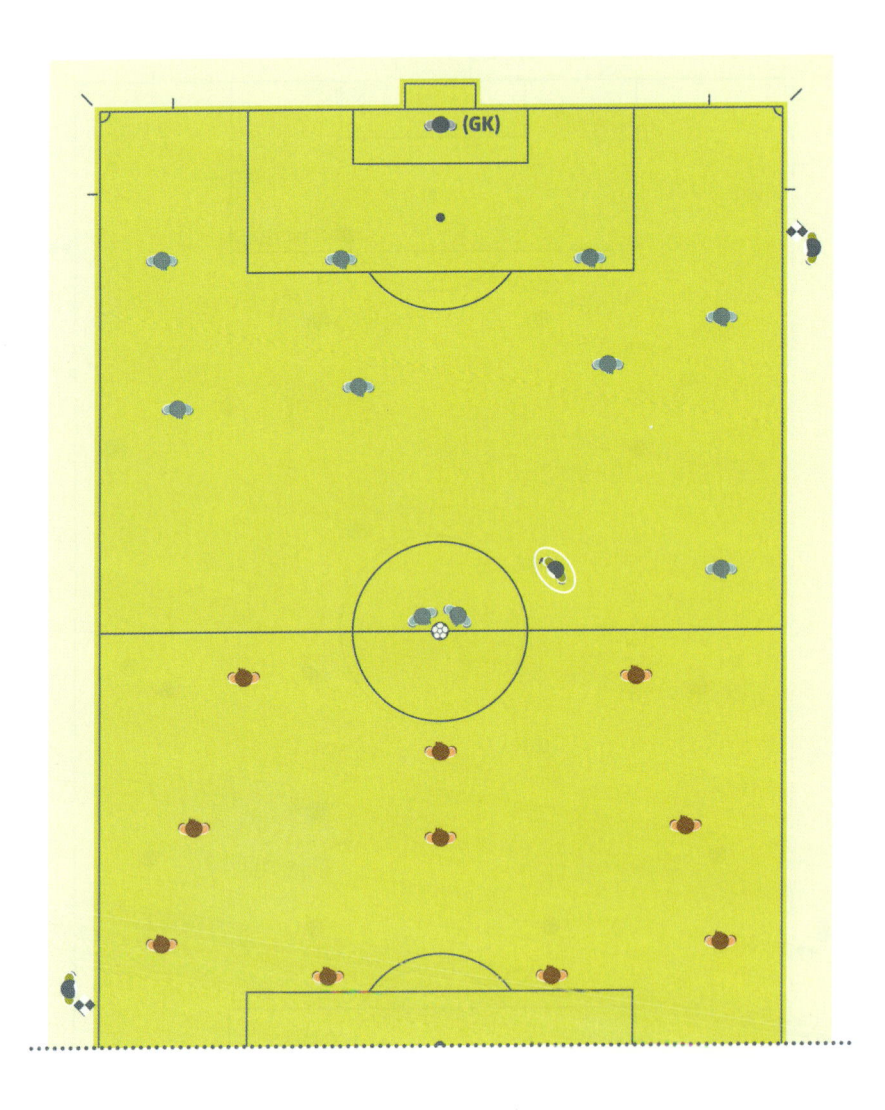

开球

助理裁判员必须与倒数第二名防守队员齐平。

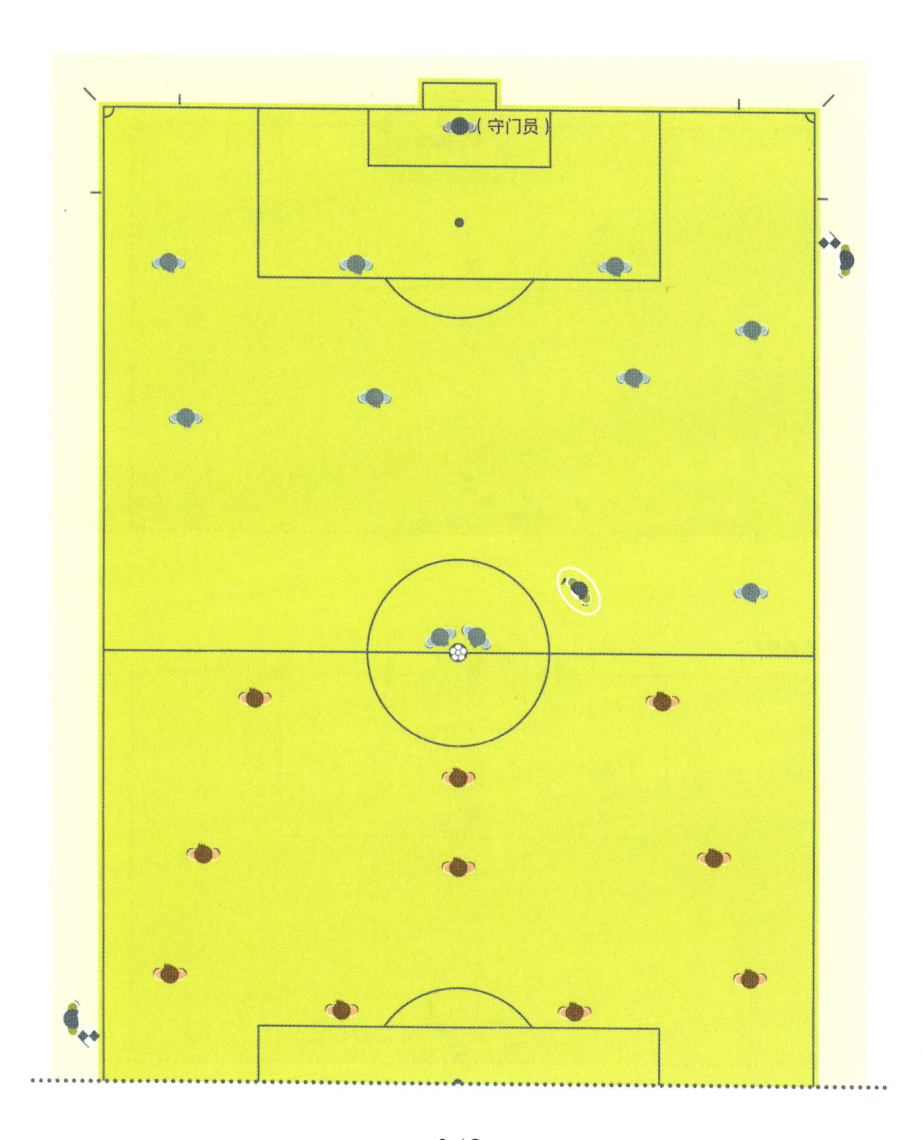

Kicks from the penalty mark

One AR must be positioned at the intersection of the goal line and the goal area. The other AR must be situated in the centre circle to control the players. If there are AARs, they must be positioned at each intersection of the goal line and the goal area, to the right and left of the goal respectively; both ARs are situated in the centre circle.

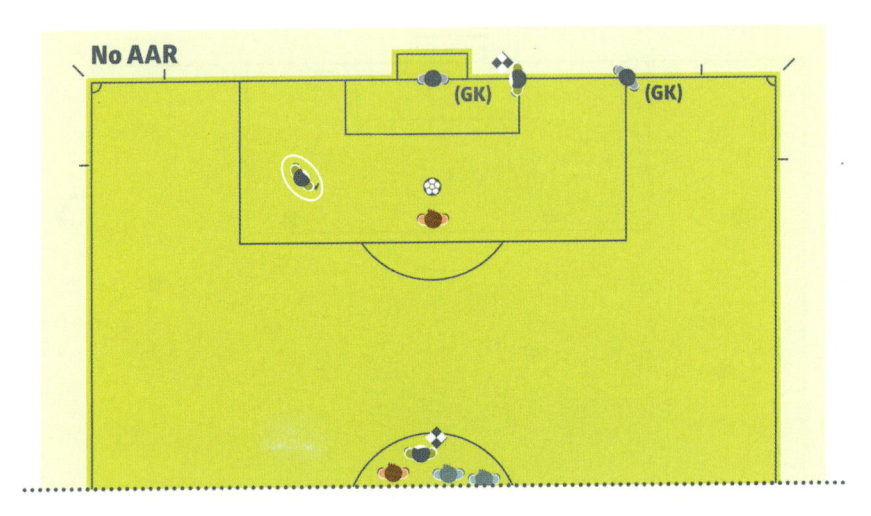

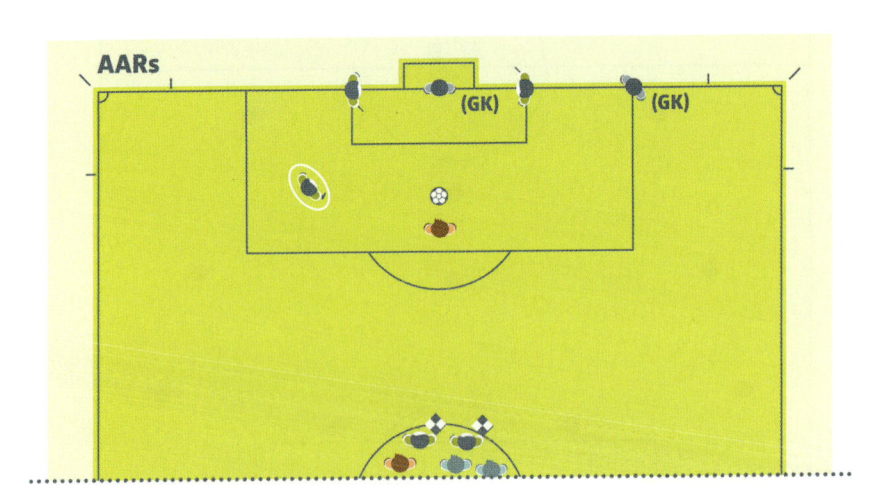

No AAR

AARs

球点球决胜

一名助理裁判员必须站在球门线与球门区线相交的位置，另一名助理裁判员必须站在中圈控制队员。如果有附加助理裁判员，则两名附加助理裁判员处于球门线与球门区线的两个交点位置，分别位于球门两侧。两名助理裁判员全部站在中圈内。

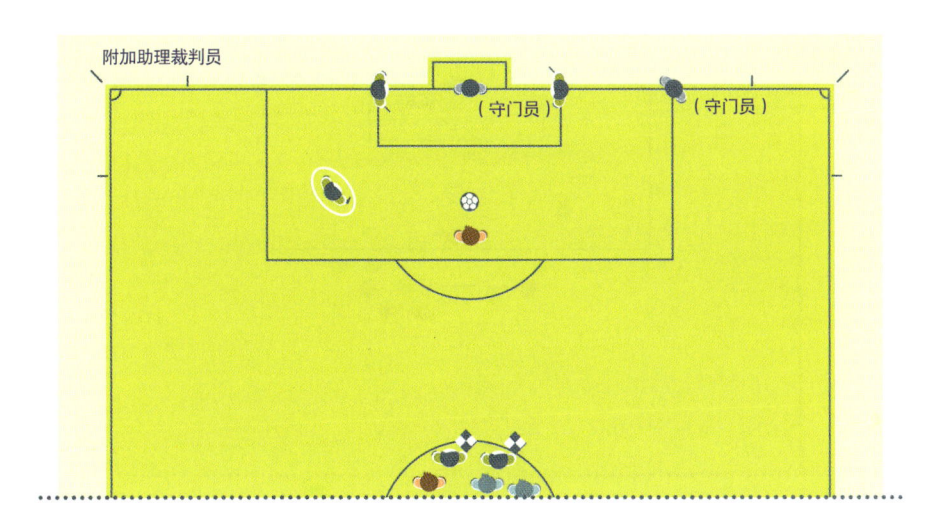

Penalty kick

The AR must be positioned at the intersection of the goal line and the penalty area.

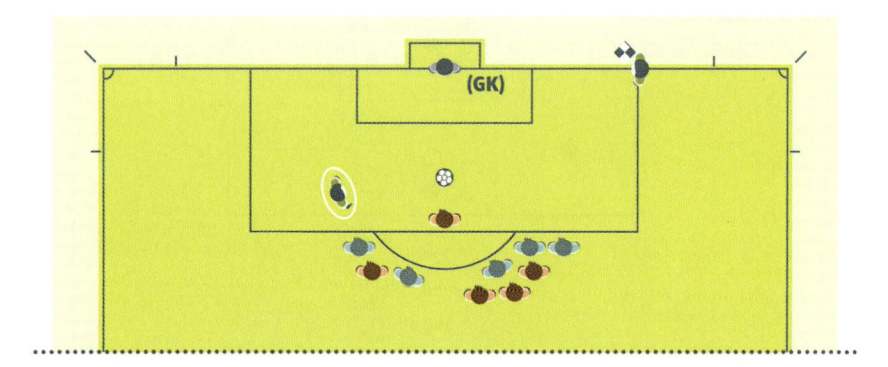

Where there are AARs the AAR must be positioned at the intersection of the goal line and the penalty area and the AR is positioned in line with the penalty mark (which is the offside line).

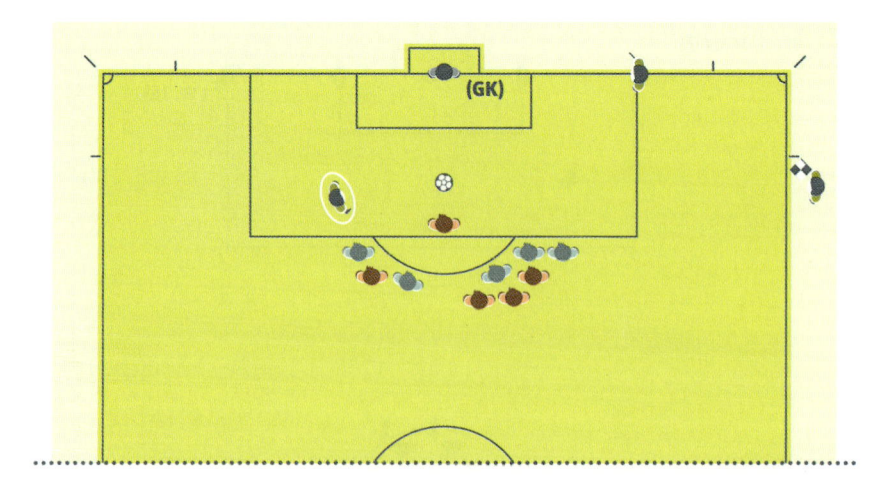

罚球点球

助理裁判员必须站在球门线与罚球区线交点的位置。

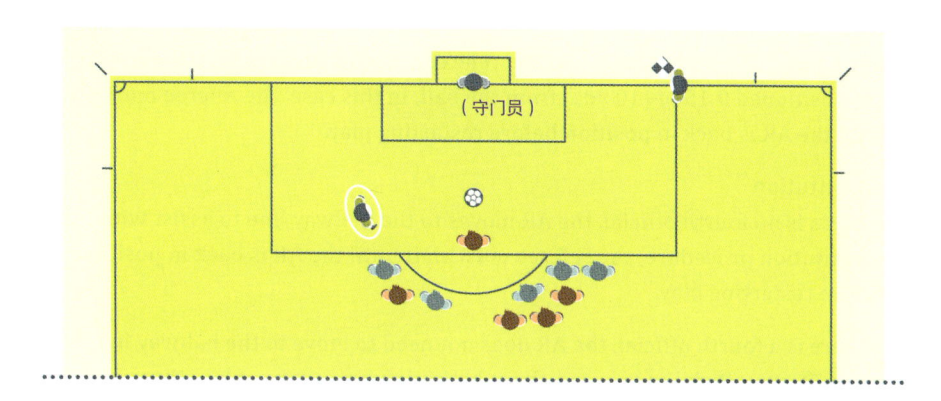

如果设有附加助理裁判员，则附加助理裁判员必须处于球门线与罚球区线交点的位置，而助理裁判员处于与罚球点齐平的边线位置（此时这里是越位线位置）。

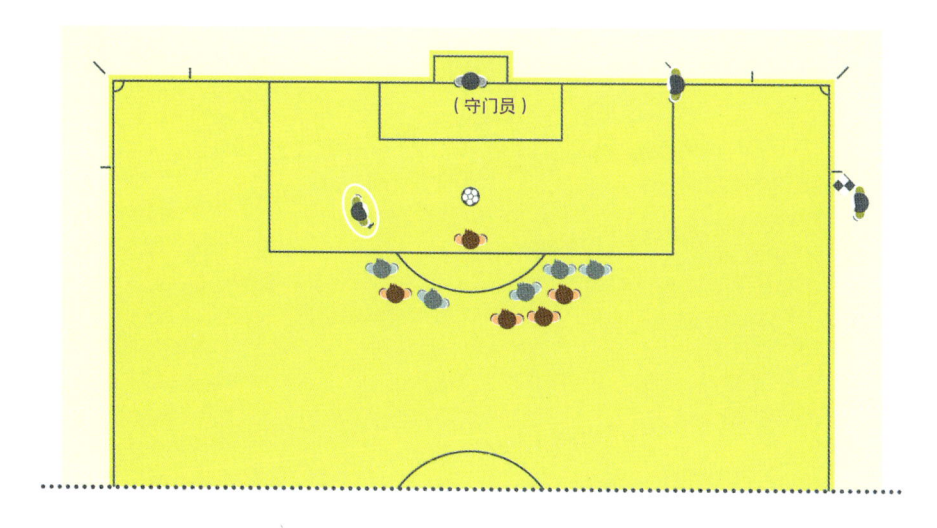

Mass confrontation

In situations of mass confrontation, the nearest AR may enter the field of play to assist the referee. The other AR must observe and record details of the incident. The fourth official should remain in the vicinity of the technical areas.

Required distance

When a free kick is awarded very close to the AR, the AR may enter the field of play (usually at the request of the referee) to help ensure that the players are positioned 9.15 m (10 yds) from the ball. In this case, the referee must wait until the AR is back in position before restarting play.

Substitution

If there is no fourth official, the AR moves to the halfway line to assist with the substitution procedure; the referee must wait until the AR is back in position before restarting play.

If there is a fourth official, the AR does not need to move to the halfway line as the fourth official carries out the substitution procedure unless there are several substitutions at the same time in which case the AR moves to the halfway line to assist the fourth official.

群体冲突

此类情况下，距事发地较近的助理裁判员可以进入比赛场地内协助裁判员；另一名助理裁判员必须观察和记录事件的细节；第四官员应留在技术区域附近。

规定距离

当罚任意球的地点距助理裁判员很近时，助理裁判员可以进入比赛场地内（通常是在裁判员的要求下）协助确保对方队员距离球至少9.15米（10码）。这种情况下，裁判员必须等助理裁判员回到常规位置后再恢复比赛。

队员替换

在没有第四官员的情况下，助理裁判员移动至中线处协助完成替换程序。裁判员必须等助理裁判员回到位置后再恢复比赛。

在有第四官员的情况下，助理裁判员不必移动至中线处，由第四官员执行替换程序。除非同一时间有多名队员进行替换时，助理裁判员可移动至中线处协助第四官员。

Body Language, Communication and Whistle

1. Referees

Body language
Body language is a tool that the referee uses to:

- help control the match
- show authority and self-control

Body language is not an explanation of a decision.

Signals
See Law 5 for diagrams of signals

Whistle
The whistle is needed to:

- start play (1st and 2nd half of normal play and extra time), after a goal
- stop play:
  - for a free kick or penalty kick
  - if the match is suspended or abandoned
  - at the end of each half
- restart play for:
  - free kicks when the appropriate distance is required
  - penalty kicks
- restart play after it has been stopped for a:
  - caution or sending-off
  - injury
  - substitution

肢体语言、沟通与哨音

1. 裁判员

肢体语言
裁判员将肢体语言作为工具运用，以：
- 协助其管理比赛。
- 显示其权威和控制力。

肢体语言不是对判罚的解释。

示意信号
详见第五章图例

哨音的使用
需要鸣哨的情况：
- 开始比赛（常规时间的上下半场和加时赛）、进球后恢复比赛。
- 停止比赛：
  - 判罚任意球或球点球。
  - 比赛需中断或中止。
  - 各半场结束。

- 恢复比赛：
  - 在需要退出规定距离的任意球罚球时。
  - 罚球点球。

- 因如下情况暂停比赛，后恢复比赛时：
  - 警告或罚令出场。
  - 受伤。
  - 替换队员。

The whistle is NOT needed to:

- stop play for a clear:
  - goal kick, corner kick, throw-in or goal
- restart play from:
  - most free kicks, and a goal kick, corner kick, throw-in or dropped ball

A whistle which is used too frequently/unnecessarily will have less impact when it is needed.

If the referee wants the player(s) to wait for the whistle before restarting play (e.g. when ensuring that defending players are 9.15m at a free kick) the referee must clearly inform the attacking player(s) to wait for the whistle.

If the referee blows the whistle in error and play stops, play is restarted with a dropped ball.

2. Assistant referees
Beep signal
The beep signal system is an additional signal which is only used to gain the referee's attention. Situations when the signal beep may be useful include:

- offside
- offences (outside the view of the referee)
- throw in, corner kick, goal kick or goal (tight decisions)

Electronic communication system
Where an electronic communication system is used, the referee will advise the ARs as to when it may be appropriate to use the communication system with, or instead of, a physical signal.

Flag technique
The AR's flag must always be unfurled and visible to the referee. This usually means the flag is carried in the hand closest to the referee. When making a signal, the AR stops running, faces the field of play, makes eye contact with the referee and raises the flag with a deliberate (not hasty or exaggerated) motion. The flag should be like an extension of the arm. The ARs must raise the flag using the hand that will be used for the next signal. If circumstances change

不需要鸣哨的情况：
- 停止比赛是为了示意：
  - 球权归属明确的球门球、角球、界外球或明显的进球。
- 以下列方式恢复比赛时：
  - 多数情况下的任意球、球门球、角球、界外球或坠球。

过于频繁或不必要的鸣哨，会在需要鸣哨时削弱哨音的作用。

如果裁判员在恢复比赛前，要求队员在其鸣哨后才可以罚球（如需要确保防守队员9.15米距离）时，必须以明确的信号告知进攻队员等待哨音。

如果裁判员错误地吹停了比赛，则以坠球恢复比赛。

2. 助理裁判员

蜂鸣信号
蜂鸣信号作为附加信号，仅用于引起裁判员注意。该信号在如下情况时能起到一定作用：
- 越位。
- 犯规（裁判员视线范围外）。
- 掷界外球、角球、球门球或进球（难以判断的情形）。

电子通讯设备
在使用电子通讯设备的情况下，裁判员可以建议助理裁判员在适当的时候使用电子通讯设备进行沟通，以取代肢体信号。

旗示技巧
助理裁判员必须始终将手旗展开，并将其保持在裁判员可见的范围内，这就意味着助理裁判员需将手旗握在最靠近裁判员的那只手中。在给出示意信号时，助理裁判员停止跑动，面向场内，与裁判员进行目光交流，随后举旗给出明确的（而非仓促、夸张的）示意信号。手旗应像手臂的延伸。助理裁判员必须用准备做出下一个信号的手举旗。如果情况发生变化而需要用另一只手，则应在腰部以下换手。如果助理裁判员

and the other hand must be used, the AR should move the flag to the opposite hand below the waist. If the AR signals that the ball is out of play, the signal must be maintained until the referee acknowledges it.

If the AR signals for a sending-off offence and the signal is not seen immediately:

- if play has been stopped, the restart may be changed in accordance with the Laws (free kick, penalty kick, etc.)
- if play has restarted, the referee may still take disciplinary action but not penalise the offence with a free kick or penalty kick

Gestures

As a general rule, the AR should not use obvious hand signals. However, in some instances, a discreet hand signal may assist the referee. The hand signal should have a clear meaning which should have been agreed in the pre-match discussion.

Signals

See Law 6 for diagrams of signals

Corner kick / goal kick

When the ball wholly passes over the goal line near to the AR, a signal should be made with the right hand (better line of vision) to indicate whether it is a goal kick or a corner kick.

When the ball wholly passes over the goal line the AR must raise the flag to inform the referee that the ball is out of play and then if it is:

- near to the AR - indicate whether it is a goal kick or a corner kick
- far from the AR - make eye contact and follow the referee's decision. The AR may also make a direct signal if the decision is an obvious one.

Fouls

The AR must raise the flag when a foul or misconduct is committed in the immediate vicinity or out of the referee's vision. In all other situations, the AR must wait and offer an opinion if it is required and then inform the referee what was seen and heard, and which players were involved.

示意比赛应该停止，则必须保持这个示意信号，直至裁判员做出反应。

如果助理裁判员示意可罚令出场的犯规，而该信号没有立即被裁判员注意：
- 如果比赛已经停止，则可以根据规则的相关规定，更改比赛恢复方式（如任意球、球点球）。
- 如果比赛已经恢复，裁判员仍可执行纪律处罚，但不得对此次犯规重新判罚任意球或球点球。

示意动作

一般情况下，助理裁判员不应使用明显的手势信号，但在某些情况下，谨慎的手势信号可以起到协助裁判员的作用。手势信号应有明确含义，并应在赛前准备时达成一致。

旗示信号

详见第六章图例。

角球/球门球

当球的整体从靠近助理裁判员的一侧完全越过球门线时，应使用右手持旗（以便拥有更好的视角）示意球门球或角球。

当球的整体完全越过球门线时，助理裁判员必须举旗示意裁判员球已经离开比赛场地，随后：
- 如果从靠近助理裁判员的一侧离开比赛场地——示意球门球或角球。
- 如果从远离助理裁判员的一侧离开比赛场地——与裁判员进行目光交流，遵从裁判员的决定。如果球权归属明显，助理裁判员也可直接给出示意信号。

犯规

当犯规或不正当行为发生在距离助理裁判员很近的区域，或裁判员视线范围外时，助理裁判员应举旗示意。对于所有其他情况，助理裁判员必须等候并在裁判员需要时给出自己的意见，告知裁判员他所看到和听到的情况，以及涉及到的队员。

Before signalling for an offence, the AR must determine that:

- the offence was out of the referee's view or the referee's view was obstructed
- the referee would not have applied the advantage

When an offence/infringement occurs which requires a signal from the AR, the AR must:

- raise the flag with the same hand that will also be used for the remainder of the signal – this gives the referee a clear indication as to who will be awarded the free kick
- make eye contact with the referee
- give the flag a slight wave back and forth (avoiding any excessive or aggressive movement)

The AR must use the "wait and see technique" to allow play to continue and not raise the flag when the team against which an offence has been committed will benefit from the advantage; it is therefore very important for the AR to make eye contact with the referee.

Fouls inside the penalty area
When a foul is committed by a defender inside the penalty area out of the vision of the referee, especially if near to the AR's position, the AR must first make eye contact with the referee to see where the referee is positioned and what action has been taken. If the referee has not taken any action, the AR must signal with the flag, use the electronic beep signal and then visibly move down the touchline towards the corner flag.

Fouls outside the penalty area
When a foul is committed by a defender outside the penalty area (near the boundary of the penalty area), the AR should make eye contact with the referee, to see the referee's position and what action has been taken, and signal with the flag if necessary. In counter-attack situations, the AR should be able to give information such as whether or not a foul has been committed and whether a foul was committed inside or outside the penalty area, and what disciplinary action should be taken. The AR should make a clear movement along the touchline towards the halfway line to indicate when the offence took place outside the penalty area.

在示意犯规前，助理裁判员必须确定：
- 犯规发生在裁判员视野范围外，或裁判员视线受到阻挡。
- 裁判员不会对此犯规掌握有利。

当发生犯规或违规，需要助理裁判员示意时，助理裁判员必须：
- 用同一只手举旗和做接下来的示意——这样能够向裁判员明确显示任意球的归属。
- 与裁判员进行目光交流。
- 前后轻微摇动手旗（避免任何过度或夸张的示意）。

当被犯规队可以从掌握有利中获益时，助理裁判员必须掌握"等和看的技巧"，允许比赛继续，不用举旗示意犯规。此时，助理裁判员和裁判员的目光交流很重要。

罚球区内的犯规

当防守方在其罚球区内犯规，且犯规处于裁判员视线外，尤其是靠近助理裁判员时，助理裁判员必须首先与裁判员进行目光交流，观察裁判员的位置和采取的行动。如果裁判员没有做出任何判罚，助理裁判员必须使用手旗蜂鸣信号，随后明确地沿边线向角旗移动。

罚球区外的犯规

当防守方在其罚球区外（靠近罚球区的边界线）犯规时，助理裁判员应与裁判员目光交流，观察裁判员的位置和采取的行动，并在必要时给出旗示信号。在某队打反击的情形下，助理裁判员应能够提供是否犯规、犯规发生在罚球区内还是罚球区外、应给予什么纪律处罚等相关信息。当出现罚球区外的犯规时，助理裁判员应明确地做出沿边线向中线移动的动作。

Goal – no goal
When it is clear that the ball has wholly passed over the goal line in the goal, the AR must make eye contact with the referee without giving any additional signal.

When a goal has been scored but it is not clear whether the ball has passed over the line, the AR must first raise the flag to attract the referee's attention and then confirm the goal.

Offside
The first action of the AR for an offside decision is to raise the flag (using the right hand, giving the AR a better line of vision) and then, if the referee stops play, use the flag to indicate the area of the field of play in which the offence occurred. If the flag is not immediately seen by the referee, the AR must maintain the signal until it has been acknowledged or the ball is clearly in the control of the defending team.

Penalty kick
If the goalkeeper blatantly moves off the goal line before the ball is kicked and a goal is not scored, the AR must raise the flag.

Substitution
Once the AR has been informed (by the fourth official or team official) that a substitution is requested, the AR must signal this to the referee at the next stoppage.

Throw-in
When the ball wholly passes over the touchline:

- near to the AR – a direct signal should be made to indicate the direction of the throw-in
- far from the AR and the throw-in decision is an obvious one – the AR must make a direct signal to indicate the direction of the throw-in
- far from the AR and the AR is in doubt about the direction of the throw-in the AR must raise the flag to inform the referee that the ball is out of play, make eye contact with the referee and follow the referee's signal

进球-未进球

当球的整体已经清晰地从球门范围内越过球门线时，助理裁判员必须与裁判员目光交流，无须给出任何附加信号。

当进球得分已经形成，但球的整体越过球门线并不明显时，助理裁判员必须举旗引起裁判员注意，然后确认进球有效。

越位

助理裁判员示意越位时的第一步骤是举旗（使用右手，以便有更好的观察视角），随后如果裁判员停止比赛，则使用手旗示意越位发生的区域。如果旗示信号没有立即被裁判员看到，则助理裁判员必须坚持举旗示意越位，直至裁判员做出反应或球已明显被防守方控制。

罚球点球

如果守门员在球被踢前，非常明显地离开了球门线，且随后球没有进门，助理裁判员必须举旗示意。

队员替换

一旦助理裁判员接到队员替换的信号（由第四官员或球队官员给出），必须在随后比赛停止时示意裁判员。

掷界外球

当球的整体越过边线时：

- 如果是在靠近助理裁判员的一侧——直接示意掷界外球的球权归属。
- 如果是在助理裁判员远端，且球权归属明确——直接示意掷界外球的球权归属。
- 如果是在助理裁判员远端，且球权归属不明确——助理裁判员必须举旗示意裁判员球已离开比赛场地，并与裁判员目光交流，跟随裁判员的示意信号。

3. **Additional assistant referees**

   The AARs use a radio communication system (not flags) to communicate with the referee. If the radio communication system fails to work, the AARs will use an electronic signal beep flagstick. AARs do not usually use obvious hand signals but, in some instances, a discreet hand signal may give valuable support to the referee. The hand signal should have a clear meaning and such signals should be agreed in the pre-match discussion.

   The AAR, having assessed that the ball has wholly passed over the goal line within the goal, must:

   - immediately inform the referee via the communication system that a goal should be awarded
   - make a clear signal with the left arm perpendicular to the goal line pointing towards the centre of the field (flagstick in the left hand is also required). This signal is not required when the ball has very clearly passed over the goal line.

   The referee will make the final decision.

3. 附加助理裁判员

附加助理裁判员使用无线通讯系统（非手旗）与裁判员进行交流。如果无线通讯系统失灵，则附加助理裁判员使用电子感应信号棒。附加助理裁判员通常不使用明显的手势信号，但在某些情况下，谨慎的手势信号可以为裁判员提供有价值的帮助。手势信号应有明确含义，并应在赛前准备时达成一致。

附加助理裁判员在确认球已经整体越过球门内的球门线时，必须：
- 立即通过无线通讯系统告知裁判员进球有效。
- 做出左臂垂直于球门线、左手持信号棒指向场地中央的明确信号。当球非常明显地越过球门线时不必做出该信号。

由裁判员做最终决定。

Other advice

1. **Advantage**

   The referee may play advantage whenever an infringement or offence occurs but should consider the following in deciding whether to apply the advantage or stop play:

   - the severity of the offence – if the infringement warrants a sending-off, the referee must stop play and send off the player unless there is a clear opportunity to score a goal
   - the position where the offence was committed - the closer to the opponent's goal, the more effective the advantage can be
   - the chances of an immediate, promising attack
   - the atmosphere of the match

2. **Allowance for time lost**

   Many stoppages in play are entirely natural (e.g. throw-ins, goal kicks). An allowance is made only when delays are excessive.

3. **Holding an opponent**

   Referees are reminded to make an early intervention and to deal firmly with holding offences, especially inside the penalty area at corner kicks and free kicks. To deal with these situations:

   - the referee must warn any player holding an opponent before the ball is in play
   - caution the player if the holding continues before the ball is in play
   - award a direct free kick or penalty kick and caution the player if it happens once the ball is in play

其他建议

1. 有利

无论是犯规还是违规违例，裁判员均可掌握有利，但应考虑如下情况决定掌握有利还是停止比赛：

- 犯规的严重程度——如果是可被罚令出场的犯规，裁判员必须停止比赛，将相关队员罚令出场，除非有明显的进球得分机会。
- 犯规发生的位置——离对方球门越近，掌握有利的效果越好。
- 能够即刻发起有效进攻的可能性。
- 当时比赛的气氛。

2. 对损耗时间的补足

比赛中的许多中断极为正常（如掷界外球、球门球等），当这些停顿延误的时间较长时才允许（针对这些停顿）补时。

3. 使用手臂等部位拉扯、阻止对方队员行动

裁判员应提早干预使用手臂等部位拉扯、阻止对方队员行动的犯规，并严格处理，尤其是在踢角球和任意球时，出现在罚球区内的此类行为。为了处理这些情况：

- 裁判员必须在比赛恢复前口头警告有此类行为的队员。
- 对比赛恢复前仍然继续此类行为的队员予以警告。
- 一旦比赛恢复，仍出现类似行为的队员，判罚直接任意球或球点球。

4. Offside

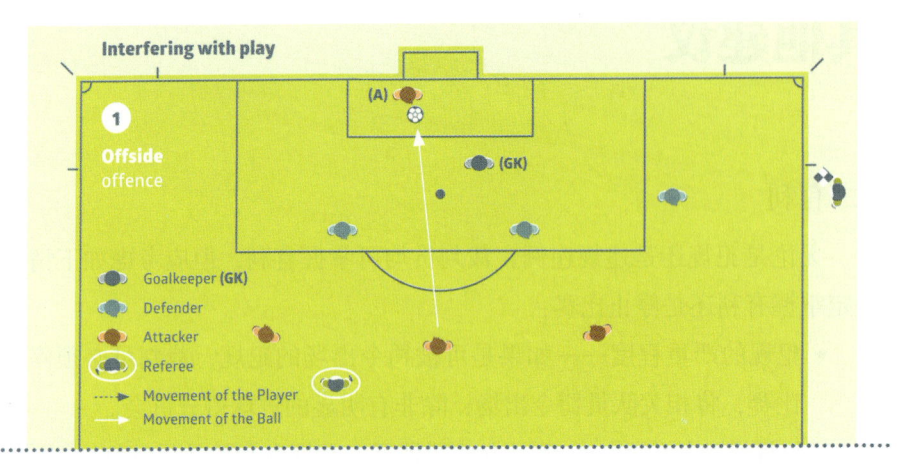

Interfering with play

1 **Offside** offence

- Goalkeeper **(GK)**
- Defender
- Attacker
- Referee
- Movement of the Player
- Movement of the Ball

An attacker **in an offside position** (A), not interfering with an opponent, **touches the ball**. The assistant referee must raise the flag when the player **touches the ball**.

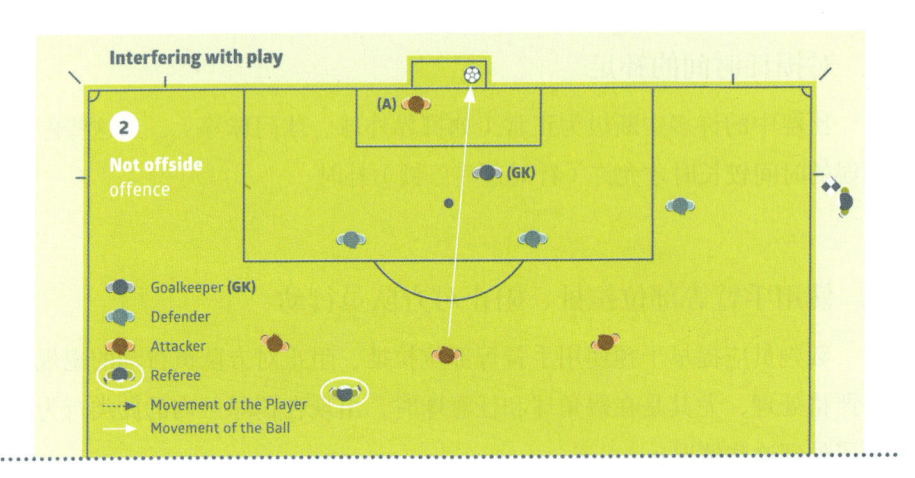

Interfering with play

2 **Not offside** offence

- Goalkeeper **(GK)**
- Defender
- Attacker
- Referee
- Movement of the Player
- Movement of the Ball

An attacker **in an offside position** (A), not interfering with an opponent, **does not touch the ball**. The player did not touch the ball, so cannot be penalised.

4. 越位

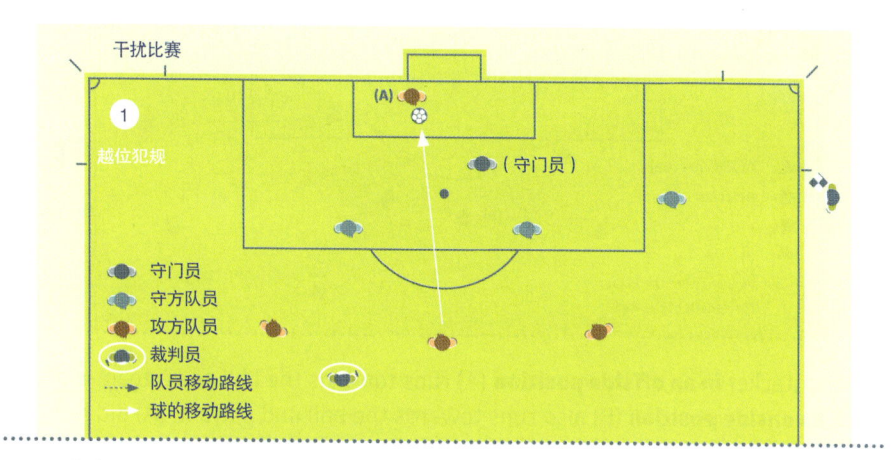

攻方队员（A）处在越位位置，并未干扰对方队员，但触到了球。助理裁判员必须在他触球时举旗示意其越位犯规。

攻方队员（A）处在越位位置，未干扰对方队员，也未触球。不能判罚其越位犯规。

Interfering with play

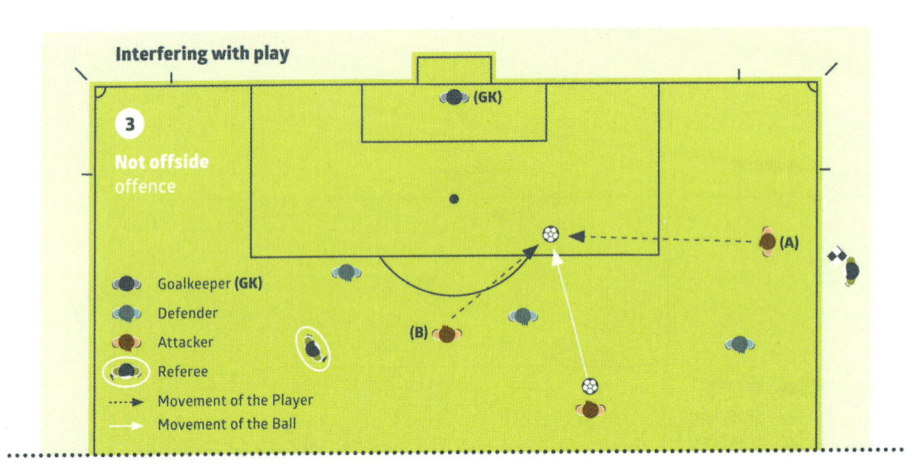

3
Not offside offence

An attacker **in an offside position** (A) runs towards the ball and a team-mate **in an onside position** (B) also runs towards the ball and plays it. (A) did not touch the ball, so cannot be penalised.

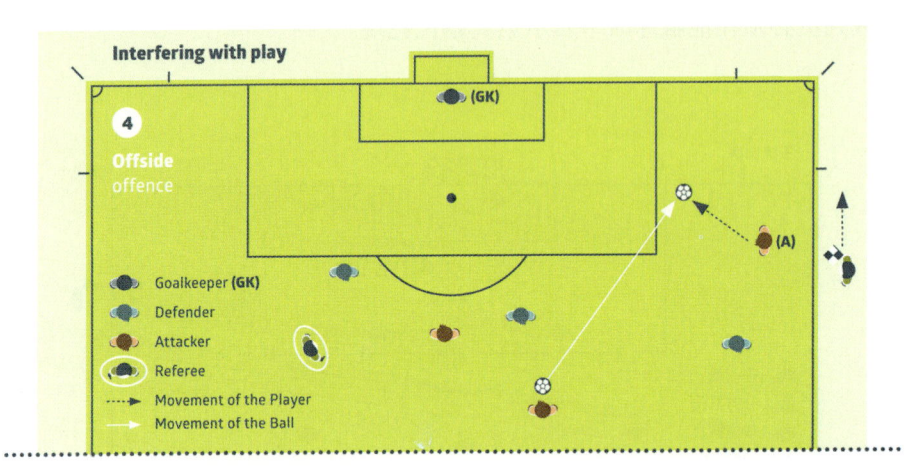

Interfering with play

4
Offside offence

A player **in an offside position** (A) may be penalised before playing or touching the ball, if, in the opinion of the referee, no other team-mate in an onside position has the opportunity to play the ball.

攻方队员（A）处在越位位置并跑向球，他的队友（B）从不越位的位置跑向球。队员（A）未触球，则不能被判罚越位犯规。

攻方队员（A）处在越位位置，如果裁判员认为不在越位位置的同队其他队员没有触球的机会，则在队员（A）触球前即可判罚其越位犯规。

Interfering with play

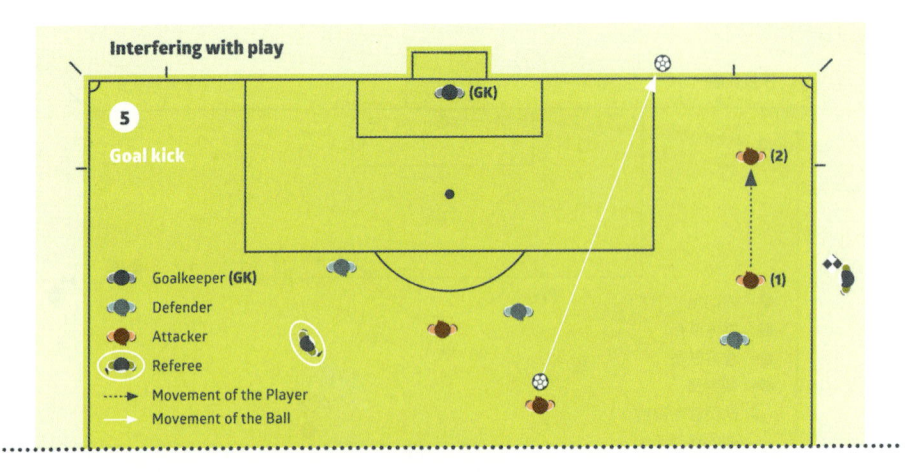

5 Goal kick

An attacker **in an offside position** (1) runs towards the ball and **does not touch** the ball. The assistant referee must signal **"goal kick"**.

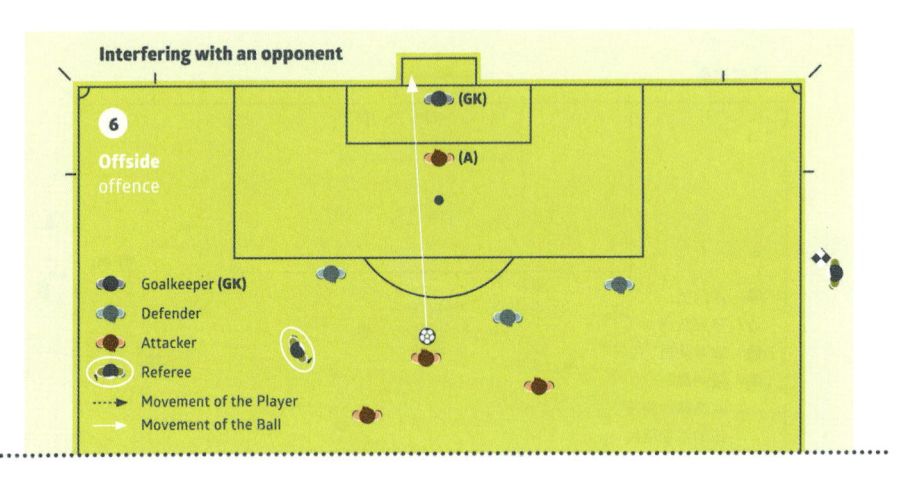

Interfering with an opponent

6 Offside offence

An attacker **in an offside position** (A) is clearly obstructing the goalkeeper's line of vision. The player must be penalised for preventing an opponent from playing or being able to play the ball.

攻方队员处于越位位置（1）并跑向球，但并未触球。助理裁判员必须示意"球门球"。

处于越位位置的攻方队员（A）明显地阻碍了守门员的视线。必须以妨碍对方队员处理球或处理球的能力为由判罚其越位犯规。

Interfering with an opponent

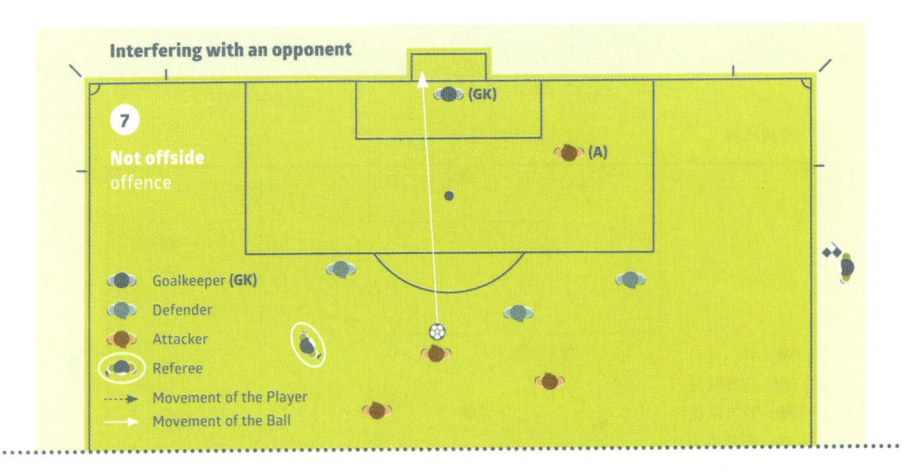

7

Not offside offence

- Goalkeeper (GK)
- Defender
- Attacker
- Referee
- ----> Movement of the Player
- → Movement of the Ball

An attacker **in an offside position** (A) is **not** clearly obstructing the goalkeeper's line of vision or challenging an opponent for the ball.

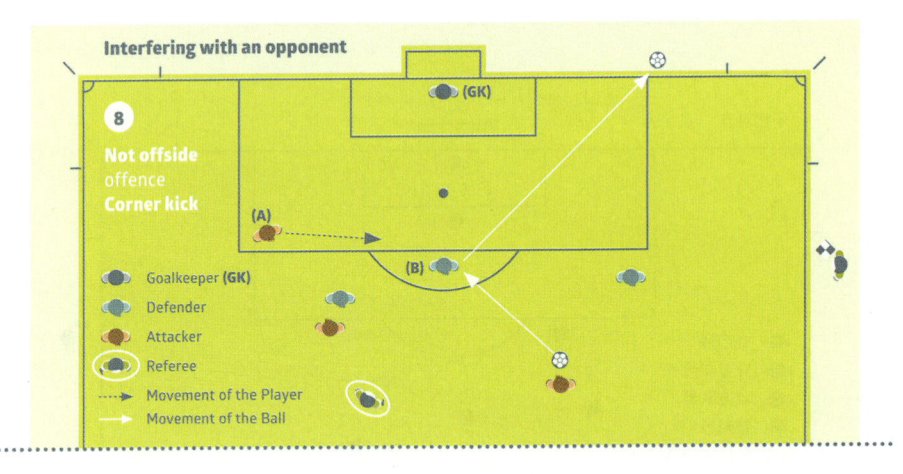

Interfering with an opponent

8

Not offside offence
Corner kick

- Goalkeeper (GK)
- Defender
- Attacker
- Referee
- ----> Movement of the Player
- → Movement of the Ball

An attacker **in an offside position** (A) runs towards the ball but does not prevent the opponent from playing or being able to play the ball.
(A) is **not** challenging an opponent (B) for the ball.

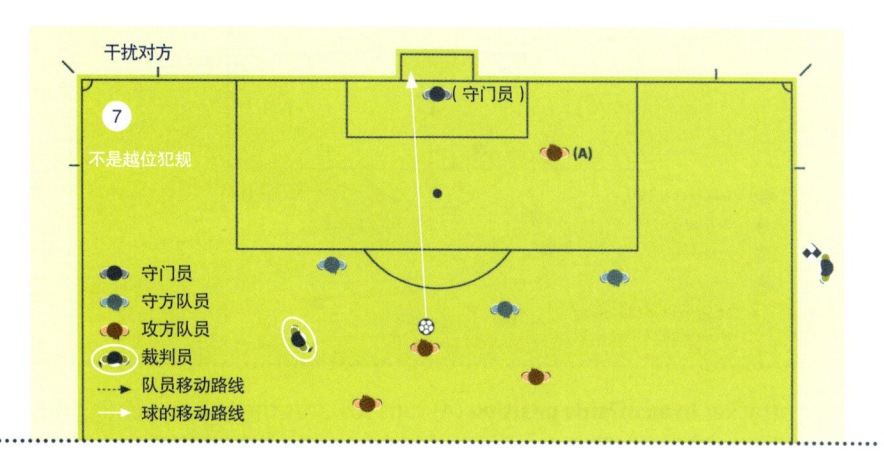

处于越位位置的攻方队员（A）没有明显地阻挡守门员的视线，也没有与对方队员争抢球。

处于越位位置的攻方队员（A）跑向球，但并未妨碍对方队员处理球或处理球的能力。队员（A）未与对方队员争抢球。

Interfering with an opponent

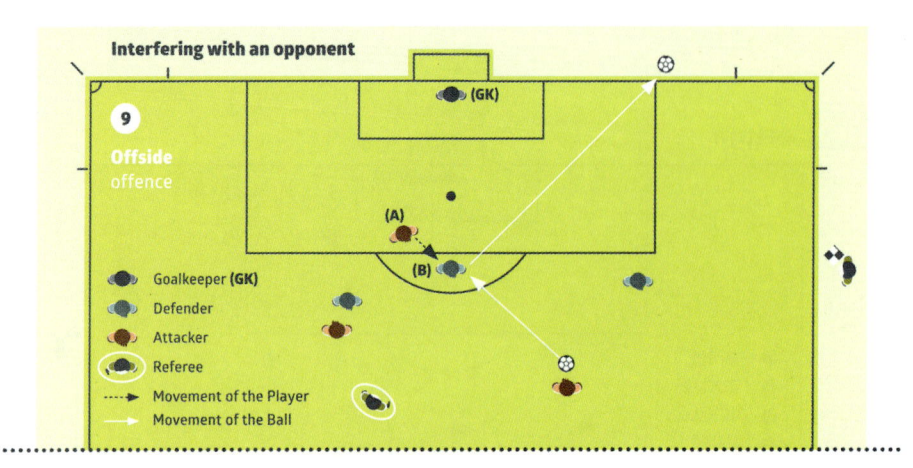

9
Offside
offence

Goalkeeper **(GK)**
Defender
Attacker
Referee
----▶ Movement of the Player
——▶ Movement of the Ball

An attacker **in an offside position** (A) runs towards the ball preventing the opponent (B) from playing or being able to play the ball by challenging the opponent for the ball. (A) is challenging an opponent (B) for the ball.

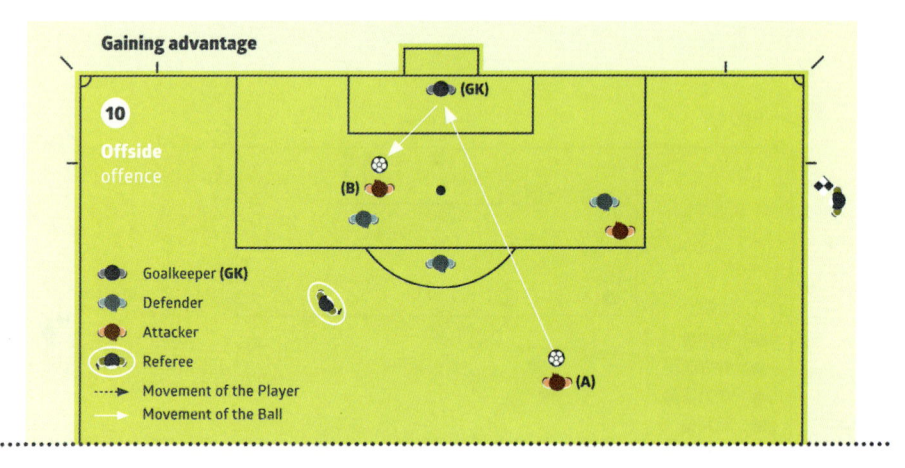

Gaining advantage

10
Offside
offence

Goalkeeper **(GK)**
Defender
Attacker
Referee
----▶ Movement of the Player
——▶ Movement of the Ball

An attacker **in an offside position** (B) is penalised for **playing or touching the ball** that rebounds, is deflected or is played from a deliberate save by the goalkeeper having been **in an offside position** when the ball was last touched or is played by a team-mate.

处于越位位置的攻方队员（A）跑向球并与对方队员争抢球，妨碍了对方队员处理球或处理球的能力。队员（A）视为与对方队员争抢球。

攻方队员（B）被判罚越位犯规，因其在同队队员传球或触球的一瞬间处于越位位置，且在球从守门员反弹、折射或经守门员有意救球后触球。

164

Gaining advantage

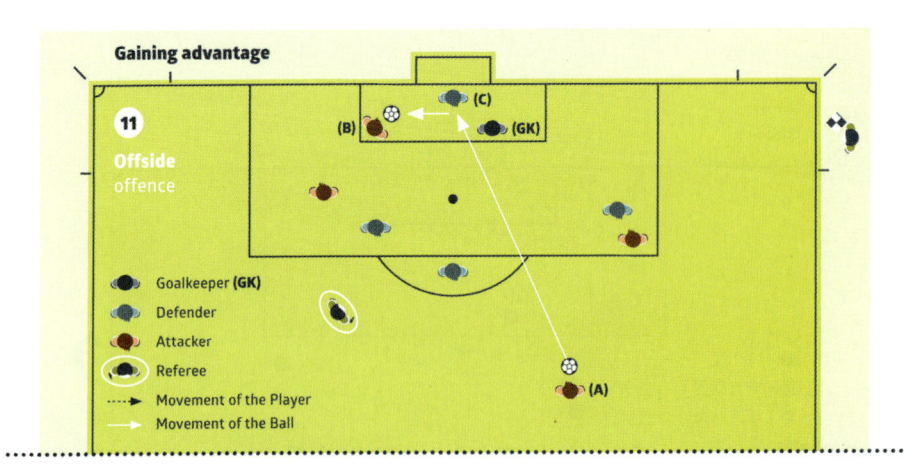

11
Offside
offence

- Goalkeeper (GK)
- Defender
- Attacker
- Referee
- ····▶ Movement of the Player
- ──▶ Movement of the Ball

An attacker **in an offside position** (B) is penalised for **playing or touching the ball** that rebounds or is deflected from a deliberate save by a player from the defending team (C) having been **in an offside position** when the ball was last touched or is played by a team-mate.

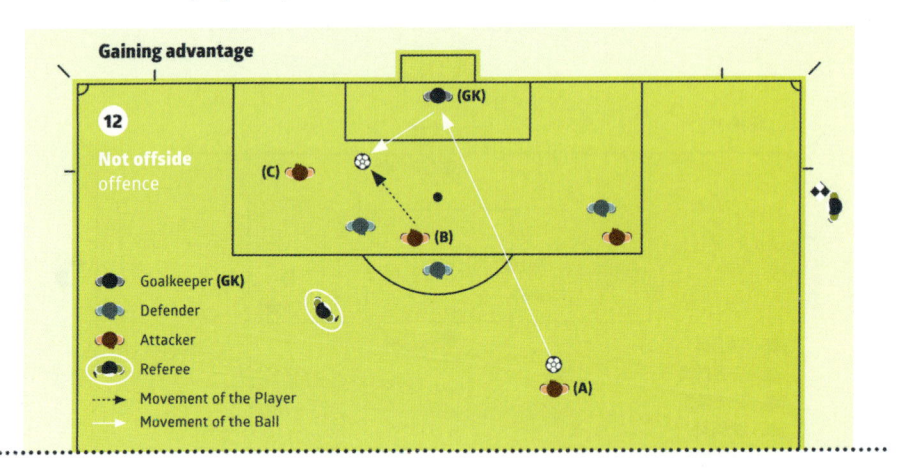

Gaining advantage

12
Not offside
offence

- Goalkeeper (GK)
- Defender
- Attacker
- Referee
- ····▶ Movement of the Player
- ──▶ Movement of the Ball

The shot by a team-mate (A) rebounds from the goalkeeper, (B) is in an onside position and plays the ball, (C) **in an offside position** is not penalised because the player did not gain an advantage from being in that position because the player did not touch the ball.

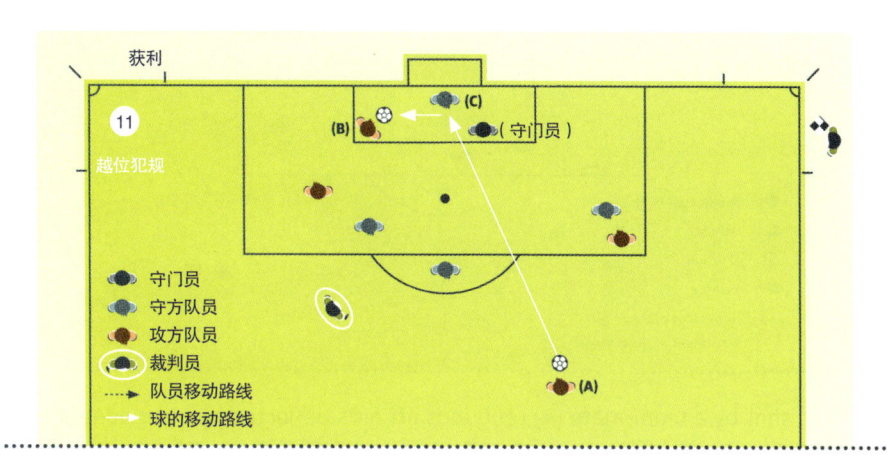

处于越位位置的攻方队员（B）被判罚越位犯规，因其在同队队员传球或触球的一瞬间处于越位位置，且在球从守方队员（C）反弹、折射或经守方队员（C）有意救球后触球。

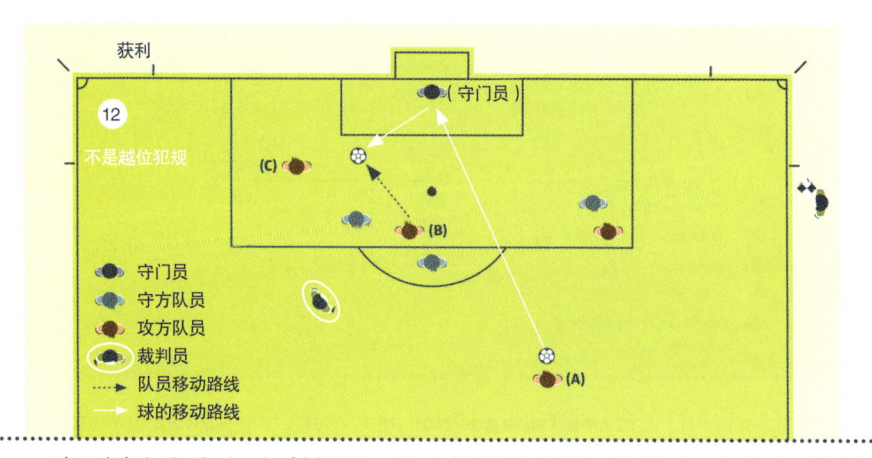

球经同队队员（A）射门后，从守门员处反弹，队员（B）处在不越位的位置，并且触球，处在越位位置的队员（C）不能被判罚越位犯规，因其未触球，并未从越位位置获利。

Gaining advantage

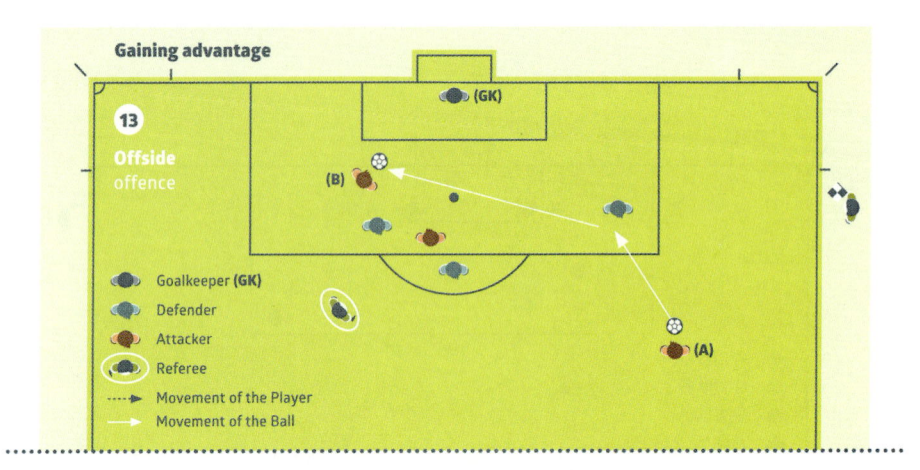

13 Offside offence

- Goalkeeper (GK)
- Defender
- Attacker
- Referee
- ----> Movement of the Player
- ⟶ Movement of the Ball

The shot by a team-mate (A) rebounds off or is deflected by an opponent to attacker (B) who is penalised for **playing or touching the ball** having previously been **in an offside position**.

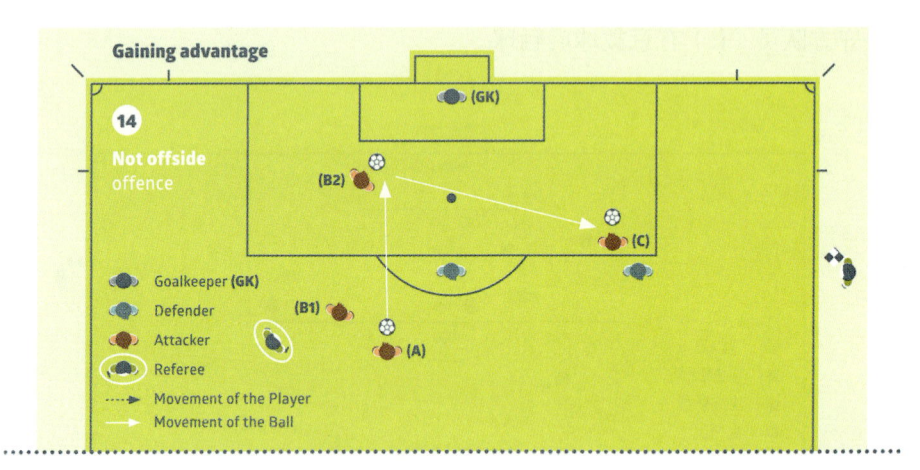

Gaining advantage

14 Not offside offence

- Goalkeeper (GK)
- Defender
- Attacker
- Referee
- ----> Movement of the Player
- ⟶ Movement of the Ball

An attacker (C) is **in an offside position**, not interfering with an opponent, when a team-mate (A) passes the ball to player (B1) in an onside position who runs towards the opponents' goal and passes the ball (B2) to team-mate (C). Attacker (C) was **in an onside position** when the ball was passed, so cannot be penalised.

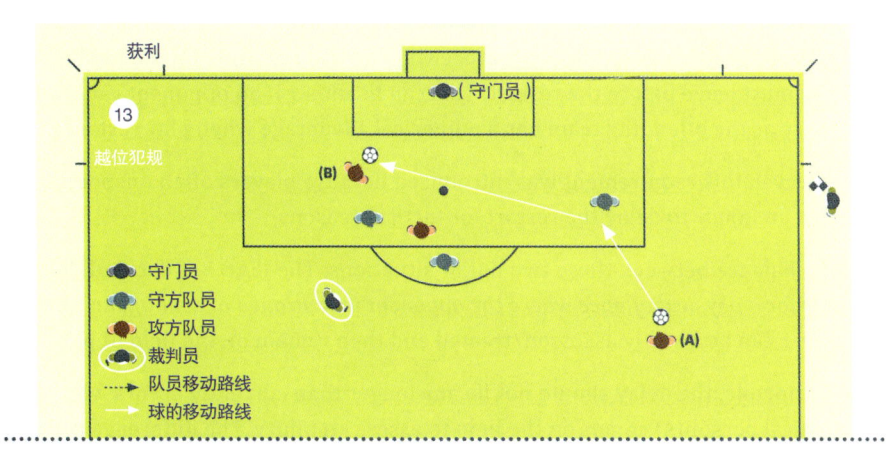

球经同队队员（A）射门后，从对方队员处反弹或折射，攻方队员（B）触球将被判为越位犯规，因其之前已处在越位位置。

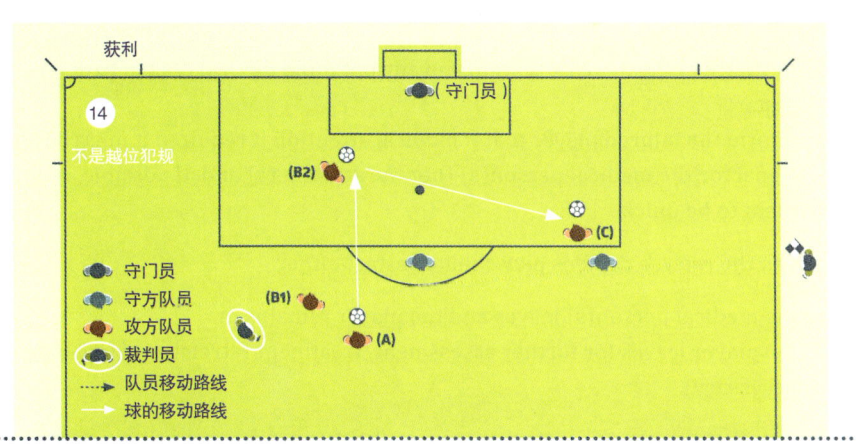

攻方队员（C）处在越位位置，未干扰对方队员。当同队队员（A）传球给处在不越位的位置，且向前插上的队员（B1），该队员在（B2）位置传球给队员（C），此时进攻队员（C）处于不越位的位置，因此不能判罚其越位犯规。

5. **Treatment/assessment after a caution/sending-off**

    Previously, an injured player who received medical attention on the field of play must leave before the restart. This can be unfair if an opponent caused the injury as the offending team has a numerical advantage when play restarts.

    However, this requirement was introduced because players often unsportingly used an injury to delay the restart for tactical reasons.

    As a balance between these two unfair situations, The IFAB has decided that *only for a physical offence where the opponent is cautioned or sent off*, an injured player can be quickly assessed/treated and then remain on the field of play.

    In principle, the delay should not be any longer than currently occurs when a medical person(s) comes on the field to assess an injury. The difference is that the point at which the referee used to require the medical person(s) and the player to leave is now the point at which the medical staff leave but the player can remain.

    To ensure the injured player does not use/extend the delay unfairly, referees are advised to:

    - be aware of the match situation and any potential tactical reason to delay the restart
    - inform the injured player that if medical attention it required it must be quick
    - signal for the medical person(s) (not the stretchers) and, if possible, remind them to be quick

    When the referee decides play should restart either:

    - the medical person(s) leaves and the player remains or
    - the player leaves for further assessment/treatment (stretcher signal may be necessary)

    As a general guide, the restart should not be delayed for more than about 20–25 seconds beyond the point when everyone was ready for play to restart.

    The referee must make full allowance for the stoppage.

5. 出现可警告/罚令出场的犯规后对受伤队员的治疗/伤势评估

在上一版本的《足球竞赛规则》中，在比赛场地内接受治疗的受伤队员必须在随后比赛恢复前离开比赛场地。然而如果受伤是由于对方的犯规造成，犯规一方在随后比赛恢复后会获得人数上的优势，这是不公平的。

这一条文的提出，是因为队员往往出于战术目的，以受伤为由不当地延误比赛恢复。

作为这两种不公平情况的平衡之法，国际足球理事会决定，仅当受伤队员在受到对方身体接触且可被警告或罚令出场的犯规时，可以在接受快速伤势评估和治疗后留在场内不必出场。

原则上，如果医护人员进入比赛场地内评估队员伤势，不应消耗更多时间。所不同的是，以往裁判员要求医护人员和受伤队员均要离开比赛场地，而现在只需医护人员离开，受伤队员仍可以留在比赛场地内。

为确保受伤队员无法以不当方式利用/延长受伤带来的时间损耗，建议裁判员：

- 留意比赛情况以及任何潜在的延误比赛的战术目的；
- 告知受伤队员，需要医护时，必须尽快完成；
- 示意医护人员（而非担架手），在可能的情况下尽快完成医护。

当裁判员作出如下决定后，比赛恢复：

- 医护人员离开比赛场地、队员留在比赛场地，或
- 队员离开比赛场地接受进一步的伤情评估/治疗（可示意担架手入场）

一般说来，当所有人员准备好恢复比赛后，延误的时间不应超过20~25秒。

裁判员必须对此类情况损耗的时间予以补足。

附录　国际足球理事会第131次年度工作会议决议

一、非体育行为

本次年度会议同意国际足联关于强调两类日渐增长的非体育行为的要求：
- 踢球门球时，防守队员故意在球未出罚球区之前触球。
- 队员故意不将界外球掷进场内。

通常队员意图故意拖延时间，他们知道在上述情况下，需要重新掷界外球/踢球门球。裁判员应对此类行为保持警觉，若队员试图用此类行为故意浪费时间，应被出示黄牌，并补回被浪费的时间。

二、对《足球竞赛规则》（2016/2017版）的解释

考虑到翻译的需要，国际足球理事会应要求对《足球竞赛规则》（2016/2017版）的部分内容进行解释说明。这些解释说明将写入《足球竞赛规则》（2017/2018版），并提交国际足球协会理事会年会审议。

第五章 裁判员

若球队的医疗人员被罚出技术区域，如果没有其他的医疗人员，其将仍被允许为队员提供医疗服务。

第十章 确定比赛结果

球点球决胜：

- 主罚队员犯规

  - 若主罚队员犯规，罚球无效（记为罚失）。

- 守门员和主罚队员均犯规

  - 若球进，主罚队员应予以警告，罚球记为罚失。

  - 若球未进，两名队员均被警告，并重新罚球。

第十二章 犯规与不正当行为

- 间接任意球

言语或手势的犯规应被罚间接任意球，即使队员被警告或罚令出场。判罚直接任意球的"对比赛官员的犯规"为直接的身体犯规（如推搡、拉拽、击打等）而非言语或手势的犯规。

- 罚令出场

- 若在进攻的最后阶段，进攻队员向角旗方向移动过掉守门员/防守队员，并且其整体移动是朝着对方球门的方向，则明显的进球得分机会仍存在。

- 通过进入场地而破坏明显的进球得分机会

- 若任何场上队员、替补队员或球队官员未得到裁判员允许而进入场地，阻止了进球或破坏了明显的进球得分机会，必须被罚令出场，即使没有其他犯规行为。

第十四章 罚球点球

- 守门员和主罚队员均犯规
  - 若球进，主罚队员应予以警告，比赛以防守方在罚球点踢间接任意球恢复。
  - 若球未进，两名队员均被警告，并重新罚球。

三、《足球竞赛规则》2017/2018版

仅有少数对《足球竞赛规则》2017/2018版的修订提议，基本均延续《足球竞赛规则》2016/2017版的修订。

另外，国际足球理事会将考虑调整《足球竞赛规则》的"修改"章节，给予国家足球协会（及他们管辖的比赛）更大的灵活性，改变竞赛规则中的一些组织部分，如比赛时长、替补人数等，以便更好地在当地推广足球运动。

四、视频助理裁判(VARs)

视频助理裁判的试验已取得重大进展，主要特征如下：

- 最少干预——最大收益：应仅用于关键的决定比赛结果的事件（进

球、球点球情况、直接红牌和错误身份）及严重的被忽视事件。这将避免频繁的中断对比赛流畅度和情感的影响。
- 裁判的决定是明显错误的吗：应仅用于纠正明显的错误。
- 同一程序——适用所有：每项比赛均使用同样的视频辅助程序，这样将令视频助理裁判试验最有可能成功。

五、电子通讯

国际足球理事会年度会议将讨论技术区域人员对电子通讯系统的使用。然而，国际足球理事会希望明确如下内容：

- 队员不得使用或穿戴任何电子或通讯设备（表现跟踪电子系统除外）。
- 球队官员可在直接关系队员安全的情况下使用电子通讯设备。

六、球网上的徽标

国家会员协会和洲际足联（及其竞赛方）应注意，竞赛规则第一章禁止球网上有任何徽标、标志或广告，即使其和球网是一体的（包括俱乐部徽标）。

图书在版编目(CIP)数据

足球竞赛规则. 2016-2017 / 中国足球协会审定. –北京：人民体育出版社，2017（2017.10.重印）
ISBN 978-7-5009-5184-1

Ⅰ. ①足… Ⅱ. ①中… Ⅲ. ①足球运动–竞赛规则–2016-2017 Ⅳ. ①G843.4

中国版本图书馆 CIP 数据核字（2017）第 125942 号

*

人民体育出版社出版发行
北京中科印刷有限公司印刷
新 华 书 店 经 销

*

787×960　16 开本　21.25 印张　380 千字
2017 年 6 月第 1 版　2017 年 10 月第 3 次印刷
印数：16,001—26,000 册

*

ISBN 978-7-5009-5184-1
定价：65.00 元

社址：北京市东城区体育馆路 8 号（天坛公园东门）
电话：67151482（发行部）　　　　邮编：100061
传真：67151483　　　　　　　　邮购：67118491
网址：www.sportspublish.cn

（购买本社图书，如遇有缺损页可与邮购部联系）